CROSS-CULTURAL BUYER BEHAVIOR

ADVANCES IN INTERNATIONAL MARKETING

Series Editor: S. Tamer Cavusgil

Recent Volumes:

ADVANCES IN INTERNATIONAL MARKETING   VOLUME 18

CROSS-CULTURAL BUYER BEHAVIOR

GUEST EDITORS

CHARLES R. TAYLOR
Villanova University, Villanova, PA, USA

DOO-HEE LEE
Korea University Business School, Seoul, Korea

ELSEVIER
JAI

Amsterdam – Boston – Heidelberg – London – New York – Oxford
Paris – San Diego – San Francisco – Singapore – Sydney – Tokyo

JAI Press is an imprint of Elsevier

HF
1009.5
.A39
VOL.18
2007

JAI Press is an imprint of Elsevier
The Boulevard, Langford Lane, Kidlington, Oxford OX5 1GB, UK
Radarweg 29, PO Box 211, 1000 AE Amsterdam, The Netherlands
525 B Street, Suite 1900, San Diego, CA 92101-4495, USA

First edition 2007

Notice
No responsibility is assumed by the publisher for any injury and/or damage to persons
or property as a matter of products liability, negligence or otherwise, or from any use
or operation of any methods, products, instructions or ideas contained in the material
herein. Because of rapid advances in the medical sciences, in particular, independent
verification of diagnoses and drug dosages should be made

British Library Cataloguing in Publication Data
A catalogue record for this book is available from the British Library

ISBN: 978-0-7623-1412-6
ISSN: 1474-7979 (Series)

For information on all JAI Press publications
visit our website at books.elsevier.com

Printed and bound in the United Kingdom

07 08 09 10 11 10 9 8 7 6 5 4 3 2 1

CONTENTS

v

LIST OF CONTRIBUTORS

Michael L. Capella	Villanova School of Business, Villanova University, Villanova, PA, USA
Dae Ryun Chang	School of Business, Yonsei University, Shinchon Dong, Seoul, Korea
Sverre Riis Christensen	TNS-Gallup, København Ø, Denmark
Sandra Diehl	Institute for Consumer and Behavior Research, Saarland University, Germany
Fabian Festge	Munich School of Management, Institute for Market-based Management, Ludwig-Maximilians-University of Munich, Munich, Germany
Ildefonso Grande	Department of Business Administration, Universidad Pública de Navarra, Pamplona, Spain
Flemming Hansen	Department of Marketing, Copenhagen Business School, Frederiksberg, Denmark
Wim Janssens	Department of Marketing, University of Antwerp, Antwerpen, Belgium
Yong Man Jung	Samsung Techwin, Changwon, Gyeongnam, Korea
Kyung Hoon Kim	Department of Business Administration, Changwon National University, Changwon, Gyeongnam, Korea

Eunju Ko   Department of Clothing and Textiles,
                                    College of Human Ecology, Yonsei
                                    University, Seodaemun-Gu, Seoul, Korea

John C. Kozup   Villanova School of Business, Villanova
                                    University, Villanova, PA, USA

Doo-Hee Lee   Korea University Business School, Seoul,
                                    Korea

Steen Lundsteen   Department of Marketing, Copenhagen
                                    Business School, Frederiksberg, Denmark

Barbara Mueller   School of Communication, San Diego
                                    State University, San Diego, CA, USA

Shintaro Okazaki   Department of Finance and Marketing
                                    Research, College of Economics and
                                    Business Administration, Universidad
                                    Autónoma de Madrid, Madrid, Spain

Yorgo Pasadeos   Department of Advertising and Public
                                    Relations, The University of Alabama,
                                    Tuscaloosa, AL, USA

Patrick De Pelsmacker   Department of Marketing, University of
                                    Antwerp, Antwerpen, Belgium

Larry Percy   Department of Marketing, Copenhagen
                                    Business School, Frederiksberg, Denmark

Joseph E. Phelps   Department of Advertising and Public
                                    Relations, The University of Alabama,
                                    Tuscaloosa, AL, USA

Manfred Schwaiger   Munich School of Management, Institute
                                    for Market-based Management, Ludwig-
                                    Maximilians-University of Munich,
                                    Munich, Germany

| *Radoslav Skapa* | Faculty of Economics and Administration, Masaryk University, Brno, Czech Republic |

| *Koo-Won Suh* | Department of Advertising, Hanyang Cyber University, Seongsong-Gu, Seoul, Korea |

| *Heewon Sung* | Human Ecology Research Institute, Yonsei University, Seoul, Korea |

| *Charles R. Taylor* | Villanova School of Business, Villanova University, Villanova, PA, USA |

| *Ralf Terlutter* | Department of Marketing and International Management, University of Klagenfurt, Austria |

| *Marcel Weverbergh* | Department of Marketing, University of Antwerp, Antwerpen, Belgium |

| *Hee-Sook Yoon* | Seoul Welfare Foundation, Jongno-Gu, Seoul, Korea |

| *Lu Zheng* | College of Communication and Information Sciences, The University of Alabama, Tuscaloosa, AL, USA |

| *Shuhua Zhou* | Department of Telecommunications and Film, The University of Alabama, Tuscaloosa, AL, USA |

LIST OF REVIEWERS

Hae-Kyong Bang	Villanova University
Michael Capella	Villanova University
Hong Cheng	Ohio University
Sejung Marina Choi	University of Texas at Austin
Maggie Geuens	Vlerek Leuven Management School
Flemming Hansen	University of Copenhagen
Ronald Paul Hill	Villanova University
Jessica Hoppner	Michigan State University
Wim Janssens	University of Antwerp
Kyung Hoon Kim	Changwon National University
Eunju Ko	Yonsei University
John Kozup	Villanova University
Wei-Na Lee	University of Texas at Austin
Tiger Li	Florida International University
Barbara Mueller	San Diego State University
Shintaro Okazaki	Autonomous University of Madrid
Hye-Jin Paek	University of Georgia
Patrick De Pelsmacker	University of Antwerp
Joseph Phelps	University of Alabama
Manfred Schwaiger	University of Munich

Ralf Terlutter	University of Klagenfurt
Shuhua Zhou	University of Alabama
Shaoming Zou	University of Missouri

PREFACE

This special volume of *Advances in International Marketing* is focused on cross-cultural buyer behavior. Specifically, it explores topics that include the impact of new technology on consumer behavior in a global context; the role emotion plays in reactions to advertising and subsequent buyer behavior; and a timely public policy issue: how prescription drug advertising influences consumer behavior in the countries where it is legal. Moreover, new perspectives of culture's impact on buyer behavior are offered. We are delighted to feature the latest research findings and insights on this topic contributed by authoritative colleagues from around the world. It is guest edited by Professors Charles R. Taylor, Villanova University and Doo-Hee Lee of Korea University Business School.

The idea for devoting a separate volume on foreign intermediaries originated from Professor Taylor. We issued a call for papers, which then attracted a variety of submissions of high quality. We owe gratitude to him for screening and evaluating these submissions, and for preparing the final set of chapters. We are also indebted to many colleagues who assisted in the review process. The resulting selections draw from a variety of perspectives and offer rich insights on foreign intermediaries.

Our thanks go to Professors Taylor and Lee for their efforts in creating this volume. At Michigan State University, I would like to recognize the professional assistance of Kathy Waldie, editorial assistant for the *Advances in International Marketing* series. Kathy carries the responsibility of corresponding with the authors, guest editors, as well as the staff of Elsevier Science at various phases of the publication process. Finally, we express our appreciation to Julie Walker, Philip Tite, Paul Penman, the production team of Macmillan India Ltd., and the other staff at JAI/Elsevier Science who saw the volume through the production process.

S. Tamer Cavusgil
Series Editor

INTRODUCTION: CROSS-CULTURAL ISSUES IN BUYER BEHAVIOR

Charles R. Taylor and Doo-Hee Lee

The theme of this issue of Advances in International Marketing is cross-cultural buyer behavior. In developing the call for papers for this issue, we intentionally defined buyer behavior in a broad sense in order to allow for papers on innovative and cutting edge issues in buyer behavior to be included. Additionally, we made a special point of publicizing the call in various parts of the world in order to ensure multiple perspectives.

Thanks to the efforts of the authors and reviewers, we are pleased that the articles included in this volume live up to these goals. Cutting edge topics including: the impacts of direct-to-consumer (DTC) prescription drug advertising on consumers; emotions in advertising; new perspectives of culture's impact on buyer behavior; and the impact of new technologies on buyer behavior. We received submissions from around the world, and contributions come from scholars who teach in and/or were educated in countries that include Australia, Austria, Belgium, China, the Czech Republic, Denmark, Germany, Japan, Korea, Spain, and the United States. The authors have a wealth of experience in researching cross-cultural issues, and include current and former Presidents of organizations such as the Korea Advertising Society, The European Academy of Advertising, and the American

Cross-Cultural Buyer Behavior
Advances in International Marketing, Volume 18, 1–5
Copyright © 2007 by Elsevier Ltd.
ISSN: 1474-7979/doi:10.1016/S1474-7979(06)18015-1

Academy of Advertising, as well as those who have played leadership roles in other marketing organizations.

Collectively, the articles in this volume are designed to make contributions to both marketing theory and practice. The first section of the volume, which focuses on prescription drug advertising has important public policy implications as well. Today, only two countries, New Zealand and the United States, allow DTC advertising. New Zealand is currently considering a ban, while several other countries are considering beginning to allow DTC advertising (Auton, 2004). As a result, it is important to understand the impact of DTC advertising on consumers. Much of the debate has focused on whether DTC advertising informs or misleads consumers. The first article in this section, by Charles R. Taylor, Michael L. Capella, and John C. Kozup, titled "Does DTC Prescription Drug Advertising Provide Information or Create Market Power: Evidence from the U.S. and New Zealand," provides a comprehensive review of the literature on DTC advertising on the issues of whether it: (a) informs consumers; (b) provides balanced information to consumers; and (c) has an impact on prices.

The second article in the Pharmaceutical Advertising section is authored by Sandra Diehl, Barbara Mueller, and Ralf Terlutter is titled, "Skepticism toward Pharmaceutical Advertising in the U.S. and Germany." The results of a survey that examines the degree to which German and U.S. consumers are skeptical of advertising of both DTC advertising and advertising of over the counter medications are reported. The authors provide a cultural explanation for differences in the degree of skepticism between U.S. and German audiences.

The theme of the second section is how emotions influence consumers in advertising and retailing contexts. The first paper in this section, by Wim Janssens, Patrick De Pelsmacker and Marcel Weverbergh is titled, "The Effect of Mixed Emotions in Advertising: the Moderating Role of Discomfort with Ambiguity." The paper examines how the personality trait of discomfort with ambiguity moderates the processing of mixed emotions. Via the use of two experiments, the authors investigate how exposure to a medium displaying one type of emotion and an ad displaying a different type of emotion impact reactions to ad. The authors find that discomfort with ambiguity does have an impact on consumers reaction to ads or medium/ad contexts in which mixed emotions are present.

The second article in the Emotions section is by Flemming Hansen, Sverre Riis Christensen, Steen Lundsteen, and Larry Percy and is titled, "Emotional Responses – A New Paradigm in Communication Research." The authors assert that advances in neurological research underscore the central role of emotions in most types of human behaviour. In a consumer behaviour context, the authors assert that emotional responses to brands can reveal intangible aspects of brand equity. Based on two studies conducted at different points in time, the authors develop and explicate a procedure for estimating the value of emotional brand equity.

The final article in the Emotions section is "Changing Consumption Values of Middle Class Korean Consumers: An Examination of Factors Associated with Trading Up," by Eunju Ko and Heewon Sung. In this study, the authors examine the "trading up" phenomenon, which refers to customers being willing to pay a price premium for products that are emotionally meaningful to them. The authors use a survey methodology to examine the various factors associated with the trading up phenomenon, including analyses of product categories, brand types, retail formats, and information sources. As with the other two articles in the emotions section, the authors provide evidence that emotions have a substantial impact on buyer behavior.

The articles in the third section examine a longstanding issue in cross-national research: the impact of culture on consumer behavior. Each of the studies in this section, however, provides a new and unique contribution to our understanding of culture's impact on buyer behavior. The first article in this section, by Dae Ryun Chang, "The "We-Me" Culture: Marketing to Korean Consumers," provides a detailed qualitative analysis of a paradoxical issue: how individualism/collectivism affects buyer behavior in a developed East Asian economy. Prior studies have shown an apparent conflict in the types of values (traditional vs. Western) represented in advertising and promotion in these societies. Chang's study provides detailed qualitative insights on how elements of both collectivism and individualism influence the buyer behavior of Koreans.

The second article in the Culture section of the volume by Lu Zheng, Joseph E. Phelps, Yorgo Pasadeos, and Shuhua Zhou is titled, "Do the Little Emperors Rule? Comparing Informativeness and Appeal Types in Chinese vs. America and French Magazine Advertising." The study provides a content analysis of the information content and types of appeals used in magazine advertising in China, France, and the United States. The authors use cultural factors as a basis for predictions and find some results that are inconsistent with expectations, suggesting a need for deeper analyses of the impact of culture on buyer behavior in specific countries.

The third article in the Cultural Factors section, titled "The Drivers of Customer Satisfaction with Industrial Goods – an International Study," by Fabian Festge and Manfred Schwaiger examines how cultural factors impact buyer behavior in the context of industrial markets. Here, the authors report the results of a survey conducted in 12 countries and examine customer satisfaction in industrial markets. Thus, the paper focuses on industrial buyer behavior and provides recommendations for enhancing satisfaction levels across cultures.

The volume's final section examines the impact of new technologies on buyer behavior in a cross-cultural context. While it took the internet a considerable period of time to become a major advertising medium in the developed world, recent trends have made it clear that the internet as well as newer technologies (e.g., SMS, MMS) will be important components of advertising in the future (e.g., Barwise & Farley, 2005; Taylor, 2005). The papers in this section examine current issues such as developing loyalty to online communities, reactions to mobile gaming and banner advertisements, and cross-national differences in website structure.

The first article in the section on New Technologies and Buyer Behavior is by Hee-Sook Yoon and Doo-Hee Lee and is entitled, "The Exposure Effect of Unclicked Banner Advertisements: A Korean Perspective." In reporting the results of a series of experiments in Korea, the authors find that mere exposure (as opposed to just click-through rates) has an impact on information processing. The authors further assert that there is an exposure effect even when an audience cannot specifically recall a banner ad on a website they navigated.

The second article in the New Technology section is authored by Kyung Hoon Kim and Yong Man Jung. It is titled, "Member Loyalty in On-Line Communities: The Relationship between Website Features and Loyalty," and details how on-line communities are used to satisfy various consumer needs. Specifically, the authors focus on what businesses can do to satisfy the needs of consumers via the use of on-line communities. The study reports the results of a major survey done in Korea and concludes that there are mere exposure ads associated with exposure to banner ads and that certain types of evaluation factors are associated with maintaining loyals buyers.

The third article in this section, by Shintaro Okazaki, Radoslav Skapa, and Ildefonso Grande is titled, "Global Youth and Mobile Games: Applying the Extended Technology Acceptance Model in the U.S.A., Japan, Spain, and the Czech Republic." As the title indicated, the authors conduct a four-country survey of the factors associated with mobile game adoption across countries. The authors build on the technology acceptance model and find some variance both some interesting similarities and difference in what drives acceptance in these countries.

In the final paper in this issue, Koo-Won Suh, Charles R. Taylor, and Doo-Hee is titled, "An Empirical Classification of Web Site Structure: A Cross-National Comparison." The study uses a content analysis of more than 350 websites to develop a typology of website structure. Additionally, the study examines whether websites in Australia and Korea vary in terms of their structure, making predictions based on cultural factors and industry types. The authors suggest that cultural factors, as well as types of product sold, help to explain differences in the structure of websites used in the two countries.

There are a few individuals who we must thank for their contribution to this project. First, we thank Tamer Cavusgil for encouraging us to edit an issue on this topic and for his advice along the way. It is Dr. Cavusgil's vision for *Advances in International Marketing* that allows these volumes to contain consistently high-quality work from leading scholars. We also thank Kathy Waldie of Michigan State University for her help in publicizing the Call for Papers. Jessica Hoppner, currently a doctoral student was very helpful to us in helping coordinate the review process and doing some preliminary editing of the paper. Additionally, Lillian Linquata's (Villanova University) assistance is gratefully acknowledged.

We greatly appreciate the efforts of Philip Tite, the production team of Macmillan India Ltd., and the staff at Elsevier in editing the manuscript. Finally, we appreciate the patience of our families as we devoted time to this project.

REFERENCES

Auton, F. (2004). The advertising of pharmaceuticals direct to consumers: A critical review of the literature and debate. *International Journal of Advertising, 23*, 5–52.

Barwise, P., & Farley, J. U. (2005). The state of interactive marketing in seven countries: Interactive marketing comes of age. *Journal of Interactive Marketing, 16*(1), 14–24.

Taylor, C. R. (2005). Moving international advertising research forward: A new research agenda. *Journal of Advertising, 34*(Winter), 7–16.

PART I:
DTC PRESCRIPTION DRUG ADVERTISING AND BUYER BEHAVIOR

DOES DTC ADVERTISING PROVIDE INFORMATION OR CREATE MARKET POWER? EVIDENCE FROM THE U.S. AND NEW ZEALAND

Charles R. Taylor, Michael L. Capella and John C. Kozup

ABSTRACT

The impact of DTC advertising of prescription drugs on consumers has been the subject of considerable debate worldwide. Proponents of DTC advertising argue that it allows patients to make more informed decisions, helps address under-treatment of some medical conditions, and improves the economic value of health care, among other benefits. In contrast, critics of DTC advertising contend that it leads to consumers paying higher prices, patients potentially being misled about risks and benefits of drugs, and patients pressuring doctors to prescribe drugs. The authors examine this debate in the context of two leading

Cross-Cultural Buyer Behavior
Advances in International Marketing, Volume 18, 9–30
Copyright © 2007 by Elsevier Ltd.
All rights of reproduction in any form reserved
ISSN: 1474-7979/doi:10.1016/S1474-7979(06)18001-1

theories on the effects of advertising – the Advertising = Information and Advertising = Market power schools of thought and review empirical studies that have examined the impacts of DTC advertising on consumers. It is found that the research evidence generally favors the Advertising = Information school, which is supportive of the idea that DTC helps patients become more informed and communicate more effectively with their doctors.

INTRODUCTION

Since its inception in the U.S. in the early 1980s, the impacts of direct-to-consumer (DTC) prescription drug advertising on consumers have been a source of controversy (Weissman, Blumenthal, Silk, & Zapert, 2003; Macias & Lewis, 2005). DTC advertising is currently legal in only two OECD countries, the U.S. and New Zealand, though it is being considered in several other countries, including Australia, Canada, the U.K., and other EU countries (Auton, 2004). Prescription drugs are a product category that has a profound impact on public health. Thus, it is particularly important to look at the economic and societal effects of prescription drug advertising.

As noted by Auton (2004), those arguing that DTC advertising is beneficial cite several benefits, including patients making more informed decisions, addressing under-treatment by informing consumers, improving the economic value of health care, improved drug treatment compliance, and improved communication between doctors and patients.

In contrast, critics of DTC advertising (e.g., Toop et al., 2003) assert that it leads to: higher industry profits rather than consumer education; increased drug prices and medical costs; patients asking doctors for drugs they do not need; patients being misled by ads that are unbalanced in disclosing benefits versus risks; pressures doctors and harms their relationship with patients; and funds being diverted from research and development.

Interestingly, this difference of opinion over DTC advertising closely mirrors the historic debate over the economic effects of advertising. As noted by Farris and Albion (1980) in their classic *Journal of Marketing* article, there are two primary schools of thought. One is the "Advertising = Market Power" school, which views advertising as a pervasive force that strongly affects consumer preferences and tastes, encourages people to buy things they do not need, raises prices, and allows large firms to create barriers to entry, thereby increasing industry concentration.

The second school of thought, "Advertising = Information" emphasizes the informative value of advertising. This school argues that advertising informs consumers about product attributes and allows them to make better choices. It also argues that better-informed consumers make better purchase decisions, as opposed to simply purchasing products they do not need. Another tenet of the "Advertising = Information" view is that consumers can compare competitive offerings and new entrants can thrive if they are able to advertise wanted features. Thus, competition is encouraged, and there is downward pressure on pricing as a result of advertising.

The purpose of this paper is to review the literature and summarize evidence related to three major points of debate relative to the impact of DTC advertising. The first of these relates to whether patients are better informed by advertising. The second investigates whether patients are misinformed by lack of balance within prescription drug ads. The final point addressed is the impact of DTC advertising on prices of pharmaceuticals. Thus, our research questions are

(1) Does DTC advertising lead to consumers being more informed about the availability of prescription drugs? Do consumers have more informed interactions with doctors, or does the advertising merely lead patients to request products they do not need?
(2) Do prescription drug ads provide adequate balance in terms of benefits versus risks, or are consumers likely to be misled by such ads?
(3) What is the impact of DTC advertising on prices of prescription drugs?

Our review of the literature will be limited to studies that have collected empirical data on DTC prescription drug advertising in the U.S. and New Zealand, as these are the only two countries in which such advertising is currently legal. The conceptual framework for the study is the differing predictions of the "Advertising = Market Power" vs. "Advertising = Information." We will assess which school's view is supported by the weight of available research evidence.

CONCEPTUAL FRAMEWORK

The debate over the economic impact of advertising has generated debate for many years. The "Advertising = Market Power" and "Advertising = Information" schools provide very different views of the role of advertising's economic and societal effects. The former school emphasizes advertising's impact on firm profitability to the possible detriment of consumers, while the latter suggests that advertising plays a largely positive role. A detailed summary of each school's view is provided below.

Advertising = Market Power

As summarized by Stanley Ornstein (1977, p. 2), the "Advertising = Market Power" is that

> In short, advertising increases industrial concentration, raises barriers to entry, and, therefore, leads to collusion and market power. The result is restricted output, raised prices, inefficient allocation of resources, long-run excess profits of monopolists, and distortion in distribution of wealth.

Adherents to the Market Power view (e.g., Kaldor, 1950; Bain, 1956; Comanor & Wilson, 1974) generally argue that advertising is so powerful that it shifts consumer preferences and tastes. This in turn creates a built-in competitive advantage that firms who advertise less or enter later simply cannot match. Thus, advertising serves as a barrier to entry and increases industry concentration ratios (Taylor, Zou, & Oszomer, 1996). Additionally, the increased brand loyalty bought by advertising makes consumers less price sensitive, and allows firms to charge higher prices. The ability to allow for high prices allows firms to make excessive profits at the expense of the consumer and allows for greater incentive to advertising the product.

Advertising = Information School

The "Advertising = Information" school also has some noted adherents, including Telser (1964) and McAuliffe (1987). This view emphasizes a positive role that advertising plays in giving the consumer information on product features, prices, and quality, thereby enhancing consumer knowledge. The increased knowledge provided by advertising, according to this school, both reduces search costs and forces producers to improve the quality of their products. With respect to industry concentration, the Information school predicts that advertising actually facilitates entry by allowing innovative products or product features to be effectively communicated to consumers (Taylor et al., 1996). By allowing new products to gain rapid acceptance if they have an advantage, firms are allowed to exploit economies of scale and offer lower prices. Thus, advertising's impact on prices is to lower them, according to the Information school.

PREDICTIONS OF THE SCHOOLS FOR THE PHARMACEUTICAL INDUSTRY

Informative Value of DTC Advertising

The Information school would clearly argue that DTC advertising plays a positive role by informing consumers about the benefits of new and existing drugs. In this view, DTC advertising helps consumers to become more knowledgeable about ailments and what treatments are available. It would follow from this logic that better informed consumers communicate more effectively with their doctors, are more prone to understand usage of the pharmaceuticals and, hence, use them more effectively. The improved communications and compliance should, in turn, lead to better health outcomes according to this view.

The Market Power school would emphasize that prescription drug advertising could lead to patients believing that they have an ailment they really do not have, or requesting a drug from their doctor that they really do not need. The idea that consumers might medicalize conditions that are really a natural part of the aging process is also consistent with this view. The Market Power school would also predict that interactions between patients and doctors might worsen due to consumers being overly assertive as a result of exposure to advertising.

Adequate Balance in What the Consumer Takes Away from an Ad

The Information school emphasizes consumer empowerment as a result of communication of product benefits. As a result, it is likely that adherents to the Information school would stress that consumers are capable of appropriately balancing risk and benefit information as provided by advertising. In contrast, the Market Power school emphasizes the empowerment of the company. This, it is likely that believers in the Market Power school would be swayed by the notion that information on benefits and risks in the ad could mislead the consumer in a way that benefits the company, but is potentially harmful to the consumer.

DTC Advertising and Prices

The predictions of the two schools on pricing are both clear and diametrically opposed. The Information school would predict that advertising allows consumers to learn about new pharmaceutical products within a category, and as such increases competition and lowers prices. In contrast, the Market Power school argues that advertising leads large firms to develop entry barriers that prevent new entrants from gaining market share and allows large firms to raise prices. Thus, the Information school would predict that advertising decreases prices, while the Market Power school predicts increased prices.

REVIEW OF THE LITERATURE

Scope and Methodology

This study is designed to provide a comprehensive review of major empirical studies of consumer perceptions of pharmaceutical advertising published in peer reviewed academic journals between 1997 and 2006. Major large-scale surveys that are cited and/or analyzed in the academic studies, including Food and Drug Administration (FDA) surveys and the Prevention magazine poll conducted by Gallup are also included in the analysis. To identify the appropriate studies, the EBSCO, Psychlit, Proquest, and Medline databases were searched.

DTC Advertising and Informing the Consumer

Over the past decade, several studies have examined the impact of DTC prescription drug advertising on consumers. Much of this work has focused on whether DTC advertising helps to better inform consumers, as opposed to having them ask for drugs they do not need. Below, we detail the empirical evidence regarding the impacts of DTC advertising on consumers and doctors, first examining U.S. studies and then studies from New Zealand. This review will be used to assess whether the research evidence is more supportive of the Information or Market Power school.

Evidence from Studies of DTC Advertising in the United States

The issue of the impact of DTC advertising on consumers has drawn widespread attention from regulators and academics alike. For example, the U.S. FDA conducted national telephone surveys in 1999 and 2002 to examine this issue. The results of these studies suggest that DTC advertising acts as a stimulus for consumers to search for more information about their health and the pharmaceutical products being advertised including the risks associated with the use of them (FDA, 1999 and 2002 – see Woodcock, 2003). For example, among those who indicated that a DTC ad had caused them to search for more information in 2002, 61 percent reported they were searching for information about side effects.

The 1999 FDA survey of 1,081 consumers included 960 who had visited a physician in the prior three months. The 2002 sample included 943 respondents who had consulted a physician within the last three months. Results of the survey indicated that approximately 45 percent of respondents in the two surveys said that an advertisement for a prescription drug had led them to seek more information. In addition, 27 percent of the survey respondents in 1999 and 18 percent in 2002 who had seen a physician indicated that the DTC advertising had caused them to discuss a medical condition they had not previously discussed with a physician.

Additionally, in an FDA survey of 500 physicians, a majority indicated that DTC advertising had a positive role in their interactions with patients. Specifically, most agreed that because of exposure to DTC advertising, patients asked more insightful questions. In addition, many physicians believed that the ads made their patients more involved in their health care. At the same time, 8 percent of physicians felt "very pressured" and 20 percent felt "somewhat pressured" to prescribe the specific brand name drug when requested by the patient. In these cases, however, most physicians suggested alternative courses of action such as prescribing a more appropriate drug due to possible side effects and/or a less expensive drug (Woodcock, 2003).

In a study using monthly time-series regression data on DTC advertising for the statin class of cholesterol lowering drugs from 1995 to 2000, Calfee, Winston, and Stempski (2002) estimated the effect of DTC advertising on demand. The authors did not find a statistically significant relationship between the level of DTC advertising and new statin prescriptions. However, the study did find that prescription drug advertising had increased the portion of cholesterol patients who were successfully treated, suggesting that increased information provided was aiding in improved treatment. In general, the authors concluded that there are no adverse effects from DTC advertising, such as unnecessary prescriptions with regard to the cholesterol-reducing drug market.

The findings of a survey conducted by Mintzes et al. (2002) also support the notion of little or no adverse impact of DTC advertising on physician prescribing behavior. Specifically, these authors examined the relationship between DTC advertising and patients' requests for prescriptions as well as the relationship between patients' requests and physician prescribing decisions. The results showed that patients requested prescriptions in 12 percent of surveyed visits. Of these requests, 42 percent were for pharmaceutical drugs advertised to consumers. Nonetheless, physicians prescribed the requested drugs to just 9 percent of patients and the requested advertised drugs to only 4 percent of patients.

In a national telephone survey of 3,000 adults conducted in 2001 and 2002, Weissman et al. (2003) reported that approximately 86 percent of consumers saw or heard a DTC advertisement in the prior year. About 35 percent of all respondents reported being prompted by a prescription drug ad to have a discussion about the advertised drug or other health concern during a physician visit. Of those persons making a physician visit, nearly one in four of these physician visits resulted in patients being given a new diagnosis for a previously untreated condition. Regarding DTC advertising, the authors failed to find large negative consequences for patients and, thus, concluded that there is no widespread adverse effect of prescription drug advertising.

A content analysis of 30 national circulation magazines conducted by Main, Argo, and Huhmann (2004) investigated whether DTC advertising presents consumers with information regarding the prescription drug, the disease it is designed to treat, as well as the drug's risks and benefits. The data came from issues of magazines published in December 1998, 1999, and 2000, resulting in a total of 195 DTC advertisements over that period. The study found that virtually all of the DTC ads did, indeed, contain information about the drug, the disease it is designed to treat, and risks and benefits. In terms of appeal type, the authors also found that the DTC advertisements relied more on emotional appeals than rational appeals.

In the largest sample of its kind, the MARS database tracks over 21,000 adults by means of a 20-page self-administered questionnaire mailed annually to a representative sample of the U.S. population. Results from 2002 and 2003 indicate that 36 and 39 percent, respectively, have made an appointment with a physician as a result of DTC advertising, presumably seeking additional information. In addition, 12 percent of respondents in 2002 and 13 percent in 2003 asked physicians to prescribe specific drugs due to prescription drug advertising (White, Draves, Soong, & Moore, 2004). These findings, as the authors conclude, are consistent with the FDA research previously mentioned that relatively little consumer pressure to prescribe specific drugs is reported by doctors.

As described by Huh and Becker (2005) in summarizing the results of prior studies, the goal of DTC advertisers is to have consumers perform one of the following four tasks: (1) seek more information about the drug; (2) discuss the drug with a physician; (3) discuss the drug with a pharmacist; or (4) communicate with family and friends about the merits of the drug. In the same article, Huh and Becker analyzed an FDA mail survey from 343 respondents and determined that DTC advertising was a strong predictor of seeking drug information, but a rather weak predictor of communication with the doctor. As a result, the authors concluded that, "consumers do not blindly rush to their doctors to get a prescription for the advertised drug but try to find more information from other sources" (p. 463).

In general, the studies that have been conducted on consumer perceptions of prescription drug advertising suggest that the public has favorable perceptions. For example, using data from the aforementioned FDA national telephone survey of 1,081 adults, Herzenstein, Misra, and Posavac (2004) found consumers were favorable toward DTC advertising, particularly when they searched for more information and discussed treatment options with their doctor. These researchers also found that the more favorable a consumer's attitude toward DTC advertising, the more likely the consumer was to search for additional information and to ask a physician about the prescription drug.

A mail survey of 288 mid-western respondents aged 21 or above by Singh and Smith (2005) also found that consumers generally have favorable perceptions of prescription drug advertising. Moreover, the authors found that consumers feel empowered by the enhanced knowledge gained by the information provided in DTC advertising. Finally, because consumers feel empowered by the prescription drug advertising, the authors indicated that there is concern about any governmental attempts to regulate prescription drug advertising.

Recent research indicates that web-based DTC advertising has educational value to consumers as well because of the ability to actively involve the consumer in their own health care management (Macias & Lewis, 2005). Indeed, the Internet offers consumers a significant benefit because of the reduced search costs involved in obtaining relevant information regarding pharmaceutical drugs. For instance, in a comprehensive review of all 90 accessible DTC prescription drug web sites as of March 2001, Macias and Lewis (2005) demonstrated that 43 percent of the web sites included a form to assist patient–doctor communication. Also, 94 percent of the web sites encouraged the patient to discuss the drug with either a doctor or pharmacist.

More recent research by Iizuka and Jin (2005) concluded that the argument that DTC advertising prompts patients to "pressure" the physician to prescribe unnecessary medications is not accurate. The authors examined data covering 151 drug classes over 72 months and found that DTC advertising does encourage more patients to seek treatment without exerting undue pressure on physicians for explicit brand named drugs. Thus, as previous research has suggested, Iizuka and Jin asserted DTC advertising has been successful in prompting patients to discuss their health conditions with physicians without prompting patients to request specific drugs (e.g., Calfee et al., 2002; Iizuka & Jin, 2005; White et al., 2004).

The aforementioned findings are further supported by a 9-year trend survey conducted by the Prevention magazine (Thomaselli, 2006) which suggests that DTC pharmaceutical advertising helps increase disease awareness, educate consumers about treatment options, increase information-seeking behavior, and encourage prescription compliance. Specifically, the national sample of 1,504 U.S. adults conducted March 2 through 19, 2006 indicated that 41 percent of consumers had talked to their doctors after seeing an advertised prescription drug, a 7 percent increase over the prior year. Furthermore, the results show DTC ads are increasing information-seeking behavior, with an 11 percent increase since 2003 in the number of respondents who saw a prescription drug advertisement that prompted them to seek out more information (Thomaselli, 2006).

In a review of the literature, Calfee (2002) suggested that DTC advertisements provide multiple benefits to consumers. For example, one is giving valuable information to consumers, including risk information for prescription drugs. Second, DTC advertising is found to induce patient information-seeking, mainly from physicians. Third, it prompts patients to communicate about conditions not previously discussed. Finally, according to Calfee, DTC advertising may improve patient compliance with drug therapy. This conclusion is not surprising, given the prior content analysis research that suggests consumers have a desire for more information about pharmaceutical products (Kopp & Bang, 2000). As a consequence, some researchers such as Calfee have concluded that DTC advertising satisfies this need for increased medical information on the part of the consumer.

Additional research has concluded that the result of increased DTC advertising has been an improvement in the under-treatment of certain diseases and an increase in drug compliance which have been associated with an overall enhancement of patient health outcomes (e.g., Auton, 2006; Calfee et al., 2002). In general, our review of the U.S. literature provides much stronger evidence in support of the Advertising = Information school of thought. There is consistent and compelling evidence that consumers are better informed about prescription drugs, have favorable attitudes about DTC advertising, and are encouraged to have constructive conversations with their doctors. Meanwhile, in contrast to the predictions of the Advertising = Market Power school, the extant research does not appear to support the argument that large numbers of consumers demand prescription drugs that they do not need or place undue pressure on physicians to prescribe pharmaceuticals that they believe they need.

EVIDENCE FROM NEW ZEALAND

Consistent with the U.S. findings, research from New Zealand suggests that while health care consumers are seeking to become more informed and better educated, there is a lack of empirical evidence to support the assertion that DTC advertising adversely affects consumers or physicians (Hoek & Gendall, 2002). Specifically, Hoek and Gendall (2002) examined the number of complaints by consumers regarding DTC advertising to measure consumers' perceptions and found a relatively small proportion of complaints were lodged against DTC advertising with the Advertising Standards Complaints Board.

Contrary findings are presented by Coney (2002) who investigated two specific examples of DTC advertisements which resulted in complaints by consumer organizations and were upheld by the Advertising Standards Complaints Board. The author concludes that DTC advertising does not provide quality health care information based on the criteria of relevance, accuracy, accessibility and acceptability, and thus does not adequately meet consumers' need for the health information they seek.

In cross-cultural research examining the U.S. and New Zealand, consumers in both countries believe DTC advertising helps them to learn about new drugs and to talk to their doctors about possible treatments, with little apparent negative impact on patient–doctor communications. Specifically, Hoek, Gendall, and Calfee (2004) surveyed 1,024 New Zealand patients and reported very high DTC recall levels of 98 percent and high levels of drug information recall at 80 percent. The biggest differences between consumers in the U.S. (based on FDA data outlined above) and New Zealand were found in the recall of risk information, with U.S. levels at approximately 80 percent and New Zealand levels at less than 30 percent.

Another New Zealand based study examined both physician and consumer responses to DTC advertising and compared results to the U.S.

Specifically, Eagle and Chamberlain (2004), used mail survey results from 262 doctors and 1,310 consumers to ascertain the effects of DTC advertising in New Zealand. The authors found that 73 percent of respondents recalled having been exposed to at least one advertisement for a prescription medicine, similar to U.S. figures. The results indicate that exposure to the DTC advertising did provide an impetus for a small number of patients, 9 percent, to consult with physicians about a medical condition not previously discussed. Another 13 percent of those exposed to DTC advertising consulted with a pharmacist regarding a medical condition not previously discussed with a doctor. Because the percentage of doctors reporting "extreme pressure" to prescribe a specific drug was less than 1 percent, these authors conclude that physicians appear to be under no substantial pressure to prescribe requested medications.

In sum, although not unanimous (see for example, Toop et al., 2003), the majority of research in both markets tend to support the notion that DTC advertising is beneficial to consumers through patient education and awareness as well as consumer empowerment (e.g., Calfee et al., 2002; Hoek & Gendall, 2002; Singh & Smith, 2005; Weissman et al., 2003). Therefore, the weight of the available empirical evidence lends support for the Advertising = Information school of thought with regard to the impact of pharmaceutical advertising in the U.S. and New Zealand.

Consumer Perceptions of Information Balance in DTC Advertising

An important facet of DTC research in the past 20 years has been the testing of information balance between product benefits, risks, and side effects. The qualifier for effective DTC communication has centered on the information in a DTC advertisement being conveyed in a clear and understandable format (DiMatteo & Friedman, 1982). From an information processing perspective, the presentation format of the advertisement could have significant effects on consumer comprehension and memory (Morris, Brinberg, Klimberg, Rivera, & Millstein, 1986). Specifically, balance is a concern, as prior research has shown, consumers are more likely to make suboptimal medical decisions when they have imperfect information on the risks and benefits of alternative options (Viscusi, Magat, & Huber, 1986). According to consumer information processing theory (CIP), consumers do not store input literally in memory, thereby leading to inferences and information modification consistent with existing knowledge and beliefs (Mandler & Johnson, 1977; Shimp & Gresham, 1983).

The FDA lists over 30 regulations for which a violation of any prescription drug may be considered misleading (Code of Federal Regulations, 2000). Of those regulations, the adequate provision of information and the doctrine of fair balance are major considerations. The FDA defines fair balance as "the presentation of true information relating to side effects and contraindications that is comparable in depth and detail with the claims for effectiveness or safety" (FDA, 2004). Further recommendations made to the U.S. Department of Health and Human Services include information specificity, scientific accuracy, objective, legible and useful. Doubts concerning the ability of DTC ads to meet fair balance requirements were cited as the primary reason for the moratorium of broadcast ads prior to 1997 (Calfee, 2002), leading the FDA to pay considerable attention to this issue.

Under the fair balance doctrine, advertisements are examined by the FDA to determine if an unbiased and balanced account of benefits and risks of drug usage are presented (Davis, 2000). The Division of Drug Marketing, Advertising and Communications (a division of FDA) reviews all proposed DTC advertising to ensure compliance with the FDA guidelines (Sheehan, 2003). If the ad is found to violate FDA standards, the agency issues a letter with a description of violations and guidance on correction.

If the FDA finds that an ad does not meet fair balance requirements in its review, it notifies the advertiser, who is given the opportunity to modify the ad. As indicated on the FDA web site, it has become quite common for advertisers to modify and ad for balance in response to an FDA review.

Based on the FDA guidelines, ad content is based on the product label and integrated with audio or both audio and visual elements. Prominence and readability play a major role in fair balance determination. For example, in a print ad context, font size and contrast are important determinants of whether the standards are met (Morris, 2001).

What Makes Disclosures of Risk More Effective in a DTC Context?

The Fair Balance Standard has been examined and scrutinized by academics and regulators for over 20 years. Researchers have experimentally manipulated information presentation formats in an effort to assess effects on consumer comprehension, memory, and retrieval. Independent variables manipulated include risk information amount (Morris, Brinberg, & Plimpton, 1984; Morris, Ruffner, & Klimberg, 1985), specificity (Davis, 2000) and format (Morris, Mazis, & Brinberg, 1989; Wogalter, Smith-Jackson, Mills, & Paine, 2002). Some findings from these studies include specific disclosure is more effective than general. For instance, dual modality messages (e.g., auditory plus visual) resulted in greater awareness of product risks; however, in several instances this greater awareness of product risks came at the expense of awareness of positive benefits.

It has also been recommended that research on format alterations emphasizing risk information should not be overly exaggerated as the consumer may view the product as more dangerous or less efficacious than warranted, thus causing unfair market "side effects" for the marketer (Morris et al., 1985). Additionally, truly balanced risk information may have positive benefits for the marketer, including increased credibility of product information as well as the perceived value of the drug (Morris et al., 1984).

The Federal Trade Commission, taking into account research findings, analyzed the DTC advertising regulations and made several recommendations to the FDA. These included: (1) modifying the brief summary requirement for broadcast ads to direct consumers to more patient friendly sources for information, (2) recommending that the brief summary requirement for print ads be made consistent with the brief summary format for broadcast ads, and (3) finding the fair balance requirement should only prohibit ads that convey a deceptive impression of the risks and benefits from the "overall" presentation of information rather than a "mechanistic" balance between risk and benefit information (FTC, 2003).

EVIDENCE FROM PERCEPTIONS OF EXISTING ADS

Studies of DTC Ads in the U.S.

In terms of the focus of the current study, the main issue of interest with respect to fair balance is the impression that actual DTC ads make on consumers. Survey research has gauged consumers' perceptions of information balance since the DTC guidelines were implemented. For example, an FDA study found that 87 percent of consumers recall viewing information on drug benefits in the last three months while 82 percent recalled viewing information on drug risks or side effects (FDA, 1999). FDA surveys conducted in 2002 also show a balanced representation of product benefits and risks as assessed by consumers. For example, when asked what kind of prescription drug information was in TV ads, 90 percent of respondents reported they saw drug benefits while 90 percent also said they saw drug risks or side effects (FDA, 2002).

A 2003 study of 29 broadcast ads found that risk information received fewer sentences and was conveyed with more difficult words (Day, 2004). In addition, viewers recalled benefits more easily than product risks. Conversely, a study of consumer comprehension of 23 DTC television ads found that the subset of ads contained 30 percent fewer benefit facts per second than risk facts per second (Kaphingst & DeJong, 2004). A follow-up comprehension study utilizing 3 of the 23 DTC ads assessed likelihood of answering objective questions concerning benefit and risk elements of the ads. Subjects reported a lower likelihood of answering risk-related questions correctly than other types of information (Kaphingst & DeJong, 2004).

In assessing whether consumers are receiving balanced information on risks and benefits, it is important to note that the surveys that have asked consumers directly about whether they recall risks and benefits have concluded that both are recalled. While the studies are somewhat mixed on the degree to which the ads appear to be designed to enhance equal comprehension, the "bottom line" appears to be that consumers are taking both risk and benefit information away from DTC ads. In terms of studies regarding specific risk-related questions, it is also important to note that there is considerably more overlap in the reported risks of various pharmaceuticals that are advertised than are the benefits. Thus, the consumer survey results appear to be more supportive of the Advertising = Information school of thought in that the preponderance of the evidence from U.S. studies shows that consumers take away useful information on both benefits and risks.

Studies of DTC Ads in New Zealand

In New Zealand, research supports improvement in the balanced presentation of information. A major difference between the U.S. and New Zealand regulation involves the concept of fair balance. Whereas the U.S. regulatory scheme couples the adequate provision of information along with the fair balance criterion, New Zealand requires the provision of specific information but lacks a fair balance criterion (Hoek & Gendall, 2004). Critics argue that the lack of a fair balance standard in New Zealand has resulted in advertisements that are weighted toward product benefits. A recent survey of New Zealand consumers found that 80 percent of respondents supported more effective risk disclosure in prescription drug advertisements (Hoek & Gendall, 2003).

Format differences between the U.S. and New Zealand illustrate the differences in regulatory standards. While the U.S. has equivalent auditory and visual disclosure mechanisms, New Zealand advertisements typically place the drug's risk profile at the last five seconds of a broadcast in a small font. Research has shown that consumers have difficulty processing the information in this format, leading to a perception that the advertisement is unbalanced (Hoek & Gendall, 2003). Format alterations including inclusion of a voiceover component have been shown to increase risk and side effect information (Anthony, Hoek, & Holdershaw, 2003). In an attempt to allay the concerns of critics, industry groups have tightened self-regulatory codes to provide greater emphasis on the risks and side effects of advertised products. The Researched Medicines Industry in New Zealand requires ads to feature cost, risk, and side effect information prominently in addition to regulating the space requirements for each piece of information.

In summary, the evidence appears to suggest that the U.S. regulatory format has been more effective than the New Zealand format in helping to ensure a balanced disclosure of benefits and risks in disclosures in order to help ensure that consumers get access to appropriate information. Specifically, New Zealand's regulatory system has received some criticism for not having a fair balance requirement, raising concern that market power might increase as consumers may be led to use prescription drugs for which they are not sufficiently familiar with the risks.

DTC Advertising and Prices

Prior studies across industries on the overall effect of advertising on consumer pricing have found seemingly conflicting results. Some research suggests that an increase in advertising leads to an increase in prices paid by consumers because of product differentiation, while other studies suggest an increase in advertising leads to a decrease in prices paid by providing information to consumers and enhancing competition (Kaul & Wittink, 1995).

Although promotional expenditures often account for 20–30 percent of pharmaceutical sales, Rizzo, writing in 1999, observed that evidence examining the competitive effects of DTC advertising on pricing had been limited and inconclusive. This was unfortunate, given the policy-related implications related to the marketing practices of the pharmaceutical industry. The "Advertising = Market Power" school would suggest greater advertising reduces price sensitivity and enables firms to raise prices. Because consumers typically have less generous insurance coverage for prescribed medicines than for other forms of health care, if DTC advertising lowers price sensitivity and raises prices in the industry, a considerable portion of the U.S. and New Zealand population could suffer undesirable consequences. Fortunately, some recent studies have begun to examine the issue of the impact on DTC advertising on prices.

In the context of branded competition, Rizzo (1999) analyzed the demand for antihypertensive drugs in the U.S. from 1988 to 1993. This author found that interactions between price and drug product class are insignificant, although detailing (personal selling directly to doctors) efforts resulted in higher prices for consumers.

In another study, Manning and Keith (2001) examined the National Institute for Health Care Management data from 2001 and found that a rank ordering of brands according to DTC expenditures shows no significant relationship with percentage increases in cost per prescription. Other research exploring advertising expenditures for branded drugs and prescription costs also support the assumption that there is little or no correlation between the level of DTC advertising and price (Masia, 2003).

The empirical evidence collected to date generally supports the hypothesis that price advertising promotes competition in the pharmaceutical industry. Thus, this finding is more supportive of the Advertising = Information school of thought. However, only a limited number of studies have been conducted on this topic, and although no research explicitly supports the implication that DTC leads to higher prices, more research is needed.

DISCUSSION

The literature review presented above suggests that, overall, the Advertising = Information school had received considerably more support from empirical studies conducted on the impact of DTC advertising of pharmaceutical products than has the Advertising = Market Power school. The first research question focused on whether DTC advertising leads consumer to be more informed about the availability of prescription drugs and have more informed interactions with doctors, as opposed to simply asking for drugs they do not really need. The empirical evidence on this topic, from both the U.S. and New Zealand strongly support the Information school. Most notably, DTC advertising provides useful information to consumers, and consumers believe they are better informed about the availability of prescription drugs (e.g., Weissman et al., 2003; Macias & Lewis, 2005; Singh & Smith, 2005; Huh & Becker, 2005). Additionally, consumers are more likely to initiate conversations with physicians and seek out other information about the advertised drugs (FDA, 2002; Herzenstein et al., 2004; Thomaselli, 2006; Weissman et al., 2003; Woodcock, 2003). Coupled with evidence that patients are more likely to discuss medications with their doctors, as opposed to directly asking for a prescription, our findings are consistent with the observation of Carey Silver, Director of Consumer and Advertising Trends for Rodale Publishing who, in reference to the impact of DTC advertising stated, "The net effect is that the doctors are still in charge, but the patient is still knowledgeable. There is also some evidence that DTC improves under-treatment of ailments and improves drug compliance" (Auton, 2006; Calfee et al., 2002).

In addition to some of the evidence of positive impacts of the information provided to consumers, the weight of the evidence appears to support a lack of significant negative impact on consumers. There is evidence doctors do not feel that they frequently face undue pressure to prescribe drugs that patients do not need and, in fact, believe that patients are asking more insightful questions (e.g., Calfee et al., 2002; Mintzes et al., 2002; Woodcock, 2003; White et al., 2004; Thomaselli, 2006). In contrast, the empirical studies are not suggestive of any kind of widespread problem with consumers mis-diagnosing themselves or unduly wasting physicians' time. It is notable that the evidence suggests that the physician's role as the learned intermediary appears to be intact, in that survey evidence demonstrates that the patients continue to rely on the physician's opinion (e.g., Calfee, 2002; Mintzes et al., 2002; Woodcock, 2003; White et al., 2004).

With respect to the second research question, which dealt with whether consumers receive balanced information which allows them to accurately assess benefits and risks, the research evidence also supports the Advertising = Information school. While there have been some concerns expressed about specific formats of presentation and relative comprehension of benefits versus risk, survey evidence from the U.S. has convincingly established that consumers exposed to DTC ads come away with comprehension of both benefits and risks associated with the drugs. Notably, the U.S. regulatory system has been found to be effective in ensuring the provision of balanced information, while New Zealand's system has not. Interestingly, while New Zealand's regulatory system has received criticism for not having a fair balance standard, a recent study of New Zealand consumers found that only 20 percent of the population favored a complete ban on DTCA while the majority favored retention of ads albeit with increased regulation (Hoek & Gendall, 2004).

Regarding the final research question, which examined the impact of DTC advertising on price, the limited evidence that exists leans toward the Advertising = Information school. However, it is clear that more research is needed, as only a limited number of studies on the impact of DTC advertising on prices of prescription drugs have been conducted.

CONCLUSION

This study set out to examine the competing predictions of the Advertising = Information vs. Advertising = Market Power schools of thought in the context of DTC prescription drug advertising. A review of empirical studies conducted to date provides convincing evidence that the benefits of DTC advertising to consumers are consistent with what is predicted by the Information school and are substantial. The evidence indicates that consumers like DTC advertising, are better informed about available drugs, are more likely to initiate conversations with their physicians, and have more effective interaction with physicians. There is also some evidence of improved compliance with drug regimens and improvement in under-treatment of some diseases. Meanwhile, there does not appear to be compelling empirical evidence of potential adverse effects, such as misinformed consumers or consumers putting excessive pressure on doctors to prescribe drugs they do not need.

One interesting outcome of this review is that the fair balance standard associated with FDA regulation of U.S. advertising appears to be quite effective in assuring balance. This standard appears to have made DTC advertising less controversial in the U.S. than it is in New Zealand and is suggestive that such a standard should be considered by countries that are considering introducing DTC advertising. While there are a few studies that dissent in terms of the effectiveness of the risk provision of U.S. DTC ads, on the whole, the evidence that the U.S. public receives balanced information on both the risks and benefits of prescription drugs is compelling.

In the area of advertising's impact on prices, while existing studies support a lack of impact of DTC advertising on prices, more research on this topic is needed. Still, on the whole, the results of this review clearly favor the Information school. Given the strength of the results, it would make sense for more countries to strongly consider legalizing DTC advertising because of the positive benefits it provides to consumers.

REFERENCES

Anthony, J., Hoek, J., & Holdershaw, J. (2003). Brand advertising of prescription medicines: A comparison of communication formats. Paper presented to the Australian and New Zealand marketing academy, University of South Australia.

Auton, F. (2004). The advertising of pharmaceuticals direct to consumers: A critical review of the literature and debate. *International Journal of Advertising, 23*, 5–52.

Auton, F. (2006). Direct-to-consumer advertising (DTCA) of pharmaceuticals: An updated review of the literature and debate since 2003. *Institute of Economic Affairs*, 24–32.

Bain, J. S. (1956). *Barriers to new competition: Their character and consequences in manufacturing industries*. Cambridge, MA: Harvard University Press.

Calfee, J. (2002). Public policy issues in direct-to-consumer advertising of prescription drugs. *Journal of Public Policy and Marketing, 21*(2), 174–193.

Calfee, J., Winston, C., & Stempski, R. (2002). Direct-to-consumer advertising and the demand for cholesterol-reducing drugs. *Journal of Law and Economics, 45*(October), 673–690.

Code of Federal Regulations (2000). *Prescription drug advertising,* 21 CFR Part 202, 72–81.

Comanor, W. S., & Wilson, T. A. (1974). Advertising, market structure and performance. *Review of Economics and Statistics, 49*(November), 423–440.

Coney, S. (2002). Direct-to-consumer advertising of prescription pharmaceuticals: A consumer perspective from New Zealand. *Journal of Public Policy and Marketing, 21*(2), 213–223.

Davis, J. J. (2000). Riskier than we think? The relationship between risk statement completeness and perceptions of direct consumer advertised prescription drugs. *Journal of Health Communication, 5*(4), 349–369.

Day, R. S. (2004). *Cognitive accessibility of drug information: Mandatory medication guides and patient package inserts.* Washington, DC: Agency for Healthcare Quality and Research.

DiMatteo, M., & Friedmen, H. (1982). *Social psychology and medicine.* Cambridge, MA: Oelgeschlager, Gunn and Hain.

Eagle, L., & Chamberlain, K. (2004). Prescription medication advertising: Professional discomfort and potential patient benefits – can the two be balanced? *International Journal of Advertising, 23*, 69–90.

Farris, P. W., & Albion, M. S. (1980). The impact of advertising on the price of consumer products. *Journal of Marketing, 44*(3), 17–35.

Federal Trade Commission (FTC) (2003). *FTC staff provides FDA with comments on direct-to-consumer prescription drug advertising.* Accessed on December 2, at http://www.ftc.gov/opa/2003/12/fdatc.htm

Food and Drug Administration (FDA) (2002). *DTC advertising.* Center for Drug Evaluation and Research, Division of Drug Marketing, Advertising and Communications. Power-point presentation of results from the 2002 consumer survey on attitudes toward direct-to-consumer promotion of prescription drugs, April 10.

Food and Drug Administration (FDA) (2004). *Code of Federal Regulations,* 21 CFR 202.1 (e)(5)(ii).

Herzenstein, M., Misra, S., & Posavac, S. S. (2004). How consumers' attitudes toward direct-to-consumer advertising of prescription drugs influence ad effectiveness, and consumer and physician behavior. *Marketing Letters, 15*(4), 201–212.

Hoek, J., & Gendall, P. (2002). Direct-to-consumer advertising down under: An alternative perspective and regulatory framework. *Journal of Public Policy and Marketing, 21*(2), 202–212.

Hoek J., & Gendall, P. (2003). *Direct to consumer advertising of prescription medicines: A consumer survey.* Department of Marketing Research Report, Massey University: Palmerston North, New Zealand, April.

Hoek, J., & Gendall, P. (2004). Regulation of prescription medicine advertising in the United States and New Zealand: A consumer perspective. *Proceedings of the 2004 WAPOR Conference*, Phoenix, AZ (pp. 1–17).

Hoek, J., Gendall, P., & Calfee, J. (2004). Direct-to-consumer advertising of prescription medicines in the United States and New Zealand: An analysis of regulatory approaches and consumer responses. *International Journal of Advertising, 23*, 197–227.

Huh, J., & Becker, L. B. (2005). Direct-to-consumer prescription drug advertising: Understanding its consequences. *International Journal of Advertising, 24*(4), 441–466.

Iizuka, T., & Jin, G. Z. (2005). The effects of prescription drug advertising on doctor visits. *Journal of Economics and Management Strategy, 14*(3), 701–727.

Kaldor, N. (1950). The economic aspects of advertising. *Review of Economic Studies, 18*, 1–27.

Kaphingst, K., & DeJong, W. (2004). The educational potential of direct-to-consumer prescription drug advertising. *Health Affairs, 23*(4), 143–150.

Kaul, A., & Wittink, D. R. (1995). Empirical generalizations about the impact of advertising on price sensitivity and price. *Marketing Science, 14*(3), 151–160.

Kopp, S. W., & Bang, H. K. (2000). Benefit and risk information in prescription drug advertising: Review of empirical studies and marketing implications. *Health Marketing Quarterly, 17*(3), 39–56.

Macias, W., & Lewis, L. S. (2005). How well do direct-to-consumer (DTC) prescription drug web sites meet FDA guidelines and public policy concerns. *Health Marketing Quarterly, 22*(4), 45–71.

Main, K. J., Argo, J. J., & Huhmann, B. A. (2004). Pharmaceutical advertising in the USA: Information or influence? *International Journal of Advertising, 23*, 119–142.

Mandler, J. M., & Johnson, N. S. (1977). Remembrance of things parsed: Story structure and recall. *Cognitive Psychology, 9*, 111–151.

Manning, R. L., & Keith, A. (2001). The Economics of direct-to-consumer advertising of prescription drugs. *Economic Realities in Health Care, 2*(1), 3–9.

Masia, N. (2003). *Economic impact of DTC advertising.* Available at http://www.fda.gov/cder/ddmac/P4Masia/index.htm (accessed on October 12, 2006).

McAuliffe, R. E. (1987). *Advertising, competition, and public policy: Theories and new evidence.* Lexington, MA: DC Heath and Company.

Mintzes, B., Barer, M. L., Kravitz, R. L., Kazanjian, A., Bassett, K., Lexchin, J., Evans, R. G., Pan, R., & Marion, S. A. (2002). Influence of direct to consumer pharmaceutical advertising and patients' requests on prescribing decisions: Two site cross sectional survey. *British Medical Journal, 324*(7332), 278–279.

Morris, L. A. (2001). Prescription drug disclosures. Powerpoint presentation at the FTC-NAD disclosure workshop, May 22.

Morris, L. A., Brinberg, D., Klimberg, R., Rivera, C., & Millstein, L. G. (1986). Miscomprehension rates for prescription drug advertisements. *Current Issues and Research in Advertising, 9*(1), 93–117.

Morris, L. A., Brinberg, D., & Plimpton, L. (1984). Prescription drug information for consumers: An experiment of source and format. *Current Issues and Research in Advertising, 1*(1), 65–78.

Morris, L. A., Mazis, M. B., & Brinberg, D. (1989). Risk disclosures in televised prescription drug advertising to consumers. *Journal of Public Policy and Marketing, 8*, 64–80.

Morris, L. A., Ruffner, M., & Klimberg, R. (1985). Warning disclosures for prescription drugs. *Journal of Advertising Research, 25*(5), 25–32.

Ornstein, S. I. (1977). *Industrial concentration and advertising intensity.* Washington, DC: American Enterprise Institute.

Rizzo, J. A. (1999). Advertising and competition in the ethical pharmaceutical industry: The case of antihypertensive drugs. *Journal of Law and Economics, 42*(1), 89–116.

Sheehan, K. B. (2003). Balancing acts: An analysis of food and drug administration letters about direct-to-consumer advertising violations. *Journal of Public Policy and Marketing, 22*(2), 159–169.

Shimp, T., & Gresham, L. (1983). An information processing perspective of recent advertising literature. *Current Issues and Research in Advertising, 6*, 39–76.

Singh, T., & Smith, D. (2005). Direct-to-consumer prescription advertising: A study of consumer attitudes and behavioral intentions. *Journal of Consumer Marketing, 22*(7), 369–378.

Taylor, C. R., Zou, S., & Ozsomer, A. (1996). Advertising and its effect on industrial concentration: A contingency perspective. *Journal of Current Issues and Research in Advertising, 18*(Spring), 35–44.

Telser, L. (1964). Advertising and competition. *Journal of Political Economy, 72*(December), 537–562.

Thomaselli, R. (2006). DTC ads prompt consumers to see physicians. *Advertising Age*, May 6.

Toop, L., Richards, D., Dowell, T., Tilyard, M., Fraser, T., & Arroll, B. (2003). *Direct to consumer advertising of prescription drugs in New Zealand: For health or for profit?* Report to the Minister of Health, New Zealand Departments of General Practice, November.

Viscusi, W. K., Magat, W. M., & Huber, J. (1986). Informational regulation of consumer health risks: An empirical evaluation of hazard warnings. *Rand Journal of Economics, 17*, 351–365.

Weissman, J. S., Blumenthal, D., Silk, A. J., & Zapert, K. (2003). Consumers' reports on the health effects of direct-to-consumer drug advertising. *Health Affairs*, (January–June), 82–95.

White, H. J., Draves, L. P., Soong, R., & Moore, C. (2004). Ask your doctor! Measuring the effect of direct-to-consumer communications in the world's largest healthcare market. *International Journal of Advertising, 23*, 53–68.

Wogalter, M. S., Smith-Jackson, T. L., Mills, B. J., & Paine, C. (2002). The effects of print format in direct-to-consumer prescription drug advertisements on risk knowledge and preference. *Drug Information Journal, 36*, 693–705.

Woodcock, J. (2003). *Direct-to-consumer advertising of prescription drugs: Exploring the consequences.* Available at http://www.fda.gov/ola/2003/AdvertisingofPrescriptionDrugs07222.html (accessed on September 28, 2006).

SKEPTICISM TOWARD PHARMACEUTICAL ADVERTISING IN THE U.S. AND GERMANY

Sandra Diehl, Barbara Mueller and Ralf Terlutter

ABSTRACT

The purpose of this investigation is to add to the body of knowledge regarding consumer skepticism toward advertising in general, and toward pharmaceutical advertising in particular. The study was conducted in the U.S. and in Germany. Skepticism toward advertising for both prescription and non-prescription pharmaceuticals was analyzed. Additional variables explored include: health consciousness, product involvement with pharmaceuticals, satisfaction with information in pharmaceutical advertising, and the importance of pharmaceutical advertising as a source of information. Furthermore, differences in the cultural value of uncertainty avoidance between U.S. and German consumers were examined and related to skepticism toward pharmaceutical advertising. Three hundred and forty-one Americans and 447 Germans were surveyed. A significant finding of this research revealed that skepticism toward pharmaceutical advertising is lower than skepticism toward advertising in general. Results also indicated that consumers showed no difference in their level of skepticism toward advertising for prescription versus non-prescription drugs. This is a particularly relevant finding as it relates directly to the ongoing discussion in Europe regarding whether or not to lift the ban on

Cross-Cultural Buyer Behavior
Advances in International Marketing, Volume 18, 31–60
Copyright © 2007 by Elsevier Ltd.
ISSN: 1474-7979/doi:10.1016/S1474-7979(06)18002-3

advertising for prescription drugs. Skepticism toward pharmaceutical advertising was found to be significantly negatively related to involvement with pharmaceuticals, to satisfaction with the informational content of the advertisements, to satisfaction with the comprehensibility of the advertisements, and to the importance placed on advertising as a source of health information. Regarding cultural differences, U.S. consumers appear to be less skeptical toward advertising in general, and toward advertising for prescription and non-prescription drugs in particular, than German consumers. This may be due to the lower degree of uncertainty avoidance in the U.S. Differences between the two countries related to the additional variables examined in the study are addressed as well. Implications for consumer protection policies are discussed, and recommendations for advertisers of pharmaceutical products are provided. The authors provide a cultural explanation for differences in the degree of skepticism between U.S. and German audiences.

STATEMENT OF PURPOSE AND BACKGROUND

Throughout the western world populations are aging. With populations on both sides of the pond graying, demand will continue to grow for a variety of medications – both over the counter (OTC) and prescription. Manufacturers of these drugs are increasingly seeking ways to communicate with consumers around the globe. While advertisements for non-prescription drugs have been directed to consumers in both the U.S. and Europe via various media for several decades, commercial messages promoting prescription drugs are a relative newcomer to the U.S. market and are still in their infancy in Europe.

In the U.S., prior to 1992, prescription drug advertising faced tight constraints regarding how information was to be presented. That year, the American Medical Association, in collaboration with the U.S. Food and Drug Administration (FDA), lifted their constraints on advertising pharmaceuticals to consumers. Advertising spending in the category increased from a mere $46 million to over $162 million within just a year (Miller, 1994). In 1997, the FDA further relaxed the rules related to the promotion of pharmaceutical products. By the end of 2004, direct-to-consumer (DTC) pharmaceutical advertising went over $4 billion (Thomaselli, 2005). As a result, American consumers have been deluged with DTC pharmaceutical ads. Surveys reveal that 85 percent of respondents reported seeing or hearing an ad for prescription drugs in 2002, up from 63 percent in 1997 (Rowl, 2003).

The United States is clearly on the cutting edge of this trend. Until quite recently, European consumers have been protected from, or deprived of (depending on one's point of view) such messages. In Europe, regulations stipulate that companies can disseminate only unbranded information in their promotional initiatives to consumers. The European Council Directive 92/28/EEC "prohibits the advertising to the general public of medicinal products which are on medical prescription only." However, "statements relating to human health or diseases, provided there is no reference, even indirectly, to medicinal products" are permitted. In other words, disease education is currently allowed (Hone & Benson, 2004). Though, it appears that the Internet may ultimately force this issue on the European Council. Thousands of medical sites worldwide are accessible from a European desktop, and many of them include branded prescription products. The number of health chat rooms, virtual pharmacies, and self-diagnosis sites are increasing. According to a recent EU survey, health is one of the most researched areas on the Internet, investigated by almost one in four Europeans (*Brand Strategy*, 2004). This flood of information makes a ban on pharmaceutical advertising for prescription drugs increasingly hard to justify.

In comparison with American consumers, Europeans still have quite limited exposure to pharmaceutical advertisements for prescription drugs. The EU is of particular attraction to pharmaceutical companies, however, as it accounts for a full one-third of global drug sales (Eagle & Kitchen, 2002). It is likely that this pressure will continue to expand DTC marketing efforts. Indeed, pharmaceutical companies have recently begun to conduct consumer-targeted campaigns which comply with current restrictions (Hone & Benson, 2004). It is expected that the European pharmaceutical DTC expenditures will experience rapid growth in the near future, as even EU leaders are arguing that the ban on pharmaceutical advertising should be lifted (*PR Newswire*, 2005a). Major regions for DTC advertising activities are Germany, France, Spain, Italy, the Netherlands, and the United Kingdom (*PR Newswire*, 2005b).

An interesting trend in the pharmaceutical industry, both in the U.S. and abroad, is the switching of drugs from prescription-only status to being sold OTCs of both pharmacies and supermarkets. With sales in 2003 estimated at $17.5 Billion, the U.S. market for OTC drugs is by far the largest in the world (*Health Insurance Week*, 2006). While the U.S. FDA has traditionally been very cautious with regard to reclassification of prescription drugs to OTC status, the rising prices of prescription drugs and pressure by both government and consumers to lower the cost of healthcare has prompted the FDA to consider more such switches. Indeed, the FDA has indicated it intends to increase OTC switches by as much as 50 percent (Monari, 2005). Europe's OTC market grew substantially in the mid-1990s following the implementation of EU legislation, which resulted in a surge of drugs switching from prescription-only status to being sold in pharmacies. While many drugs have switched to being sold in pharmacies, many more have also moved into the general sales list where they are sold by non-prescription retailers (*Brand Strategy*, 2004). As a point of explanation, in Europe, as in the U.S., prescription drugs must be obtained from a pharmacist; many OTC drugs in Europe can only be purchased in pharmacies, however. Drugs on the general sales list, however, can be purchased from retailers, such as supermarkets. As more drugs in both markets make the jump from prescription to OTC, healthcare will increasingly be in the hands of consumers and the boundaries between prescription and non-prescription pharmaceutical advertising will continue to blur.

It is of importance to examine pharmaceutical advertising from an international as well as a national perspective. Regulation of pharmaceutical advertising varies significantly around the globe. Currently, DTC advertising is only allowed in the U.S. and in New Zealand, but is banned in Europe and the rest of the world. A cross-cultural analysis of skepticism toward pharmaceutical advertising in two countries with differing legal regulations is expected to reveal interesting results. As the debate on whether to lift the ban on prescription drug advertising continues in Europe, the U.S.'s experiences with prescription drug advertising may prove valuable in evaluating the arguments of proponents and opponents. Research on attitudes toward pharmaceutical advertising is of significant interest to the pharmaceutical industry as well. Leading manufactures in the pharmaceutical industry are all multinational enterprises. For such firms, knowledge of differences in attitudes toward pharmaceutical advertising in various countries is vital, in order to effectively communicate with consumers worldwide.

While some research has been conducted over the past decade exploring attitudes toward pharmaceutical advertising in the U.S., there is a paucity of such research in the European Union. Virtually no studies have been conducted from a cross-cultural perspective to date. Given cultural differences between Americans and Germans, and given the differing regulatory environments with regard to prescription drug advertising, one might ask whether German consumers perceive and judge promotional communications for pharmaceuticals in the same manner as American consumers and also inquire as to what variables may explain the difference.

When comparing attitudes toward pharmaceutical advertising among consumers from different countries, variations in the perception and evaluation of such messages may well be due to differences in cultural values. While cultural dimensions that may prove useful for advertising purposes are manifold, one cultural dimension that has direct relevance to the discussion of skepticism toward pharmaceutical advertising is uncertainty avoidance (Hofstede, 1980, 2001; House, Hanges, Javidan, Dorfman, & Gupta, 2004). In this study, the cultural dimension of uncertainty avoidance is explored as it relates to skepticism toward pharmaceutical advertising.

LITERATURE REVIEW

Skepticism toward Advertising

Skepticism toward advertising is defined as the tendency to disbelieve advertising claims (Obermiller & Spangenberg, 1998). Obermiller, Spangenberg, and MacLachlan (2005) regard ad skepticism as an individuals' willingness to believe advertising claims. The general construct of skepticism may have several meanings and may consist of several dimensions (Ford, Smith, & Swasy, 1990). A person may be skeptical of the literal truth of an advertising claim, of the motives of the advertisers, of the value that the information has to oneself or to society, or of the appropriateness of advertising toward a specific audience, such as children (Obermiller & Spangenberg, 1998). The definition employed in this study is limited to the consideration of skepticism as a disbelief of ad claims, that is the tendency to regard ad claims as more or less believable. This construct definition separates ad skepticism from more general attitudes toward advertising (Obermiller & Spangenberg, 1998). A person may dislike advertising because the person is skeptical of it; however, a person may also dislike advertising yet believe the ad claim and have little skepticism of the information contained within the ad. Ad skepticism and general attitude toward advertising are conceptually separate (Obermiller & Spangenberg, 1998).

Analyzing a large number of U.S. public opinion polls, Calfee and Ringold (1994) concluded that there is ample empirical evidence to suggest that skepticism toward advertising is widespread among consumers. Roughly two-thirds of American consumers claim that they doubt the truthfulness of advertising. The opinion that advertising attempts to persuade people buy things that they neither need nor want is widespread. In their study on skepticism toward television advertising in the U.S., Boush, Friestad, and Rose (1994) reported relatively high scores of skepticism toward advertising, as well. A study conducted by *IMAS International* (2004) in Germany revealed that roughly two-thirds of all consumers think that there is too much advertising. An investigation by the *GfK* (*Gesellschaft für Konsumforschung, 2003*) in 21 European countries, with 21,178 respondents, revealed that in Germany, about 78 percent of respondents find advertising annoying. Nonetheless, many consumers also believe that advertising provides useful information (Calfee & Ringold, 1994; *GfK*, 2003).

Overall, skepticism toward advertising may be closely related to skepticism toward advertising for a particular product category – such as pharmaceuticals. We hypothesize that high skepticism toward advertising in general is expected to correlate with high skepticism toward commercial messages for pharmaceutical products and vice versa.

Hypothesis 1. Skepticism toward advertising in general and skepticism toward pharmaceutical advertising are positively related.

Given that pharmaceutical advertising targets an individual's health and well-being, one might expect consumers to be particularly cautious regarding pharmaceutical advertising and distrustful of claims made on behalf of such products. Several investigations have, however, indicated that responses to pharmaceutical messages among American consumers are generally not negative. One poll of 1,200 consumers found that 74 percent believe these ads help them become more involved in their own health care while 67 percent say the ads teach them about the risks and benefits of drugs (Steyer, 1999). A 2003 Prevention Magazine survey on consumer reactions to such advertising found that 84 percent of respondents noted that drug ads tell people about new treatments, 83 percent said ads encouraged them to find out more about the condition a drug treats and 80 percent said the ads alert people to symptoms of a condition they might have (*Medical Marketing & Media*, 2003).

Further, recent research by Mueller (2006) has shown, at least in the U.S., that while consumers are significantly less likely to believe advertiser's claims for low-involvement products (such as shampoo), they are significantly more likely to believe claims made on behalf of high-involvement products and, in particular, claims for health-related products. Obermiller et al. (2005) found that involvement with a product tends to mitigate the negative effects of higher skepticism toward advertising.

Consumers may well believe that pharmaceutical advertising faces much stricter regulatory controls than it actually does. Bell, Kravitz, and Wilkes (1999) revealed substantial misconceptions among U.S. consumers regarding governmental regulation of DTC advertising. Though no such regulation exists, 50 percent of the subjects surveyed believed that drug companies must submit copies of all prescription drug ads to the federal government for approval before those ads can be disseminated. Forty-three percent incorrectly believed that only drugs that have been found to be completely safe are allowed to be advertised in the U.S. Twenty one percent erroneously believed that only extremely effective drugs could be advertised, and 22 percent mistakenly believed that the advertising of prescription drugs with serious side effects had already been banned in the U.S. These false beliefs regarding advertising regulation could lead to the perception that pharmaceutical advertising is more strictly controlled than regular advertising. In Germany, all non-prescription pharmaceutical advertisements directed at consumers must include the following statement: "For risks and side effects read the package insert and ask your physician or pharmacist." Such copy has the potential of creating a misconception that all informational claims in such advertisements are scrutinized by governmental bodies (which is not the case). In Germany and in the U.S., overestimation on the part of consumers regarding the degree of regulatory control may increase the believability of, and also reduce the skepticism toward, pharmaceutical advertising. Hence, we hypothesize that skepticism toward pharmaceutical advertising is *lower* than skepticism toward advertising in general.

Hypothesis 2. Subjects are less skeptical of advertising for pharmaceutical advertising than of advertising in general.

In contrast to commercial messages for OTC medications, advertising for prescription drugs typically addresses health issues that are of a more serious nature and therefore may be perceived as more important and more involving by consumers. Consumers may also expect a higher level of governmental oversight of prescription drug advertising than for non-prescription drug advertising. With regard to the level of skepticism toward advertising for non-prescription versus prescription medications, we expect consumers to be less skeptical of commercial messages for prescription drugs than for non-prescription drugs. Hence, we hypothesize:

Hypothesis 3. Subjects are less skeptical of advertising for prescription than for non-prescription pharmaceuticals.

Uncertainty Avoidance and Skepticism toward Pharmaceutical Advertising

When comparing attitudes toward pharmaceutical advertising among consumers from two different countries, differences in perception and evaluation of such messages may be due to discrepancies in cultural values. One cultural dimension that has direct relevance to the discussion of attitudes toward healthcare advertising is uncertainty avoidance. Uncertainty avoidance has been highlighted as an important construct in two different frameworks: Hofstede (1980, 2001) and, more recently, in a typology proposed by House et al. (2004). According to Hofstede (2001), uncertainty avoidance is related to the level of stress in a society in the face of an unknown future. Depending on the level of tolerance of uncertainty, individuals pursue strategies and behaviors to avoid insecurity. According to House et al. (2004), uncertainty avoidance is the extent to which members of a society strive to avoid uncertainty by relying on established social norms, rituals, and bureaucratic practices.

Uncertainty avoidance focuses on the degree to which society does or does not reinforce uncertainty and ambiguity. According to Hofstede, the U.S. culture ranks relatively low in uncertainty avoidance (Uncertainty Avoidance Index (UAI) score = 46). In contrast, a number of European countries rank relatively high on Hofstede's Uncertainty Avoidance Index, including Germany (UAI = 65, *note*: countries range from 8 to 112). Similarly, House et al. (2004), found that Germans score much higher on uncertainty avoidance (country score of societal practices of 5.19), compared with Americans (country score of 4.15, *note*: countries range from 2.88 to 5.37). Hence, both typologies report much lower levels of uncertainty avoidance in the U.S. than in Germany.

People in countries that scored low in uncertainty avoidance are relatively comfortable with ambiguity. Weak uncertainty avoidance cultures believe more in generalities and common sense. Consumers in such cultures more readily accept change and take on greater risks. In terms of health care advertising, consumers in low uncertainty avoidance countries may be more likely to believe commercial messages and rely upon them. Where uncertainty avoidance is high, however, there is a need for rules, regulations, and controls. Formality and structure are central. This often translates into a search for truth and a belief in experts. The implication for communication is that uncertainty reduction requires explicit, logical, and direct information on the part of the communicator. Consumers in high uncertainty avoidance cultures focus on low risk and value safety features.

It is expected that individuals scoring higher on uncertainty avoidance are more likely to doubt the truthfulness of pharmaceutical advertising than lower scoring individuals and are therefore more skeptical of pharmaceutical advertising. As U.S. consumers are expected to score lower on uncertainty avoidance than German consumers, we assume that U.S. consumers will be less skeptical of pharmaceutical advertising than German consumers.

This should prove particularly true for prescription drug advertising, as this category of advertising is currently not allowed in Germany.

Hypothesis 4. U.S. consumers will be less skeptical of pharmaceutical advertising than German consumers.

Health-Related Variables and Skepticism toward Pharmaceutical Advertising

A number of additional variables are deemed worthy of examination as they relate to the development of skepticism toward pharmaceutical advertising. These include the consumer's overall level of health consciousness, the degree of involvement with pharmaceutical products, and the level of satisfaction with information provided in pharmaceutical advertising. Furthermore, the degree of importance of pharmaceutical advertising as a source of health information is included in the analyses.

Health consciousness: Research conducted by Gould (1988) suggests that some consumers may take a more scientific approach to health care and prevention than others. Further, demographics, health status, and health consciousness are partial predictors of that consumer's approach. Gould explored the role of health consciousness and found that individuals who are more health conscious tend to be more evaluative of health claims and information, are more preventative in their outlook, and have somewhat more open attitudes toward unorthodox health care alternatives than do consumers who are generally less health conscious. Gould (1990) tested the relationship between a large number of different health-related behaviors and health consciousness. He revealed that health consciousness and various healthy behaviors were positively related. For instance, health conscious individuals tend to read labels, listen to radio programs dealing with health issues, read more health-related magazines and books, and shop more frequently in health food stores than less health conscious individuals. According to Gould (1990), health conscious consumers perceive these behaviors as means of expanding their health-related knowledge and contributing toward healthy behaviors. These findings suggest that health conscious consumers may well perceive advertisements for pharmaceutical products as a welcome source of information on health issues and may therefore be more accepting of such messages. Hence, we expect that health consciousness and skepticism toward pharmaceutical advertising are negatively related.

Hypothesis 5. Health consciousness and skepticism toward pharmaceutical advertising are negatively related.

Product involvement with pharmaceuticals: The concept of involvement has been addressed in the advertising literature from a variety of perspectives (Zaichkowsky, 1986). Involvement ranges on a continuum from low to high. Low-involvement goods tend to be package goods of a relatively low price, which are purchased frequently by the consumer. Here, consumers require minimal product information. High-involvement goods are those which generally tend to be higher in price, purchased relatively infrequently, and which require extensive information searching by the consumer – for example, automobiles. Pharmaceuticals, in particular, can be considered highly involving because they deal with a consumer's well-being.

Results reported by Mueller (2006) and Obermiller et al. (2005) indicate that a higher level of involvement might have positive effects on responses to advertising for pharmaceutical products. Hence, we hypothesize that a higher degree of involvement with pharmaceuticals and skepticism toward pharmaceutical advertising are negatively related.

Hypothesis 6. Involvement with pharmaceuticals and skepticism toward pharmaceutical advertising are negatively related.

Satisfaction with information in pharmaceutical advertising: "Americans appear to want as much information as they can get when it comes to managing their health care," notes Fariba Zamaniyan, VP and spokesperson, Ipsos-Insight health practice. American consumers increasingly see pharmaceutical ads as a useful source of information. Zamaniyan notes that Americans want advertising because they expect to be informed by any medium that is feasible and easy to understand. In addition to providing disease education, the American public expects drug manufacturers to inform them of the drug discovery process and the availability of treatment alternatives to achieve positive health outcomes and support longevity (*Med Ad News*, 2005). Regardless, a major area of concern relates to the information quality of such messages as well as the potential for consumer confusion. A survey of 1,500 U.S. adults asked what consumers wanted to know from drug advertising. The respondents most often said they wanted ads to clearly state all risks associated with the medicine (84 percent), followed by wanting all the needed information (76 percent) (*Pediatrics*, 1999). However, other surveys revealed that 61 percent of consumers noted that the ads caused confusion about risks and benefits (Steyer, 1999) and 60 percent felt that advertisements for prescription drugs did not provide enough information about risks (Aikin, Swasy, & Braman, 2004). Bell, Wilkes, and Kravitz (2000) found the educational value of U.S. magazine advertisements (published over a 10-year period, 1989–1998, in the U.S.) to be minimal. Sixty-four percent of the advertisements failed to explain how the drug worked, 71 percent made no mention of any other possible treatments, 73 percent did not mention any causes or risk factors of the treated condition, 76 percent made no mention of other helpful activities, such as exercise or diet, and 91 percent did not mention the likelihood of treatment success.

Both, satisfaction with informational content and satisfaction with comprehensibility of the information in the pharmaceutical advertisements are addressed in the literature (e.g., Aikin et al., 2004; Bell et al., 2000). If consumers fail to understand the information provided in pharmaceutical advertisements, this will likely lead to increased skepticism toward pharmaceutical advertising. Similarly, if consumers perceive the informational content in such messages to be insufficient, this will also lead to increased skepticism toward pharmaceutical advertising. A higher level of satisfaction will, however, be negatively related to skepticism toward pharmaceutical advertising. Hence, the following hypotheses are proposed.

Hypothesis 7. Skepticism toward pharmaceutical advertising and satisfaction with the informational content of such ads are negatively related.

Hypothesis 8. Skepticism toward pharmaceutical advertising and satisfaction with the comprehensibility of information provided in such ads are negatively related.

Importance of pharmaceutical advertising as a source of information: Obermiller et al. (2005) reported that skeptical consumers do not rely significantly on advertisements in their decision-making process. They found that advertising skepticism influences a set of responses to advertising, one of which is to bypass advertising all together. In terms of skepticism toward pharmaceutical advertising, the following hypothesis is proposed.

Hypothesis 9. Skepticism toward pharmaceutical advertising is negatively related to the importance placed on advertising as a source for health information in the purchase-making decision process for such products.

RESEARCH DESIGN AND METHODOLOGY

In order to test the above stated hypotheses, a survey in the U.S. and Germany was carried out. A structured questionnaire was developed which

included questions on skepticism toward advertising in general, and skepticism toward pharmaceutical advertising (both for non-prescription and
prescription drug advertising). In addition, the cultural dimension of uncertainty avoidance was measured, as well as health consciousness, product
involvement with pharmaceuticals, satisfaction with information in pharmaceutical advertising, and importance of pharmaceutical advertising as a
source of information. A translation/back-translation procedure was applied in the development of the questionnaires. Bilingual speakers translated
the questionnaires and different bilingual speakers then back-translated the
questionnaires.

A total of 788 respondents in the USA and Germany took part in the
survey (341 Americans and 447 Germans), 55.3 percent of the respondents
were female and 44.7 percent were male. The average age of respondents was
30.4 years. 55.2 percent were non-students and 44.8 percent were university
students. Respondents either completed the questionnaire independently, or
it was administered by a trained interviewer. For the non-student sample,
two German interviewers collected data in Germany and two American
interviewers collected the data in the U.S. All interviewers were female. In
order to ensure comparable interviewing situations in both countries, all
interviewers received extensive training and were provided with a standardized text to employ in approaching subjects. The non-student subjects
were approached on public property, for instance, along public streets, at
the entrance to walking/jogging trails and parks, on public transportation
(trains), as well as in cafes. Interviewers explained to subjects that the investigation dealt with consumer responses to advertising. Subjects were informed that participation was completely voluntary and that all responses
would remain anonymous. The majority of respondents completed the
questionnaire independently, minimizing interviewer influence. The survey took approximately 10 min to complete.

As the questionnaire addressed health-related issues, the health status of
subjects was controlled, using a single item scale "I am in good physical
health." Subjects could answer on a five-point scale ranging from
$5 =$ "strongly agree" to $1 =$ "strongly disagree."

The majority of respondents indicated a good health status. The average
agreement with the statement was 4.08. The majority of respondents either
agreed or strongly agreed that they are in a good physical health (for details
see Table 1). With regard to the U.S. and Germany, there were no significant
differences with regard to health status (Table 2).

In addition, subjects were asked to provide their body height and the
body weight. Based on the height and weight, their body mass index (BMI)

Table 1. Health Status: "I am in Good Physical Health".

	Strongly Agree				Strongly Disagree
Scale value	5	4	3	2	1
Respondents	265	370	116	27	10

Table 2. Mean Value: Health Status.

Variable	U.S.	Germany	F-Value
Health status	4.07	4.09	0.186 (ns)

Note: ns = not significant.

was calculated. The BMI is the most widely used measurement to define those who are overweight or obese. BMI is measured as body weight in kilograms divided by body height in meter square (European definition). According to the *WHO* (*World Health Organization*), a BMI of 18.50–24.99 is recommended. A BMI of under 18.50 is underweight, a BMI of 25.00–29.99 is regarded as overweight, and a BMI higher than 30.00 is regarded as obese (www.euro.who.int). Of the sample, 5 percent were underweight, 67 percent were normal weight, 22 percent were overweight, and 6 percent were obese. With regard to the U.S. and Germany, no significant differences were found with regard to the BMI. The average BMI of the U.S. subjects was 23.45, the average BMI of the German subjects was 23.47 ($F = 0.062$, $p > 0.05$).

The data reveals that respondents in both countries were relatively equal in terms of health status and BMI. Differences in the importance of health-related variables between U.S. and German subjects are therefore not due to differences in the health of the respondents of the two countries.

MEASURES

Skepticism toward advertising in general and skepticism toward pharmaceutical advertising: Obermiller and Spangenberg (1998) developed and validated a 9-item, Likert-type scale to measure the construct of ad skepticism (SKEP), and then demonstrated empirical support for this construct. Skepticism is a basic marketplace belief, which varies across individuals and is related to the consumer's tendency of persuasability. In this investigation the original SKEP scale was employed for the measurement of skepticism toward advertising in general, and adapted for the measurement of skepticism toward pharmaceutical advertising. For instance, subjects were asked to rate the SKEP scale statement "We can depend on getting the truth in most advertising" and the adapted version for the measurement of skepticism toward pharmaceutical advertising, "We can depend on getting the truth from most ads for medications." Subjects were asked to indicate the extent to which they agreed or disagreed with the statements on a five-point scale.

Uncertainty avoidance: Conceptualization of uncertainty avoidance as a cultural dimension was based on the work of Hofstede (1980, 2001) and House et al. (2004). However, as neither the measurement of uncertainty avoidance by Hofstede nor the one by House et al. was deemed appropriate for this investigation, three items were developed with the intention to semantically represent the concept of uncertainty avoidance. The items read (1) "I attempt to avoid taking risks in my life," (2) "I tend to respond to innovation with caution," and (3) "I tend to stick with things that have stood the test of time." Subjects were asked to indicate their agreement with these statements on a five-point scale.

Health consciousness: Health consciousness was measured using the nine-item scale developed by Gould (1988, 1990). Based on his research, Gould (1988) identified four factors relating to health consciousness: overall alertness (HA), self-consciousness (HCSC), involvement (HI) and self-monitoring (HSM) of one's health. Gould noted that it is possible to sum the individual item scores to form an overall health consciousness score. Subjects were asked to indicate the extent to which they agreed or disagreed with statements on a five-point scale (e.g., "I am alert to changes in my health" and "I am very involved with my health").

Involvement with pharmaceuticals: Level of involvement with pharmaceuticals was measured in this investigation via two items (adapted from Obermiller et al., 2005; Laurent & Kapferer, 1985). They were (1) "Medications are an interesting product category to me" and (2) "Medications are a very important product category for me personally." Subjects were asked to indicate their agreement with these statements on a five-point scale.

Satisfaction with information in pharmaceutical advertising: Satisfaction with the information provided in advertising for pharmaceutical products was measured via two questions. The questions asked for satisfaction with the information content of advertisements for medications in general, and for satisfaction with the comprehensibility of the information. The questions read (1) "Overall, how satisfied are you with the informational content of advertisements for medications?" and (2) "In general, how satisfied are you with the comprehensibility of the information in advertisements for medications?" Subjects indicated their level of satisfaction on a five-point scale.

Importance of advertising as a health information source: Various advertising media were explored as sources of information in this investigation: (1) TV –advertising, (2) Print advertising (in newspapers or magazines), and (3) Internet advertising (banner ads or pharmaceutical web sites). Subjects were asked to rate the importance of each information source in their purchase decision process for pharmaceutical product on a five-point scale.

RESULTS

Consumer skepticism toward advertising: Principal component analysis revealed that the nine items measuring consumer skepticism toward advertising by Obermiller and Spangenberg (1998) loaded on one single factor. Likewise, skepticism toward non-prescription drug advertising and skepticism toward prescription drug advertising also both loaded on a single factor. The measures of skepticism toward advertising in general, as well as the measures toward pharmaceutical (non-prescription and prescription) advertising are shown in Tables 3 and 4. The values of Cronbach's α (Cronbach, 1951) were 0.924 (SKEP scale), 0.935 (skepticism toward non-prescription pharmaceutical advertising), and 0.943 (skepticism toward prescription pharmaceutical advertising), demonstrating high internal consistency of the scales.

Hypothesis 1 states that skepticism toward advertising in general and skepticism toward pharmaceutical advertising are positively related. Correlation analyses of skepticism toward advertising in general and skepticism toward advertising for non-prescription pharmaceuticals clearly support Hypothesis 1 ($r^2 = 0.673$, $p < 0.01$). Likewise, the correlation between skepticism toward advertising in general and skepticism toward advertising for prescription pharmaceuticals is significant as well ($r^2 = 0.616$, $p < 0.01$). With regard to the U.S. and Germany, results are similar (Table 5).

Hypothesis 2 states that subjects are less skeptical of advertising for pharmaceutical advertising than of advertising in general. Mean comparisons of the different skepticism scales lend support to Hypothesis 2. The mean value of skepticism toward advertising in general in the joint dataset of U.S. and German subjects is 2.85, whereas the mean value of skepticism toward advertising for non-prescription pharmaceuticals is 2.63 (Tables 3 and 4). The mean difference is significant ($t = 9.826$, $p < 0.01$). The results of the mean comparison of skepticism toward advertising in general and

Table 3. Measurement of Skepticism toward Advertising in General
(SKEP Scale).

	Mean Values		
	Total Sample	U.S.	Germany
We can depend on getting the truth in most advertising (0.788)	3.08	2.83	3.27
Advertising's aim is to inform the consumer (0.685)	2.53	2.56	2.50
I believe advertising is informative (0.770)	2.38	2.14	2.57
Advertising is generally truthful (0.824)	2.92	2.65	3.13
Advertising is a reliable source of information about the quality and performance of products (0.845)	2.94	2.69	3.13
Advertising is truth, well told (0.749)	3.17	3.07	3.24
In general, advertising presents a true picture of the product being advertised (0.837)	2.90	2.78	3.00
I feel I have been accurately informed after viewing most advertisements (0.842)	2.95	2.65	3.18
Most advertising provides consumers with essential information (0.798)	2.67	2.47	2.83
Factor	2.85	2.66	3.00

Note: Mean ratings are based on a five-point scale (5 = strongly agree and 1 = strongly disagree), all items reverse coded. *Higher* values indicate *higher* skepticism. Loadings from factor
are in parentheses.

skepticism toward advertising for prescription pharmaceuticals (mean value
of 2.61) show significant differences as well ($t = 9.076$, $p < 0.01$). Hence,
Hypothesis 2 is supported by the data.

The results are stable in both sub data sets. In the U.S., the mean value of
skepticism toward advertising in general is 2.66, compared to 2.44 toward
non-prescription and 2.41 toward prescription advertising. Both differences
are significant ($t = 6.777$, $p < 0.01$ and $t = 6.371$, $p < 0.01$). In the German
dataset, the mean value of skepticism toward advertising in general is 3.00,
compared to 2.77 toward non-prescription and 2.76 toward prescription
drug advertising. Again, both differences are significant ($t = 7.124$, $p < 0.01$
and $t = 6.503$, $p < 0.01$).

Hypothesis 3 states that subjects are less skeptical of advertising for prescription than for non-prescription pharmaceuticals. However, data revealed that neither of the differences are significant (neither within the entire
data set, within the U.S., nor with German subsets). Hypothesis 3 is not

Table 4. Measurement of Skepticism toward Pharmaceutical Advertising (Non-prescription and Prescription).

	Mean Values					
	Non-prescription			Prescription		
	Sample	U.S.	Germany	Sample	U.S.	Germany
We can depend on getting the truth from most ads for medications (0.800 and 0.802)	2.66	2.50	2.78	2.61	2.43	2.74
The aim of advertising for medications is to inform the consumer (0.716 and 0.748)	2.36	2.24	2.45	2.35	2.22	2.45
I believe advertising for medications is informative (0.796 and 0.812)	2.31	2.04	2.52	2.34	2.07	2.54
Advertising for medications is generally truthful (0.829 and 0.840)	2.55	2.33	2.71	2.50	2.28	2.66
Advertising for medications is a reliable source of information about the quality and performance of the product (0.854 and 0.878)	2.69	2.47	2.86	2.65	2.45	2.81
Advertising for medications is truth, well told (0.778 and 0.810)	2.90	2.77	3.00	2.86	2.68	2.99
In general, advertising for medications presents a true picture of the product being advertised (0.854 and 0.885)	2.72	2.52	2.88	2.70	2.50	2.86
I feel I have been accurately informed after viewing most ads for medications (0.835 and 0.842)	2.78	2.45	3.03	2.79	2.50	3.02
Most ads for medications provide consumers with essential information (0.829 and 0.847)	2.51	2.33	2.65	2.53	2.34	2.67
Factor	2.63	2.44	2.77	2.61	2.41	2.76

Note: Mean ratings are based on a five-point scale (5 = strongly agree and 1 = strongly disagree), all items reverse coded. *Higher* values indicate *higher* skepticism. Loadings from factors are in parentheses.

Table 5. Correlations (r^2) between Skepticism toward Advertising in General (SKEP) and Skepticism toward Advertising for Pharmaceutical Products.

	Skepticism toward Advertising for ...	
	Non-prescription Drugs	Prescription Drugs
Total sample	0.673**	0.616**
U.S.	0.652**	0.611**
Germany	0.660**	0.588**

**$p < 0.01$.

supported by the data. Rather, the results indicate that consumers do not differentiate between prescription and non-prescription drug advertising. One reason might be that consumers do not explicitly think about whether the ads they see are for prescription or non-prescription medications. The reader is also reminded that prescription drug advertising does not yet exist in Germany in the form, and to the extent, to which it exists in the United States.

Uncertainty avoidance: When subjected to an exploratory factor analysis, the three items designed to measure uncertainty avoidance loaded on one single dimension (Table 6). The value α was 0.710.

Based on the work of Hofstede (1980, 2001), and House et al. (2004), it was expected that U.S. subjects would score lower on uncertainty avoidance than German subjects. Table 7 reveals that the U.S. subjects indeed showed a significantly lower level of uncertainty avoidance than German subjects. The mean uncertainty avoidance score for the German sample was 0.113, while the mean score for the U.S. sample was −0.150 ($F = 13.322$, $p < 0.01$, *note*: mean values are factor scores). As expected, U.S. subjects tolerate ambiguity and uncertainty to a higher degree than German subjects.

Hypothesis 4 analyzes differences in skepticism toward pharmaceutical advertising in the two countries. Based on the cultural dimension of uncertainty avoidance, it was hypothesized that U.S. consumers would have a lower level of skepticism toward pharmaceutical advertising than German consumers. The results in Table 4 support Hypothesis 4. The mean values of U.S. consumers are 2.44 (non-prescription) and 2.41 (prescription), versus respective values of 2.77 and 2.76 for the German consumers. The differences are significant ($F = 37.871$, $p < 0.01$, and $F = 32.825$, $p < 0.01$). The same discrepancies are applicable to skepticism toward advertising in general (U.S. mean value 2.66, Germany 3.00, $F = 40.934$, $p < 0.01$; Table 3).

Table 6. Measurement of Uncertainty Avoidance.

	Mean Values	
	U.S.	Germany
I attempt to avoid taking risks in my life (0.763)	2.94	3.36
I tend to respond to innovation with caution (0.844)	2.96	2.92
I tend to stick with things that have stood the test of time (0.781)	3.34	3.62

Note: Mean ratings are based on a five-point scale (5 = strongly agree and 1 = strongly disagree). Loadings from factor are in parentheses.

Table 7. Mean Value: Uncertainty Avoidance.

Variable	U.S.	Germany	*F*-Value
Uncertainty avoidance	−0.150	0.113	13.322**

Note: Values are factor means.
**$p < 0.01$.

Health consciousness: The nine items designed to measure health consciousness, based on the work of Gould (1988), were subjected to principal component analysis. The analysis extracted two basic dimensions of health consciousness (Table 8). Factor one consisted of five items and was labeled "health self-consciousness." This factor also included health involvement. Factor two was comprised of four items and was labeled "health self-monitoring." The α value of the health self-consciousness (HCSC) dimension was 0.797. The value of the health self-monitoring (HSM) dimension was 0.822. In our study, the four factors of health consciousness described in Gould (1988) merged into only two dimensions. Health self-consciousness suggests that individuals are generally aware of their health and are concerned with it. These individuals can be said to be highly involved with their health. Yet, this dimension should be seen as more of a basic attitude toward health, rather than a pre-occupation with health issues. In contrast, health self-monitoring refers to individuals who are actively involved in examining their health throughout the course of the day. They constantly monitor changes in their health status and their health is generally always on their mind.

Hypothesis 5 states that health consciousness and skepticism toward advertising for pharmaceutical products are negatively associated. Principal component analysis has shown that subjects perceived two distinct dimensions of health consciousness, (1) health self-consciousness and (2) health

Table 8.   Measurement of Health Consciousness.

	Factor Loadings		Mean Values	
	HCSC	HSM	U.S.	Germany
Health self-consciousness (HCSC)				
I am very self-conscious about my health	0.84	0.03	3.60	3.78
I am very involved with my health	0.71	0.22	3.60	3.98
I am generally attentive to my inner feelings about my health	0.66	0.38	3.66	3.57
I reflect about my health a lot	0.58	0.44	3.74	3.25
I am usually aware of my health	0.56	0.46	4.01	3.77
Health self-monitoring (HSM)				
I notice how I feel physically as I go through the day	0.10	0.88	4.07	3.08
I am aware of the state of my health as I go through the day	0.22	0.83	3.66	3.12
I am constantly examining my health	0.46	0.62	3.28	2.61
I am alert to changes in my health	0.50	0.59	3.96	3.57

Note: Mean ratings are based on a five-point scale (5 = strongly agree and 1 = strongly disagree).

self-monitoring (Table 8). Tables 9 and 10 present the results of correlation analyses carried out for the different variables.

Results presented in Tables 9 and 10 indicate moderate negative correlations between skepticism toward advertising for pharmaceutical products and health self-monitoring. This is only applicable to the German data subset, lending some support for Hypothesis 5; however, no significant correlations were found between health self-consciousness and skepticism toward advertising for pharmaceutical products. It appears that the variable of health self-consciousness has no close relationship to the level of skepticism toward pharmaceutical advertising. While health self-consciousness can result in a healthy lifestyle (e.g., sports, activities, no alcohol), it is not necessarily correlated with either a positive or negative attitude to pharmaceutical advertising. That health self-monitoring is significantly negatively correlated with skepticism toward pharmaceutical in Germany, but not in the U.S., is rather difficult to interpret. Overall, Hypothesis 5 is not supported by the data.

The data revealed that the U.S. subjects are significantly less self-conscious regarding their health than the German subjects (mean in the U.S. -0.205, in Germany 0.157, $F = 26.145$, $p < 0.01$). Health self-monitoring,

Table 9. Correlations (r^2) between Health Self-Consciousness and Skepticism toward Advertising for Pharmaceutical Products.

	Skepticism toward Advertising for ...	
	Non-prescription Drugs	Prescription Drugs
Total sample	0.016	0.056
U.S.	−0.100	−0.023
Germany	0.038	0.056

Note: All correlations not significant.

Table 10. Correlations (r^2) between Health Self-Monitoring and Skepticism toward Advertising for Pharmaceutical Products.

	Skepticism toward Advertising for ...	
	Non-prescription Drugs	Prescription Drugs
Total sample	−0.197**	−0.153**
U.S.	0.062	0.100
Germany	−0.214**	−0.166**

**$p < 0.01$.

however, is significantly higher among the U.S. consumers than among the German consumers (U.S. 0.553, Germany −0.422, $F = 239.755$, $p < 0.01$) (Table 11). This suggests that while Germans may be more involved in their health in general sense, Americans may be more actively concerned with the status of their health on a daily basis.

Involvement with pharmaceuticals: Principal component analysis revealed that the two items related to involvement with pharmaceuticals loaded on one single factor (Table 12). The underlying dimension of product involvement indicates the general importance of medications to the individual. The dimension is labeled involvement with pharmaceuticals. The value α for the involvement with pharmaceuticals is 0.847.

Hypothesis 6 analyzes the relationship between level of involvement with pharmaceuticals and skepticism toward pharmaceutical advertising. It stated that the variables are negatively correlated. It was hypothesized that high involvement with pharmaceuticals related to lower skepticism toward advertising for pharmaceutical products. Results of correlation analysis indicate moderate negative yet significant associations between involvement with pharmaceuticals and skepticism toward pharmaceutical advertising,

Table 11. Mean Value: Health Consciousness.

Variable	U.S.	Germany	F-Value
Health self-consciousness	−0.205	0.157	26.145**
Health self-monitoring	0.553	−0.422	239.755**

Note: Values are factor means.
**$p<0.01$.

Table 12. Measurement of Involvement with Pharmaceuticals.

	Mean Values	
	U.S.	Germany
Medications are an interesting product category to me (0.93)	2.81	2.12
Medications are a very important product category for me personally (0.93)	2.58	1.97

Note: Mean ratings are based on a five-point-scale (5 = strongly agree and 1 = strongly disagree). Loadings from factor are in parentheses.

based on the entire dataset, as well as on the U.S. and on the German subsets (Table 13). Hence, the data supports Hypothesis 6.

Compared with health self-consciousness (which included overall health involvement), involvement with pharmaceuticals as a product category is more closely correlated to skepticism toward pharmaceutical advertising. Consequently, product specific levels of involvement have more diagnostic and prognostic relevance for advertising purposes.

The level of involvement with pharmaceuticals is significantly higher in the U.S. than in Germany (Table 14). The finding that U.S. consumers have a higher level of involvement with pharmaceuticals is validated by their subjective perception that they consume drugs significantly more often than German consumers. Based on the question, "in a typical year, how often do you use OTC medications/prescription medications" (five-point scale with 1 = very seldom and 5 = very often), U.S. consumers used both categories significantly more often than German consumers. The mean value of U.S. subjects with regard to OTC medications was 3.06 versus 2.44 for Germans ($F = 49.372$, $p<0.01$). The mean value of U.S. subject with regard to prescription medications was 3.38 versus 2.11 for Germans ($F = 179.721$, $p<0.01$).

Table 13. Correlations (r^2) between Involvement for Pharmaceuticals and Skepticism toward Advertising for Pharmaceutical Products.

	Skepticism toward Advertising for ...	
	Non-prescription Drugs	Prescription Drugs
Total sample	−0.224**	−0.181**
U.S.	−0.196**	−0.179**
Germany	−0.157**	−0.095*

*p<0.05.
**p<0.01.

Table 14. Mean Value: Involvement for Pharmaceuticals.

	U.S.	Germany	*F*-Value
Involvement for pharmaceuticals	0.324	−0.248	68.339**

Note: Values are factor means.
**p<0.01.

Satisfaction with information in pharmaceutical advertising: Both satisfaction with informational content and satisfaction with comprehensibility of the information in the pharmaceutical advertisement are addressed in the literature (e.g., Aikin et al., 2004; Bell et al., 2000). They were treated separately and not factor analyzed. The mean value of satisfaction with informational content in the U.S. was 2.68, while the mean value in Germany was 2.40 ($F = 19.650$, $p<0.01$). The mean value of satisfaction with the comprehensibility of the information in pharmaceutical advertising in the U.S. was 2.83 and in Germany it was 3.04 ($F = 8.649$, $p<0.01$). Whereas satisfaction with the informational content is higher in the U.S. than in Germany, satisfaction with the comprehensibility is lower in the U.S. than in Germany. One possible explanation might be that more information is provided in pharmaceutical advertising in the U.S. than in Germany. Therefore, U.S. consumers may report greater levels of satisfaction with the information content. However, it is difficult to convey complex medical information in a comprehensible manner in an advertisement. As a result, there may be a trade off between the number of information cues contained in an ad, and the comprehensibility of the information. It could well be that with greater information, the likelihood that consumers become confused increases. There is also a higher probability that technical terminology used in pharmaceutical messages is not comprehensible to the average consumer. Satisfaction with the level of informational content in pharmaceutical ads was lower than the level of satisfaction with the comprehensibility of such information.

Hypothesis 7 states that skepticism toward pharmaceutical advertising and satisfaction with the informational content of the ads are negatively associated. Correlation analyses revealed that the data strongly support Hypothesis 7, for all data sets (Table 15).

Hypothesis 8 states that skepticism toward pharmaceutical advertising and satisfaction with the comprehensibility of information provided in the ads are negatively associated. Again, this hypothesis is supported in all datasets (Table 16).

Importance of advertising in the decision-making process for medications: Principal component analysis revealed that the three items designed to

Table 15. Correlations (r^2) between Satisfaction with the Informational Content of the Ads and Skepticism toward Advertising for Pharmaceutical Products.

	Skepticism toward Advertising for ...	
	Non-prescription Drugs	Prescription Drugs
Total sample	-0.580^{**}	-0.577^{**}
U.S.	-0.553^{**}	-0.578^{**}
Germany	-0.577^{**}	-0.553^{**}

$^{**}p<0.01.$

Table 16. Correlations (r^2) between Satisfaction with the Comprehensibility of Information Given in the Ads and Skepticism toward Advertising for Pharmaceutical Products.

	Skepticism toward Advertising for ...	
	Non-prescription Drugs	Prescription Drugs
Total sample	-0.315^{**}	-0.320^{**}
U.S.	-0.454^{*}	-0.463^{**}
Germany	-0.276^{**}	-0.274^{**}

$^{*}p<0.05.$
$^{**}p<0.01.$

Table 17. Measurement of Importance of Advertising in the Decision-Making Process for Medications.

	Mean Values	
	U.S.	Germany
TV advertising (0.89)	2.08	1.67
Print advertising (in newspapers or magazines) (0.90)	2.24	1.72
Internet advertising (banner ads or pharmaceutical web sites) (0.82)	1.91	1.43

Note: Mean ratings are based on a five-point scale (5 = very important and 1 = not at all important). Loadings from factor are in parentheses.

Table 18. Correlations (r^2) between Importance Placed on Advertising as a Source of Health Information and Skepticism toward Advertising for Pharmaceutical Products.

	Skepticism toward Advertising for …	
	Non-prescription Drugs	Prescription Drugs
Total sample	−0.409**	−0.410**
U.S.	−0.334*	−0.336**
Germany	−0.413**	−0.419**

*p < 0.05.
**p < 0.01.

measure the importance of the advertising medium in the decision-making process for medications loaded on one single factor (Table 17). The α value for the importance of advertising in decision process of medications is 0.841. The mean values indicate that consumers in the U.S. place more importance on advertising in the decision-making process for medications than German consumers.

Hypothesis 9 states that skepticism toward pharmaceutical advertising relates negatively to the importance placed on advertising as a source for health information. Correlation analyses support Hypothesis 9 in the dataset as a whole, as well as in the U.S. and German datasets (Table 18).

DISCUSSION

The results of this investigation add to the body of research in both the marketing of health care products and international advertising.

Skepticism toward pharmaceutical advertising: Overall skepticism toward advertising, and skepticism toward pharmaceutical advertising in particular, was found to be positively related. Furthermore, and more importantly, results indicate that skepticism toward pharmaceutical advertising is lower than skepticism toward advertising in general. There are several possible rationales for this finding. First, pharmaceuticals are typically more highly involving products for consumers as they directly relate to personal health and well-being. Pharmaceutical advertising is also an additional source of information and serves consumers' need for health-related data. Second, consumers expect stronger governmental regulations in the area of pharmaceutical advertising and thus anticipate a higher degree of accuracy in the informational claims made in these advertisements. This misconception regarding the level of governmental oversight likely leads to lower levels of skepticism toward pharmaceutical advertising, compared to advertising in general. Third, pharmaceutical advertisements generally contain a good deal more technical information than general advertisements, thus proving more informative to the audience. Even if an individual did not read all the information in a specific advertisement, he or she would likely note that additional information was available. The typically higher level of information in pharmaceutical advertising likely lowers the level of skepticism toward pharmaceutical advertising.

The fact that consumer skepticism toward pharmaceutical advertising is lower than it is toward advertising in general suggests that such advertising has some form of built-in "trust factor" – an important finding with policy implications. Lower skepticism toward pharmaceutical advertising most likely leads to higher persuasibility of these advertisements. Does this suggest a call for stricter governmental regulation of pharmaceutical advertising?

On the one hand, one can argue that stricter regulations are mandatory in order to protect consumers. On the other hand, existing governmental regulations may also be the primary source of consumers' confidence in oversight of the area. While consumers recognize that governmental guidelines exist, they overestimate the level of protection provided in the area of pharmaceutical advertising. If governmental regulation of pharmaceutical advertising were instead *loosened*, and if the consumers were made aware of this, they might, in fact, become *more* skeptical of pharmaceutical advertising. Consumers may begin to question the informational claims made in such messages to a greater extent than they do today. At the very least, consumers should be informed that governmental regulations in the area of pharmaceutical advertising are less stringent than consumers believe them to be.

Another important result of this investigation is that consumers showed no difference in their level of skepticism toward advertising for non-prescription drugs and for prescription drugs. One explanation might be that consumers may not know whether an advertised product or brand is a prescription or non-prescription drug. Often, this information is not immediately recognizable to the audience of such messages. Additionally, many pharmaceuticals shift from prescription status to non-prescription status, potentially further confusing the consumer. In Germany, where DTC advertising for prescription drugs is not yet allowed in the form, and to the extent to which it is employed in the U.S., there might be a methodological explanation as well. German subjects may have had difficulty in hypothetically evaluating their level of skepticism toward commercial messages for prescription drugs and, therefore, were not able to differentiate between advertising for prescription and non-prescription drugs. Clearly, this methodological explanation is less relevant when one considers that in the U.S., where prescription drug advertising is allowed, subjects still did not differentiate between prescription and non-prescription advertising.

The finding that neither Germans nor Americans showed significant differences in their level of skepticism toward advertising for prescription versus non-prescription pharmaceuticals leads to the assumption that consumers do not differentiate between the two types of pharmaceutical advertising. This is especially interesting as advertising for prescription drugs is allowed in the U.S., whereas it is currently not allowed in Germany. From a consumers' perspective, the discussion of whether to treat prescription drug advertising differently from non-prescription drug advertising (in particular, the discussion of whether to maintain or to loosen the ban on prescription drug advertising in Europe) seems to be of little relevance. Consumers likely do not mind being confronted with prescription drug advertising, as the results from the U.S. indicate. This interpretation is based only on the results of this investigation as it relates to the variable of skepticism toward pharmaceutical advertising. Other considerations in the decision whether to loosen or maintain the ban play an important role as well, but are not addressed here.

Health-related variables and skepticism toward pharmaceutical advertising: Variables in this investigation with a significant negative relationship to skepticism toward pharmaceutical advertising include involvement with pharmaceuticals, satisfaction with the informational content and with the comprehensibility of the advertisements, and importance placed on advertising as a source of health information. No relationship was found for the health consciousness variable, except with regard to health self-monitoring among German subjects. Satisfaction with the informational content and with the comprehensibility of the information showed strong correlations with skepticism toward pharmaceutical advertising. By pre-testing the comprehensibility of messages, as well as the level of satisfaction with an advertisements' informational content, advertisers can effectively reduce skepticism toward pharmaceutical advertisements.

Cultural differences between the U.S. and Germany: U.S. consumers are less skeptical toward advertising in general and toward advertising for prescription and non-prescription drugs than German consumers. They also place a higher importance on advertising as a source for health information. As discussed above, this might be due to differences in the cultural value of uncertainty avoidance. U.S. consumers score lower on uncertainty avoidance, whereas Germans score higher. Given the fact that they are less skeptical toward advertising for pharmaceutical products, it is plausible that U.S. consumers attribute significantly more importance to advertising in their decision-making process regarding medications than Germans. Germans, however, may prefer information from sources other than advertising, which are perceived to be more neutral.

Germans tend to be more health self-conscious and to have a higher general level of health involvement. Americans are more involved with health self-monitoring, suggesting that they are more involved with their health throughout the course of the day. This finding has implications for advertising design. In Germany, it may be of greater importance to demonstrate that the advertised product supports a healthy lifestyle, whereas in the U.S. it may be more relevant to show that pharmaceutical products help the individual throughout the course of the day. For example, in the U.S., a headache remedy could be positioned as helping to cope with the various situations throughout the day, such as loads of work in the morning, meetings in the afternoon, or dinner with friends in the evening. Despite this, the health consciousness variable (health self-consciousness and health self-monitoring) turned out to be less important overall than the variable of involvement with pharmaceuticals in terms of skepticism toward pharmaceutical advertising.

U.S. consumers show a significantly higher level of involvement with pharmaceuticals than German consumers. This may be one reason for their lower level of skepticism toward pharmaceutical advertising, as skepticism and involvement are negatively correlated. The finding that U.S. consumers have a higher level of involvement for pharmaceuticals is supported by their subjective perception that they take pharmaceuticals significantly more often than German consumers. In addition, the higher degree of privatization of the health care system in the U.S., when compared with Germany, may also contribute to the higher involvement with pharmaceuticals for U.S. consumers.

The above findings can prove useful to pharmaceutical advertisers in lowering the degree of skepticism toward advertising for pharmaceutical products among audiences in diverse markets. Further research is necessary to determine whether the significant differences in skepticism toward pharmaceutical advertising, as well as variations in health-related variables between Americans and Germans, would require that manufacturers of pharmaceutical products tailor their advertisements based on nationality rather than communicating with consumers in a standardized fashion. Additionally, results of this and of other investigations may well determine whether regulatory bodies around the globe will turn back the clock on pharmaceutical advertising or loosen restrictions even further.

REFERENCES

Aikin, J. K., Swasy, J. L., & Braman, A. C. (2004). *Patient and physician attitudes and behaviors associated with DTC promotion of prescription drugs – summary of FDA survey research results.* U.S. Department of Health and Human Services, Food and Drug Administration, Center for Drug Evaluation and Research, Final Report November 19.

Bell, R. A., Kravitz, R. L., & Wilkes, M. S. (1999). Direct-to-consumer prescription drug advertising and the public. *Journal of General Internal Medicine, 14,* 651–657.

Bell, R. A., Wilkes, M. S., & Kravitz, R. L. (2000). The educational value of consumer targeted prescription drug print advertising. *Journal of Family Practice, 49*(12), 1092–1098.

Boush, D. M., Friestad, M., & Rose, G. M. (1994). Adolescent skepticism toward TV advertising and knowledge of advertiser tactics. *Journal of Consumer Research, 21,* 165–175.

Brand Strategy (2004). Design for self diagnosis. London, June, p. 24.

Calfee, J. E., & Ringold, D. J. (1994). The seventy percent majority – enduring consumer beliefs about advertising. *Journal of Public Policy and Marketing, 13,* 228–238.

Cronbach, L. J. (1951). Coefficient alpha and the internal structure of tests. *Psychometrika, 16*(3), 297–334.

Eagle, L., & Kitchen, P. (2002). Direct consumer promotion of prescription drugs: A review of the literature and the New Zealand experience. *International Journal of Medical Marketing, 2*(4), 293.

Ford, G. T., Smith, D. B., & Swasy, L. J. (1990). Consumer skepticism of advertising claims – testing hypotheses from economics of information. *Journal of Consumer Research, 16,* 433–441.

GfK (Gesellschaft für Konsumforschung) (2003). Einstellung zur Werbung in Europa, www.gfk.de

Gould, S. J. (1988). Consumer attitudes toward health and health care: A differential perspective. *Journal of Consumer Affairs, 22*(1), 96–118.

Gould, S. J. (1990). Health consciousness and health behavior: The application of a new health consciousness scale. *American Journal of Preventive Medicine, 6*(4), 228–237.

Health Insurance Week (2006). *Research and markets; U.S. has the largest over-the-counter drug market in the world, according to new report.* March 5, 98.

Hofstede, G. (1980, 2001). *Culture's consequences: International differences in work-related values* (1st and 2nd eds). Beverly Hills, CA: Sage.

Hone, F., & Benson, R. (2004). DTC: European style. *Pharmaceutical Executive, Eugene, 24*(3), 96.

House, R. J., Hanges, P. J., Javidan, M., Dorfman, P. W., & Gupta, V. (2004). *Culture, leadership and organizations: The globe study of 62 societies.* Beverly Hills, CA: Sage.

IMAS International (2004). *Werbeakzeptanz.* Juli 2004, www.imas-international.de

Laurent, G., & Kapferer, J.-N. (1985). Measuring consumer involvement profiles. *Journal of Marketing Research, 22,* 41–53.

Med Ad News (2005). *The new face of consumer advertising* (Vol. 24(6), p. 1). London, June.

Medical Marketing and Media (2003). *Damned if it works, damned if it doesn't* (Vol. 38(4), p. 38). April.

Miller, C. (1994). Drug firms boost pitch directly to consumers. *Marketing News,* November 21, p. 1.

Monari, G.-L. (2005). Proceed with caution. *Med Ad News* (Vol. 24(3), p. 4). London, March.

Mueller, B. (2006). The role of product involvement in advertising message perception and believability. In: S. Diehl & R. Terlutter (Eds), *International advertising and communication: New insights and empirical findings* (pp. 3–22). Wiesbaden, Germany: Gabler.

Obermiller, C., & Spangenberg, E. (1998). Development of a scale to measure consumer skepticism toward advertising. *Journal of Consumer Psychology, 7*(2), 159–186.

Obermiller, C., Spangenberg, E., & MacLachlan, D. (2005). Ad skepticism. *Journal of Advertising, 34*(3), 7–17.

Pediatrics (1999). *Prescription drug ads in magazines and on television* (Vol. 104 (1), p. 99). July.

PR Newswire (2005a). *EU leaders argue ban on pharmaceutical advertising should be lifted.* New York, February 2.

PR Newswire (2005b). *Frost & Sullivan: Pharmaceutical direct-to-consumer to evolve holistically.* New York, August 15.

Rowl, C. (2003). Drug ads deliver a few side effects; firms reap rewards. *Boston Globe,* June 12.

Steyer, R. (1999). Do drug ads educate or mislead consumers. *St. Lewis Post-Dispatch,* June 20, p. A-9.

Thomaselli, R. (2005). Pharmaceutical industry issues DTC guidelines. *AdAge.com,* August 2, www.adage.com/news.cms?newsID = 45698

Zaichkowsky, J. L. (1986). Conceptualizing involvement. *Journal of Advertising, 15,* 4–14.

PART II:
EMOTIONS AND THEIR IMPACT
ON CONSUMERS

THE EFFECT OF MIXED EMOTIONS IN ADVERTISING: THE MODERATING ROLE OF DISCOMFORT WITH AMBIGUITY

Wim Janssens, Patrick De Pelsmacker and
Marcel Weverbergh

ABSTRACT

The purpose of this research is to study the moderating role of the personality trait Discomfort With Ambiguity (DWA) on the processing of mixed emotions in advertising. Two experiments were conducted. In the first experiment, the emotions between the medium context and the embedded advertisement were mixed. In the second experiment, the emotions in an advertisement were mixed by manipulating emotions in the text and picture. Results indicate that DWA, being a proxy for how well people are able to deal with mixed emotions, has a moderating effect on advertising processing. Individuals having a high DWA appear to respond less positively to mixed emotions.

Cross-Cultural Buyer Behavior
Advances in International Marketing, Volume 18, 63–92
Copyright © 2007 by Elsevier Ltd.
ISSN: 1474-7979/doi:10.1016/S1474-7979(06)18003-5

INTRODUCTION

Research into the effect of emotional appeals in advertising is substantial (e.g., Aaker & Williams, 1998; Burke & Edell, 1986; Edell & Burke, 1987; Holbrook & Batra, 1987). However, as indicated by Williams and Aaker (2002), little research exists on the effect of the use of mixed emotions in persuasion appeals in a consumer behavior context. A typical example of this type of persuasion appeal are fear appeals with a recommendation. For example, a TV advertisement in which a widow and children are shown grieving over the loss of their husband and father, also simultaneously expressing a sense of comfort and security thanks to the deceased's life insurance policy (actual advertisement, ca. 2001 as described in Williams & Aaker, 2002).

The term 'simultaneous emotions' must be used with care. As Plutchick (1980) notices, it may be impossible to experience two bipolar (opposite) emotions at exactly the same time. Moreover, Lazarus (1991) and Ortony, Clore, and Collins (1988) argue that emotions are presumably tied to different cognitive appraisals of a situation. Because these cognitive appraisals cannot be experienced simultaneously, the emotions they elicit cannot be experienced simultaneously either. In that sense, experiencing mixed emotions 'simultaneously' must rather be interpreted as experiencing emotions in close temporal proximity.

However, there is also an opposite perspective. Following Cacioppo, Gardner, and Berntson (1997) and Larsen, McGraw, and Cacioppo (2001), Williams and Aaker (2002, p. 636) argue that "[...] emotional valence is represented by two independent dimensions. Thus not only can one simultaneously experience conflicting emotions, such joint experience may be natural and frequently occurring." Hence, dependent of the perspective, the concept 'mixed' must be seen as 'in close temporal proximity' or as 'simultaneous.' It must also be noted that Williams and Aaker (2002) use the term mixed emotions, although it may, in fact, be a mix of affective meanings rather than a mix of emotions. However, following Williams and Aaker (2002) we will use the term 'mixed emotions' in the remainder of this paper.

The mixing of emotions may not be solely embedded in the advertisement itself. The combination of the medium context with an embedded advertisement can also result in a mixed emotion. For example, there is a combination of emotions when a fund-raising advertisement shows a poor child, although the advertisement is embedded in a story about the happiness of a family. The extent to which mixed emotions in advertising or in a context/ advertisement situation lead to specific consumer responses may depend on specific consumer characteristics.

The purpose of this paper is to extend previous research on the response to mixed emotions in advertising in two directions. The moderating influence of the personality trait Discomfort With Ambiguity (DWA) is studied. This moderating influence on the response to mixed emotions is also tested within advertisements and between advertisements along with the contexts in which they are embedded. These two settings were chosen as they are the same in terms of execution style and because they are both realistic. At the same time, however, they are different because a different viewing behavior can be expected, as an advertisement is a more focused stimulus whereas in a context/advertisement setting the context and the advertisement are two different and substantial parts. If similar results are found this will add to the overall robustness of the findings. The study is applied to advertisements for a fictitious, non-profit organization. A fictitious organization has an advantage in that there is no effect of prior experience. The non-profit organization was chosen because this is part of a larger research project.

MIXED EMOTIONS AND DISCOMFORT WITH AMBIGUITY

Mixed Emotions in a Medium Context/Advertisement Setting

Medium context can be defined as the characteristics of the content of the medium in which an advertisement is inserted. According to the priming principle, a specific context can serve as a primer. Being primed, a consumer can become more susceptible to a subsequent advertisement and, thus, process it more intensively (Herr, 1989; Yi, 1990, 1993). Much attention has been devoted to affective priming resulting in mood effects. Mood can be defined as a feeling state, though it is less intense and is less attention-getting than emotions (Gardner, 1985). A first line of research focuses on the effect of a positive mood-eliciting context on subsequent advertisement effectiveness.

Goldberg and Gorn (1987) stated that an advertisement placed in a television program that elicited a positive mood generated better advertisement responses when compared to a situation where the advertisement was embedded in a negative mood-eliciting television program. As indicated by De Pelsmacker, Geuens, and Anckaert (2002), a number of theories are put forward to explain this effect. The excitation, or affect transfer, hypothesis (Cantor, Zillman, & Bryant, 1975) states that the positive effect of the context is transferred to the advertisement, leading to a more positive evaluation of the advertisement. Another theory is the hedonic contingency theory (e.g., Lee & Sternthal 1999), which states that people who are in a positive mood engage in a more profound elaboration of extra information because they expect that the outcome will be favorable. Aylesworth and MacKenzie (1998) stipulate that when people are in a good mood, they will process an advertisement more centrally. Conversely, when in a bad mood, people will continue to process the program that elicited the bad mood more centrally, leaving no room to process the subsequent advertisement centrally.

A second line of research focuses on the congruency between the medium context and the embedded advertisement. Instead of stating that an advertisement performs better when embedded in a positive mood context, these theories postulate that an advertisement must be placed in a mood-congruent context (implying, for instance, that a sad advertisement placed in a sad context can perform better than when placed in a joyful context). In his research based on the semantic network theory, Bower (1981, p. 147) points out that "people attend to and learn more about events that match their emotional state." Lord, Burnkrant, and Unnava (2001, p. 3) states the mood-congruency hypothesis:

> [...] holds that the greater availability of mood-consistent information in memory facilitates the encoding of information that is affectively consistent with the prevailing mood state. It does this by making available more concepts in memory that can be linked to the incoming information. Consequently, this leads to greater elaboration of mood-congruent information, and this facilitates subsequent retrieval of that information.

Kamins, Marks, and Skinner (1991) call this process the Consistency Effects Model. They compare it with the (confusingly termed) Mood Congruency Model (Goldberg & Gorn, 1987), which indicates that commercials in a happy program context were seen as more effective compared with ads embedded in a sad program context. However, in this case (and also in other studies, e.g., Axelrod, 1963; Edell & Burke, 1987; Srull, 1983), the focus was on the effect of a happy or sad mood context on advertisement responses without taking the affective valence of the commercial itself into account. Kamins et al. (1991) found that the Consistency Effects Model outperformed the Mood Congruency Model, indicating that context and advertisement should match in order to achieve the most positive advertisement responses. Hence, the recommendation was to embed a happy advertisement in a happy context and a sad advertisement in a sad context.

Results of studies on mood congruency are mixed. Many studies offer support for the mood-congruency hypothesis (e.g., Gardner & Wilhelm, 1987; Kamins et al., 1991; Perry et al., 1997; Lord et al., 2001). Some authors, however, have found partial or no effects, and other authors have even recommended placing an advertisement in a contrasting context (e.g., Isen, Shalker, Clark, & Karp, 1978; Hasher, Rose, Zacks, Sanft, & Doren, 1985; Cantor & Venus, 1980; Murphy, Cunningham, & Wilcox, 1979; Derks & Arora, 1993). A possible explanation for the effectiveness of this contrast strategy lies in the unexpectedness of the information (e.g., an advertisement), given its context, consequently leading to increased attention (Goodstein, 1993; Juntunnen, 1995). In terms of catching the attention of consumers, the contrast idea may be extended toward a mood contrast: a mood-breaking advertisement can be more remarkable, hence leading to more advertisement attention and to more positive advertisement responses.

Some researchers have tried to identify factors that moderate the responses to ads in congruent or in contrasting contexts. For instance, De Pelsmacker et al. (2002) found that low-involvement individuals perceived that ads embedded in a congruent context resulted in more positive responses. Hence, the extent to which an (in)congruent context is 'suitable' may depend upon certain individual differences.

Mixed Emotions in Ads

Most of the research on the use and the effects of emotions in advertising is one-dimensional, i.e., the emotions are not mixed, e.g., humor (e.g., Spotts, Weinberger, & Parsons, 1997), eroticism (e.g., Smith, Haugtvedt, Jadrich, & Anton, 1995), warmth (e.g., Aaker, Stayman, & Hagerty, 1986), and fear (e.g., LaTour, Snipes, & Bliss, 1996). Emotional appeals are mostly used to evoke a positive feeling in the consumer, which is subsequently transferred to the attitude toward the advertisement and directly, or indirectly, to the attitude toward the brand/company/institution and to the behavioral intention. However, in practice, many ads use a combination of emotions. An example of such an appeal is a fear appeal with a recommendation of hope. Olsen and Pracejus (2004) investigated the integration of affective stimuli with opposite valence. In one study, a radio advertisement text consisting of a positive and negative text in a specific order was accompanied by positive music and negative music, respectively. Hence, this was a 2(information order) × 2(positive music present versus absent) × 2(negative music present versus absent) design. With respect to the global advertisement evaluation, they found an interaction effect between the presentation order and the presence of positive music. Positive music increased evaluations only if it was played after receiving negative information and not when it occurred at the outset. However, no difference was made between subjects differing on their proclivity to accept duality.

Williams and Aaker (2002) found that the processing of mixed emotions within one advertisement depended on culture among other factors. They found that Asian people could deal more easily with mixed emotions than Western people. This was attributed to the fact that Western cultures are more influenced by Enlightenment and Christianity, as well as by Aristotelian logic. Because of its principles, Aristotelian logic is responsible for a tendency to experience difficulty in engaging in dialectical processing. In addition, the law of identity (things are what they are and nothing else), especially the law of the excluded middle (a statement is either true or false), and the law of non-contradiction (no statement can be true and false at the same time) focus on a strongly dualistic way of thinking. Conversely, Asian cultures are often based on Confucian and Buddhist philosophies, in which the ideas of a constantly changing environment and of holism are key elements, implying that contradictions are perceived as both natural and as common.

Age also appears to be a relevant variable in dividing people into low and high acceptors of duality. The more mature and wiser a person becomes (normally increasing with age), the greater his/her ability to harmonize contradictions (Basseches, 1980; Baltes & Staudinger, 1993). In other words, some groups of people are more dualistic than others. Here, dualism is defined as the extent to which one sees things in a bipolar way (e.g., good versus bad and strong versus weak).

Discomfort with Ambiguity

Williams and Aaker (2002) operationalize groups accepting duality in two ways. On the one hand, they focus on the intercultural differences affecting the acceptance of duality (Anglo-Americans vs. Asian Americans, low versus high propensity to accept duality, respectively). On the other hand, they define duality groups by age (the older the person, the higher the propensity to accept duality). Although measuring duality in this way makes results more operational, this procedure may be biased, for instance, as a result of potential confounds due to socioeconomic background. Western countries may have a focus on Aristotelian ideas and, in a later phase, on Enlightenment, but these ideas are not reflective of the whole of Western philosophy. For instance, Arthur Schopenhauer (1788–1860) was the first important

Western philosopher to incorporate Eastern philosophical ideas into Western philosophy. Moreover, in a period where movements such as the New Age movement gain attraction and where Western people are more open to holism, proclivity to accept duality will also be greater for certain people in Western culture. With respect to age, it is clear that certain personal life experiences may make people wiser or more mature as compared to their contemporaries. Therefore, individual differences instead of socio-demographic categories may be more appropriate.

An appropriate personality trait to measure duality at the personal level is DWA. DWA is a subconstruct of the Need for Closure Scale (NFCL). Need for closure reflects a person's desire for clear, definite, or unambiguous knowledge that will guide perception and action, as opposed to the unde-sirable alternative of ambiguity and confusion. Need for closure is a mo-tivation to draw a conclusion quickly and to terminate cognitive information processing related to the issue (Webster & Kruglanski, 1994). For instance, in a study by Klein and Webster (2000) on the influence of need for closure on information processing of a persuasive message con-taining both heuristic cues and systematic arguments, high-NFCL people tended to use the peripheral, or heuristic, route (providing quick, easy clo-sure), while low-NFCL people used the central or systematic route. The DWA subscale measures the discomfort produced by ambiguity. Individuals who score high on this construct are expected to have a low proclivity to accept duality in messages, and individuals who have a low score are able to process mixed emotions and messages more easily. The DWA scale has affective as well as cognitive oriented items and some items are a mixture of both. For example, the statement 'I feel uncomfortable when someone's meaning or intentions are unclear to me' stresses the feelings aspect (feeling uncomfortable). Also, the cognitive characteristics of the DWA scale are appropriate given the above-mentioned cognitive appraisal mechanism with respect to experiencing emotions, indicating that emotions are seen as being tied to the different cognitive appraisals of a situation (Lazarus, 1991; Ortony et al., 1988). Moreover, in cognitive psychology, subjective feelings, such as moods, and emotions are conceptualized in terms of encoding, storage, and retrieval processes (Bower, 1981). In addition, research (Schwarz, 1990; Schwarz & Clore, 1983, 1988) indicates that affect can also be seen as information when making evaluative judgments. In this 'affect-as-information' model, people evaluate their feelings while imagining a target situation and use this information in their judgment. This "How-do-I-feel-about-it" heuristic posits that positive or negative feelings about the target's representation will lead to a positive or negative evaluation of the target itself, respectively. Therefore, DWA, containing a mixture of cognitively and affectively oriented items, is an appropriate variable for measuring the proclivity to accept emotional duality in stimuli, i.e., a higher score on DWA reflects a higher level of dualism. Individuals with a low DWA do not necessarily like ambiguity. Low DWA scores simply mean not having any problems with ambiguity. Individuals with a higher DWA are less comfortable with ambiguity.

The personality trait DWA can be expected to have a moderating effect on the processing of mixed emotions, both in a single advertisement and in a mixed emotions advertisement/context situation. On the basis of the foregoing, the following hypotheses can be developed:

H1a. Individuals scoring low on DWA generate equal responses (attitude towards the advertisement, attitude towards the organization, and behavioral intention) whether emotions in the advertisement and medium context are mixed or not mixed.

H1b. Individuals scoring high on DWA, as opposed to individuals scoring low on DWA, generate more positive responses in the case of non-mixed emotions in the advertisement and the medium context than in the case of mixed emotions.

H2a. Individuals scoring low on DWA generate equal responses (attitude towards the advertisement, attitude towards the organization, and behavioral intention) whether emotions in the advertisement are mixed or not mixed.

H2b. Individuals scoring high on DWA, as opposed to individuals scoring low on DWA, generate more positive responses in the case of non-mixed emotions in the advertisement than in the case of mixed emotions.

Hypotheses 1 and 2 are examined in Experiments 1 and 2, respectively. In the next section, the selection of an appropriate set of emotions to be mixed is discussed. Based on this set of two emotions, the effect of mixed emotions in an advertisement-medium context setting are examined (Experiment 1) as well as the effect of mixed emotions in a single advertisement (Experiment 2).

DETERMINING AN APPROPRIATE SET OF
OPPOSITE EMOTIONS

Although Plutchik's theory of emotions may be criticized for its strong basis in evolutionary psychology and for its lack of cognitive elements (Cafferata & Tybout, 1989), it remains a popular and a frequently cited theory. In his 'wheel of emotions,' Plutchik (1980) distinguishes eight primary emotions. These emotions can be split into four bipolar couples: Acceptance–Disgust, Fear–Anger, Anticipation–Surprise, and Joy–Sadness. Although Plutchik indicates that people can experience a blend of emotions (first, second, and third dyad), he postulates that opposite emotions cannot be experienced at the same time. He further categorizes these eight emotions into positive (joy, acceptance, anticipation, and surprise) and negative emotions (anger, fear, disgust, and sadness). For the purpose of our study, we want to mix the most opposite two emotions, thus inducing the strongest emotional tension.

The four emotional bipolarities were presented to a sample of 30 persons. They were asked to indicate for each couple the extent to which they experienced the stated emotions as opposite. Answers were given on a five-point Likert type scale ranging from 1 (totally not opposite) to 5 (strongly opposite). Mean scores and standard deviations are reported in Table 1. Repeated measures analysis of variance indicated that the null hypothesis of equal means was rejected (Wilk's $\lambda(3,27) = 0.163$, $p < 0.001$). The Joy–Sadness couple was seen as the most opposite ($M = 4.17$, $SD = 0.87$). Pairwise comparisons indicated significant differences at the $p < 0.001$ level except for the comparison between Joy–Sadness and Acceptance–Disgust (still significant at $p = 0.007$), and the comparison between Acceptance–Disgust and Anticipation–Surprise ($p = 0.156$). From this analysis, it appeared that the emotions of Joy and of Sadness were seen as the most opposite. Hence, the development of stimuli was based on these two emotions.

Table 1. Indicated Extent of Oppositeness between Emotions.

Opposite Emotions	M^a	SD
Joy–sadness	4.17	0.87
Acceptance–disgust	3.40	0.77
Anticipation–surprise	2.90	1.03
Fear–anger	2.20	0.81

[a]Score on five-point Likert type scale (1 = totally not opposite to 5 = strongly opposite).

EXPERIMENT 1: MIXED EMOTIONS BETWEEN MEDIUM CONTEXT AND ADVERTISEMENT

Design

Stimuli

Two experimental ads (which later had to be embedded in contexts) were created. We created an advertisement for a fictitious fundraising organization, 'Children in need,' in order to exclude effects of prior knowledge that could bias attitudes and intentions. The advertisement was A5 sized with the left half consisting of a picture. A short text was written on the right half (centered, surrounded by white space). A message was written at the bottom of the right part (the same for all ads): Support 'Children in need' (http://www.cin.be). An account number was added, and it was mentioned that gifts were tax deductible. A jury of two collected 10 joyful and 10 sad pictures. These pictures were randomized and all presented to 30 respondents who had to indicate on a seven-category semantic joyful/sad differential how joyful/sad they experienced each picture. A repeated measure analysis indicated that the null hypothesis of equal means was rejected (Wilk's $\lambda(19,11) = 0.004$, $p < 0.001$). A jury of three selected a pair of pictures from the top four of the sad and joyful pictures that differed the least in terms of picture layout and concept (two pictures of a child were chosen), but that still showed a significant difference on the semantic differential (joyful picture ($M = 6.43$, SD $= 1.01$), sad picture ($M = 2.53$, SD $= 0.86$), $t(29) = 18.03$, $p < 0.001$). For the selection of the texts, a similar procedure was followed. Again, the null hypothesis of equal means was rejected (Wilk's $\lambda(19,11) = 0.004$, $p < 0.001$). The happiest and saddest texts that were acceptable in terms of matching with the pictures were withheld (joyful text ($M = 6.37$, SD $= 0.85$), sad text ($M = 1.37$, SD $= 0.49$), $t(29) = 28.92$, $p < 0.001$). The joyful text read: 'If every person would make one other person joyful, then the whole world would be joyful.' The sad text read: 'In Africa, every ten seconds a child dies from hunger.' Hence, a joyful advertisement (joyful text and picture) as well as a sad advertisement (sad text and picture) were created. In a second step, these ads were embedded in an emotional context. For each emotional combination (joyful/sad advertisement and joyful/sad newspaper content), a double mock newspaper page was created, each page with 85% context (articles) and 15% advertisement space. For the newspaper content, joyful and sad articles were gathered from newspapers and from the Internet that were published during the months before the experiment took place. A jury of two persons made a selection from these articles, taking into account that the newspaper, as a whole, should look realistic (e.g., no articles with a specific date included or referring to a specific period as 'last week').

Independent Variables

Three independent variables were used: emotion type of the context (joyful/ sad), emotion type of the advertisement (joyful/sad), and DWA. The emotion type of the context and the advertisement were checked by means of a self-reported, seven-category semantic differential scale (1 = very sad, 7 = very joyful). There was a significant difference between the contexts indicating successful manipulation of the sad context ($M = 2.02$, SD $= 0.96$) and of the joyful context ($M = 5.51$, SD $= 1.00$, $t(189) = 24.54$, $p < 0.001$). There was also a significant difference between the two advertisement types indicating successful manipulation of the sad advertisement ($M = 2.23$, SD $= 1.02$) and of the joyful advertisement ($M = 4.33$, SD $= 0.94$, $t(189) = 14.64$, $p < 0.001$). DWA was measured by means of a five-item seven-point scale (Vermeir, 2003; Webster & Kruglanski, 1994) at the end of the survey. As shown in Table 2, Cronbach's α indicated an acceptable reliability (0.69) (Hair et al., 1998).

Dependent Variables

Three dependent variables were measured: attitude toward the advertisement, attitude toward the organization, and behavioral intention. Table 2 shows the three dependent variables with their reliability and corresponding items. Cronbach's α indicates acceptable reliability for each of the constructs.

Participants and Procedure

The sample consisted of 191 undergraduate students, and the study was conducted during class time. Each respondent received one of the four newspaper versions with an embedded advertisement. Participants were told that the research was about a test for a new newspaper. It was stressed that the focus of the test was on the evaluation of the newspaper, and that they should look at the full context of the newspaper as they would normally do. After two minutes, they were instructed to turn over the double-sided newspaper, which was then collected. Persons who needed less than two minutes were instructed to turn over the newspaper and wait until the

Table 2. Reliability of Attitudes, Intentions, and DWA (Experiments 1 and 2) with Corresponding Items.

Attitude toward the advertisement (Aad) (Cronbach's α in Experiment 1: 0.80; Experiment 2: 0.78)
This advertisement is well made
This advertisement attracts attention
This advertisement is remarkable
This advertisement appeals to me

Attitude toward the organization (Cronbach's α in Experiment 1: 0.80; Experiment 2: 0.82)
I think this is a good organization
This organization looks to me as better than other similar organizations
This organization arouses trust in me
This organization appeals to me
This organization knows what it stands for

Behavioral intention (Cronbach's α: in Experiment 1: 0.80; Experiment 2: 0.81)
After watching this ad, I consider making a deposit to this organization
I would rather deposit money to this organization than to another similar organization
After watching this ad, I am going to inform myself better about the operations and targets of this organization
By watching this ad, I am prompted to make an effort to help this organization

Discomfort with ambiguity (Cronbach's α: in Experiment 1: 0.69; Experiment 2: 0.63)
I feel uncomfortable when someone's meaning or intentions are unclear to me
I do not like it if I do not understand why someone makes a particular statement
I always want to know why certain people make certain decisions
I do not like it when people make statements that can be interpreted in different ways
I always like to know immediately what people mean when they say something

two minutes were over. Finally, they were instructed to open an envelope containing the questionnaire. They were allowed as much time as they needed to complete it.

Analytical Method
Moderated regression analysis was chosen as an analytical tool.[1] Mixing of emotions was manipulated by combining the emotion (joyful/sad) in the newspaper content and the emotion in the advertisement (joyful/sad). Two types of analysis were carried out. Analysis 1 was a parsimonious one in which the combination of emotions was taken together, i.e., emotions were mixed (joyful advertisement/sad context or sad advertisement/joyful context) or not mixed (joyful advertisement/joyful context or sad advertisement/sad context). Hence, the first analysis for Experiment 1 is as follows (a separate regression analysis was carried out for each dependent

variable: attitude toward the advertisement, attitude toward the organization, and behavioral intention):

$$Y = a + b \times \text{mixed\_emotions} + c \times \text{DWA}$$
$$+ d \times [\text{mixed\_emotions} \times \text{DWA}] + \text{error} \qquad (1)$$

where Y = three variables measuring advertisement effectiveness; mixed_emotions, a dichotomous variable (mixed emotions or no mixed emotions, $-1/1$ coded); and DWA, a mean centered interval variable.

We expected the coefficient of the second-order interaction term to be significant, indicating a moderating effect of DWA on the processing of mixed emotions. Analysis 2 was a more extended analysis, where the emotions reflected in advertisement and context were treated as separate variables:

$$Y = a + b \times \text{emotion\_ad} + c \times \text{emotion\_context} + d \times \text{DWA}$$
$$+ e \times [\text{emotion\_ad} \times \text{emotion\_context}]$$
$$+ d \times [\text{emotion\_ad} \times \text{DWA}] + e \times [\text{emotion\_context} \times \text{DWA}]$$
$$+ f \times [\text{emotion\_ad} \times \text{emotion\_context} \times \text{DWA}] + \text{error} \qquad (2)$$

where Y = three variables measuring advertisement effectiveness; emotion_ad and emotion_context, dichotomous variables (sad or joyful, $-1/1$ coded); and DWA, a mean centered interval variable.

We expected the coefficient of the third-order interaction effect to be significant, indicating a moderating effect of DWA on the combination of emotions presented. Analysis 1 is nested in Analysis 2, i.e., the results of Analysis 2 are more nuanced and go beyond the results of Analysis 1, although the latter is more parsimonious.

Results

For each of the dependent variables in Experiment 1 (shown in Table 2), a moderated regression analysis was conducted for Analysis 1 (Eq. (1)) as well as for Analysis 2 (Eq. (2)). The results for Analysis 1 (Eq. (1)) are shown in Table 3. We found partial support for Hypotheses 1a and 1b. For behavioral intention, a moderately significant second-order interaction effect was found ($t(187) = 1.74$, $p = 0.084$).

The graphical representation (Fig. 1) shows that individuals with a high DWA show a significantly more positive behavioral intention as a result of exposure to non-mixed emotions compared to mixed emotions. The

Table 3. Summaries of Moderated Regression Analysis, Experiment 1, Analysis 1, Eq. (1).

	Attitude toward the Ad	Attitude toward the Organization	Behavioral Intention
Model	3.094**	2.956**	10.437***
Intercept	3.885***	4.135***	2.817***
	(0.079)	(0.055)	(0.068)
Mixed emotions	0.048	0.042	0.089
	(0.079)	(0.055)	(0.068)
DWA	0.297***	0.184**	0.444***
	(0.100)	(0.069)	(0.086)
Mixed emotions × DWA	0.002	−0.059	0.149*
	(0.100)	(0.069)	(0.086)

Note: Numbers in columns represent unstandardized regression coefficients (standard errors are in italic between parentheses) for a moderated regression analysis employing the dependent variable at the top of the column and the independent variables in the far left column. For the model, the F value is reported. All tests of main effects and interactions are based on $t(187)$. The test for the corrected model is based on $F(3, 187)$.
*$p < 0.10$.
**$p < 0.05$.
***$p < 0.01$.

Behavioral intention towards the organization

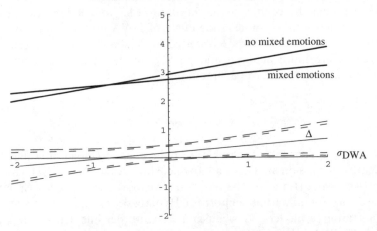

Fig. 1. Graphical Representation of the Interaction Effect of Mixed Emotion (Newspaper) × DWA, Experiment 1, Analysis 1. *Note:* Scores are shown in bold line, lines with small and large dashes represent confidence intervals for difference at 90 and 95% confidence, respectively.

confidence interval for the difference shows that this difference is significant for mean-corrected DWA values higher than 0.5 standard deviation. In other words, the scores for individuals with low DWA are not significantly different in the case of mixed and of non-mixed stimuli. Hypotheses 1a and 1b were, therefore, supported. In Table 4, the regression results for Analysis 2 (Eq. (2)) are presented. For behavioral intention, a significant third order interaction effect was found ($t(183) = 1.74$, $p = 0.030$), again supporting Hypothesis 1.

Inspection of the graphical representation in Fig. 2 shows crossover interaction effects in the case of a joyful as well as of a sad context. Scores for individuals with low DWA are not significantly different for mixed and non-mixed emotions. The confidence intervals for the differences also show that

Table 4. Summaries of Moderated Regression Analysis, Experiment 1, Analysis 2, Eq. (2).

	Attitude toward the Ad	Attitude toward the Organization	Behavioral Intention
Model	2.572**	2.576**	5.228***
Intercept	3.890***	4.139***	2.817***
	(0.079)	(0.054)	(0.068)
Ad	−0.099	−0.073	0.068
	(0.079)	(0.054)	(0.068)
Context	−0.161**	−0.096*	0.104
	(0.079)	(0.054)	(0.068)
DWA	0.258**	0.163**	0.439***
	(0.105)	(0.072)	(0.091)
Ad × context	0.051	0.049	0.100
	(0.079)	(0.054)	(0.068)
Ad × DWA	−0.006	0.025	−0.013
	(0.105)	(0.072)	(0.091)
Context × DWA	0.166	0.138*	0.115
	(0.105)	(0.072)	(0.091)
Ad × context × DWA	0.030	−0.035	0.199**
	(0.105)	(0.072)	(0.091)

Note: Numbers in columns represent unstandardized regression coefficients (standard errors are in italic between parentheses) for a moderated regression analysis employing the dependent variable at the top of the column and the independent variables in the far left column. For the model, the *F* value is reported. All tests of main effects and interactions are based on $t(183)$. The test for the corrected model is based on $F(7, 183)$.
*$p < 0.10$.
**$p < 0.05$.
***$p < 0.01$.

Behavioral intention towards the organization if context = sad

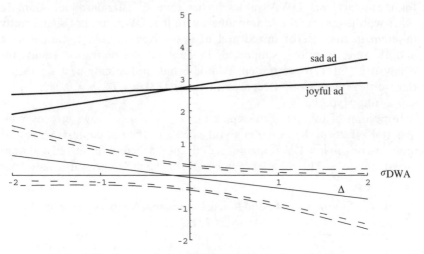

Behavioral intention towards the organization if context = joyful

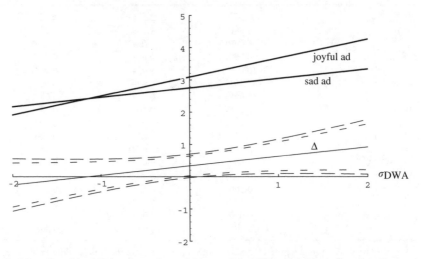

Fig. 2.   Graphical Representation of Interaction Effect Ad (Emotion 1) × Context (Emotion 2) × DWA, Experiment 1, Analysis 2. *Note:* Scores are shown in bold line, lines with small and large dashes represent confidence intervals for difference at 90 and 95% confidence, respectively.

the interaction effect was only significant in the case of a joyful context. In case of a joyful context, people having difficulties with ambiguity prefer a joyful advertisement. Hence, Hypothesis 1a was supported and Hypothesis 1b was partially supported. No significant interaction effects for attitude toward the advertisement and attitude toward the organization were found. A significant main effect of DWA was also detected for all three dependent variables.

EXPERIMENT 2: MIXED EMOTIONS IN A SINGLE ADVERTISEMENT

Design

Stimuli

In this experiment, emotions were mixed by attributing a joyful/sad emotion to the pictorial part or to the textual part of the advertisement, using the stimuli developed in Experiment 1. Four experimental ads were created (joyful picture, joyful text; joyful picture, sad text; sad picture, joyful text; sad picture, sad text).

Independent Variables

Three independent variables were used in this experiment: emotion type of the advertisement text (joyful/sad), emotion type of the advertisement picture (joyful/sad), and DWA. Manipulation of the emotion type of advertisement text and advertisement picture was checked by a self-reported, seven-category semantic differential scale ($1 =$ very sad, $7 =$ very joyful). A significant difference between the pictures was found ($t(237) = 24.01$, $p < 0.001$), hence, a successful manipulation of joyful picture ($M = 5.62$, $SD = 1.34$) and sad picture ($M = 1.86$, $SD = 1.05$) was established. For the advertisement text, a significant difference was also found ($t(237) = 11.21$, $p < 0.001$), indicating an acceptable manipulation of the joyful text ($M = 4.21$, $SD = 1.41$) and the sad text ($M = 2.29$, $SD = 1.22$). Although the score on the joyful text is relatively low, the score is above the neutral score of 4 (hence, more joyful). For DWA, the same scale as in Experiment 1 was used (Table 2) and was administered at the end of the survey. The reliability measure Cronbach's α (0.63) was still above the lower limit of acceptability of 0.60 (Hair et al., 1998).

Dependent Variables
The same three dependent variables as in Experiment 1 were measured: attitude toward the advertisement, attitude toward the organization, and behavioral intention. Reliabilities of these constructs are shown in Table 2. The lowest Cronbach's α was 0.79, indicating good reliability.

Participants and Procedure
The sample consisted of 239 graduate students, and the study was conducted during class time. The procedure was similar to the one used in Experiment 1, but here, each respondent randomly received one of the four ads and a questionnaire in an envelope, which they were not allowed to open at the beginning. The briefing stated that they were involved in an advertising test, and they were instructed to look at the advertisement just as they would look at an ordinary advertisement.

Analytical Method
Two analyses were carried out as in Experiment 1. Analysis 1 was a parsimonious approach in which the combination of the emotions expressed by text and picture was dichotomized, i.e., emotions were mixed (joyful picture/sad text or sad picture/joyful text) or not mixed (joyful picture/joyful text or sad picture/sad text). Hence, Analysis 1 for Experiment 2 was as follows:

$$Y = a + b \times \text{mixed\_emotions} + c \times \text{DWA}$$
$$+ d \times [\text{mixed\_emotions} \times \text{DWA}] + \text{error} \qquad (3)$$

where $Y =$ three variables measuring advertisement effectiveness; mixed_emotions, a dichotomous variable (mixed emotions or no mixed emotions, $-1/1$ coded); and DWA, a mean centered interval variable.

As in Experiment 1, we expected the coefficient of the second-order interaction term to be significant, indicating a moderating effect of DWA on the processing of mixed emotions.

Analysis 2 was a more extended one in which the emotions reflected in text and in picture were treated as separate variables:

$$Y = a + b \times \text{emotion\_picture} + c \times \text{emotion\_text} + d \times \text{DWA}$$
$$+ e \times [\text{emotion\_picture} \times \text{emotion\_text}]$$
$$+ d \times [\text{emotion\_picture} \times \text{DWA}] + e \times [\text{emotion\_text} \times \text{DWA}]$$
$$+ f \times [\text{emotion\_picture} \times \text{emotion\_text} \times \text{DWA}] + \text{error} \qquad (4)$$

where $Y =$ three variables measuring advertisement effectiveness; emotion_picture and emotion_text, dichotomous variables (sad or joyful, $-1/1$ coded); and DWA, a mean centered interval variable.

We expected the coefficient for the third-order interaction effect to be significant, indicating a moderating effect of DWA on the combination of emotions presented. As in Experiment 1, Analysis 1 is nested in Analysis 2.

Results

For each of the three dependent variables, a moderated regression analysis was carried out for Analysis 1 (Eq. (3)) and Analysis 2 (Eq. (4)). The results in Table 5 partially support Hypothesis 2. For the attitude toward the organization, there was a moderately significant interaction effect ($t(235) = 1.72$, $p = 0.087$) between the type of advertisement (mixed emotion or not) and DWA.

Fig. 3 shows that individuals scoring high on DWA reported a more positive attitude toward the organization when exposed to consistent (non-mixed) emotions, than when exposed to mixed emotions. The confidence

Table 5. Summaries of Moderated Regression Analysis, Experiment 2, Analysis 1, Eq. (3).

	Attitude toward the Ad	Attitude toward the Organization	Behavioral Intention
Model	1.864	3.004**	3.28**
Intercept	4.404***	4.128***	2.92***
	(0.071)	(0.054)	(0.064)
Mixed emotions	0.044	0.073	0.149**
	(0.071)	(0.054)	(0.064)
DWA	0.230**	0.182**	0.179*
	(0.105)	(0.079)	(0.095)
Mixed emotions × DWA	0.097	0.136*	−0.017
	(0.105)	(0.079)	(0.095)

Note: Numbers in columns represent unstandardized regression coefficients (standard errors are in italic between parentheses) for a moderated regression analysis employing the dependent variable at the top of the column and the independent variables in the far left column. For the model, the F value is reported. All tests of main effects and interactions are based on $t(235)$. The test for the corrected model is based on $F(3, 235)$.
*$p < 0.10$.
**$p < 0.05$.
***$p < 0.01$.

Attitude towards the organization

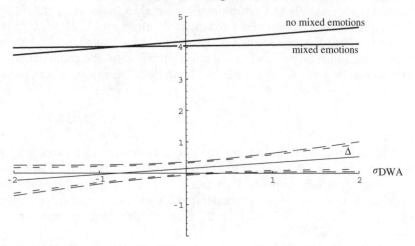

Fig. 3. Graphical Representation of the Interaction Effect of Mixed Emotion (Ad) × DWA, Experiment 2, Analysis 1. *Note:* Scores are shown in bold line, lines with small and large dashes represent confidence intervals for difference at 90 and 95% confidence, respectively.

interval for the difference shows that this difference is significant for positive values of mean corrected DWA (values higher than 0.3 standard deviation) only. Consequently, the attitude of low DWA individuals does not differ between mixed and non-mixed emotion. These findings support Hypotheses 2a and 2b.

The results of the more extended regression analysis (Eq. (4)) are presented in Table 6. A significant third-order interaction effect for attitude toward the organization was found ($t(231) = 1.95, p = 0.084$). Fig. 4 shows that high DWA people prefer affective congruent texts and pictures in an advertisement. Similarly to Experiment 1, the confidence intervals for the differences show that this congruency effect was only significant in the case of a joyful text with a joyful picture for positive values of mean corrected DWA (values above 0.5 standard deviation). Consequently, the attitude of low DWA individuals was not significantly different between mixed and non-mixed emotions. High DWA individuals react more positively to non-mixed advertisement emotions; however, the latter is only the case when both picture and text are joyful. Again, support for Hypothesis 2a and partial support for Hypothesis 2b was found. The interaction effects on attitude toward the advertisement and the behavioral intention were not

Table 6. Summaries of Moderated Regression Analysis, Experiment 2, Analysis 2, Eq. (4).

	Attitude toward the Ad	Attitude toward the Organization	Behavioral Intention
Model	0.97	1.68	1.93*
Intercept	4.406***	4.131***	2.919***
	(0.071)	(0.054)	(0.064)
Picture	−0.008	0.023	−0.036
	(0.071)	(0.054)	(0.064)
Text	−0.065	0.003	0.104
	(0.071)	(0.054)	(0.064)
DWA	0.236**	0.176**	0.182*
	(0.107)	(0.080)	(0.096)
Picture × text	0.046	0.070	0.147**
	(0.071)	(0.054)	(0.064)
Picture × 10 DWA	0.074	0.003	−0.004
	(0.107)	(0.080)	(0.096)
Text × DWA	0.036	0.126	0.079
	(0.107)	(0.080)	(0.096)
Picture × text × DWA	0.100	0.157*	−0.009
	(0.107)	(0.080)	(0.096)

Note: Numbers in columns represent unstandardized regression coefficients (standard errors are in italic between parentheses) for a moderated regression analysis employing the dependent variable at the top of the column and the independent variables in the far left column. For the model, the F value is reported. All tests of main effects and interactions are based on $t(231)$. The test for the corrected model is based on $F(7, 231)$.
*$p<0.10$.
**$p<0.05$.
***$p<0.01$.

significant. Again, a significant main effect of DWA was found for all three dependent variables.

DISCUSSION

Partial support was found for the hypothesis that DWA plays a moderating role in the processing of mixed emotions when emotions are mixed within ads as well as when they are mixed between advertisement and medium context. The moderating effect of cultural and age differences on the processing of mixed emotions (Williams & Aaker, 2002) can be extended to the individual difference DWA. Our findings extend present knowledge on

Attitude towards the organization if picture = sad

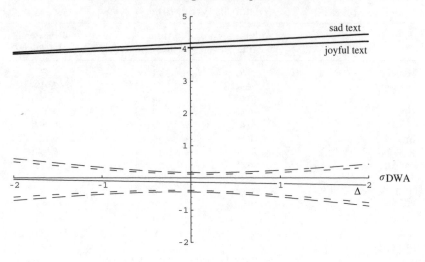

Attitude towards the organization if picture = joyful

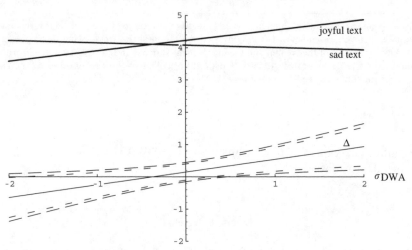

Fig. 4.   Graphical Representation of the Interaction Effect of Picture (Emotion 1) ×
Text (Emotion 2) × DWA, Experiment 2, Analysis 2. *Note:* Scores are shown in bold
line, lines with small and large dashes represent confidence intervals for difference at
90 and 95% confidence, respectively.

contrast or on congruency effects in medium context effects by indicating that the extent to which people feel comfortable with ambiguity determines which of the two theories applies. The analysis of the advertisement-context setting indicated that congruency outperforms incongruency for high DWA people, but that this effect was only significant in a joyful context, i.e., when placed in a joyful context, a joyful advertisement outperforms a sad advertisement. For a sad context, a similar pattern was found, but this was not significant. For the within-advertisement setting, the results are similar. High DWA people appear to prefer no mixed emotions in the advertisement, and when a joyful picture was used, a joyful text outperforms a sad text for high DWA subjects. Another interesting finding is that the crossover interaction effects are mostly attributable to the moderating effect of DWA in the case of context-congruent ads rather than in the case of opposite-valenced ads. Hence, when a joyful advertisement is placed in a sad context or when a sad advertisement is placed in a joyful context, the level of DWA has little influence on responses. However, when a sad advertisement is placed in a sad context or when a joyful advertisement is placed in a joyful context, advertisement responses are very different for people scoring low and high on DWA. This means that the moderating effect of DWA on the use of mixed emotions is more apparent when using the same valence, than when using mixed emotions. Moreover, it appears from the results that the moderating effect of DWA leads to significant differences, but only when DWA scores are above average (i.e., for high DWA individuals).

Assuming that the context is processed before the advertisement, our results mitigate the findings of Aaker et al. (1986), who stipulated that when an emotional advertisement with a positive valence is placed after an advertisement of the same emotion, it elicits more negative evaluations compared with when it is placed after an advertisement of a different emotion. Of course, in our study, the advertisement is not placed after another advertisement but is placed after an affect-eliciting context. We find that two succeeding affective stimuli of the same valence (especially in the joyful–joyful condition) outperform mixed-emotion combinations for people scoring high on DWA. Previous research (e.g., Loewenstein & Prelec, 1993) pointed out that consumers prefer a positive affect to occur after a negative affect (final trend improvement). Our findings (sad context setting) show no significant support for this proposition. There are, however, indications for such a support, but only for people scoring low on DWA. People scoring high on DWA apparently do not need the affect improvement to report more positive responses.

In the two experiments, only some of the advertisement responses were significantly affected. In the single-advertisement experiment, the significant

Table 7.   Average Ad Response Scores for Experiments 1 and 2[a].

Ad Responses	Experiment 1	Experiment 2	Difference (*p*-value)
Attitude toward the ad	3.89	4.41	0.52
			(<0.001)
Attitude toward the organization	4.14	4.13	0.00
			(0.963)
Behavioral intention	2.82	2.91	0.09
			(0.354)

[a]Scores on seven-point Likert type scale.

effects were measured on the dependent variable 'attitude toward the organization,' whereas in the advertisement-context experiment, the significant effects were found on the variable 'behavioral intention toward the organization.' In search for an explanation for these findings, mean scores for the three dependent variables in each experiment are reported in Table 7.

In the within-advertisement setting a significantly higher Aad score (4.41) was attained compared to the advertisement-context setting (3.89, $t = 4.836$, $p < 0.001$). This might have resulted from the fact that in the within-advertisement setting, people had a deeper processing of the advertisement because it was the only stimulus, contrary to the advertisement-context setting where there was also a newspaper that embedded the advertisement. Possibly, the higher Aad score resulted in a more favorable attitude toward the organization. Maybe because of the less realistic setting (a standalone advertisement), the effects found for attitude toward the organization were not transferred to the behavioral intention, i.e., respondents can have a positive attitude toward the organization, but, because of the less realistic setting, these effects were not found for behavioral intention. Contrary, in the advertisement-context setting, Aad scores were relatively lower. It might be possible that due to the context, less attention was paid to the advertisement. As such, rather than focusing on the organization, focus was on the essence of the advertisement message (giving money for children suffering from starvation), leading to more significant effects for behavioral intention and not for attitude toward the organization. Another difference in the two settings has to do with the difference in temporal proximity of exposure to the two emotions. The temporal proximity between the picture and the text is probably higher than the temporal proximity between the context and the advertisement. Of course, it is not possible to look at the picture and the text at exactly the same time and in a certain order (scan path) is followed. This procedure, however, can be expected to occur in a limited amount of time, or at least in a narrower time frame than when the context and advertisement is processed. It is unclear to what extent this difference in temporal proximity may relate to differences found in the two settings. Further research is needed to corroborate and/or refine the different results in the two settings. Regardless, as an advertisement is mostly embedded in a medium context, it means that our findings for the advertisement setting must be interpreted with caution because the embedding medium context may have a moderating effect.

Although no hypotheses were formulated for the main effect of DWA (found in both experiments), a possible explanation is available. Compared to the misery of the topic in the advertisement (children suffering form starvation), all respondents live in a relatively luxurious world. It might very well be the case that high DWA people are more sensitive to the ambiguity that may arise from these two perspectives (misery and luxury). This may result in a more positive attitude toward the problem, and, subsequently, in more favorable advertisement responses.

CONCLUSION

DWA appears to play a moderating role in the processing of mixed emotions, both when the emotions are mixed within an advertisement and when they are mixed between the medium context and the advertisement. The latter finding refines the discussion about contrast or congruency medium context effects in advertising, as it shows that they appear to be moderated by the proclivity to accept duality. The affective priming principle and similar frameworks, such as the affect transfer hypothesis and the hedonic contingency theory, mainly focus on the positive effect of context-elicited positive mood on advertisement responses. Our results indicate that this seems the case only when a joyful advertisement is used for individuals scoring high on DWA. Thus, it seems that a joyful context will not always have a positive effect on advertisement effectiveness. The crossover interaction effects suggest that high DWA people prefer congruent emotions. This is significantly true for joyful–joyful conditions, although some non-significant indications are also found for a sad–sad setting. This might suggest that people who prefer to have non-dualistic cognitive and affective information prefer to hold a well-specified, affective tone of information. An implication of these results may be that the kind of combination of emotions to be used in advertising or in advertisement/context combinations has to depend on the profile of the target group. Rather than focusing solely on specific sociodemographics, it might be better to gain insight into more specific and relevant personality profiles. This information can then be linked to socio-demographic profiles.

Only the joy–sadness emotion couple set was used in this study. Further research could concentrate on other emotional sets, for instance, those less opposite yet bipolar and those less bipolar. One could expect that in taking lesser opposite emotions, the stimulus ambiguity would diminish. The expected effect on the moderating role of DWA in this situation is unclear. On the one hand, it may be expected that DWA will have a weaker moderating effect as the extent of having to deal with mixed emotions diminishes. However, the strongest bipolar emotional combination is possibly so opposite that dealing with mixed emotions in this way may be even hard for people with a low DWA; hence the moderating influence of DWA could be stronger with less opposite emotional couples.

The target advertisement was an advertisement for a good cause ('children in need'). Linked to this target, some extra personality traits may be taken into account in future research. For example, it is possible that taking into account the involvement of people with 'good causes' may nuance the present findings. It might be hypothesized that high 'good cause' involvement people will process such advertisements more centrally and that the role of the peripheral medium context diminishes. For low 'good cause' people, the process may be reverse, meaning that the medium context will be of relatively more importance.

Another limitation of this study is that it only took into account the valence of emotions. Future research could also examine the role of arousal. The potential influence of the arousal level on the moderating role of DWA is not straightforward. A high-arousal combination of mixed emotions might increase the moderating role of DWA because of the higher perceived ambiguity. At the same time, however, higher arousal could elevate the ambiguity in such a way that it may even impair low-DWA people's ability to deal with the mixed emotions. Moreover, it is not clear how the addition of arousal must be handled. Is it the arousal levels of the distinct emotions or the resulting arousal of the emotional combination that is important? In any case, the impact of arousal levels should be further explored.

NOTE

1. A common approach to analyze experiments of this kind is by means of an ANOVA $2 \times 2 \times 2$ full factorial design (emotion in advertisement × emotion in context × level of DWA). As discussed, in our study, DWA was measured by means of a five-item seven-point scale (Vermeir, 2003; Webster & Kruglanski, 1994). The score

of a scale variable is often transformed into a categorical variable, for example, by means of a median split. However, Irwin and McClelland (2001) indicate that this approach can influence the statistical significance of the interaction and that it can decrease the statistical power to detect interaction. McClelland (1997) points out that dichotomizing a variable with a median split can be equivalent to discarding about half of the data. Hence, they recommend using moderated regression analysis. They also indicate that, in contrast to additive regression analysis, it is important to include all components of the product terms in the regression model. It is important to include all terms, even if these terms are non-significant or meaningless, to enable proper partialling of the product. In regression analysis, multicollinearity can inflate the standard errors of the regression coefficients (Jaccard, Turrisi, & Wan, 1990). Cronbach (1987) suggests mean-centering the scale variables before forming the multiplicative term because multiplicative terms in moderated regression analysis can cause high levels of multicollinearity. Mean-centering improves the multicollinearity diagnostics, although it has no substantive impact on the results. "This transformation will tend to yield low correlations between the product term and the component parts of the term" (Jaccard et al., 1990, p. 31).

ACKNOWLEDGEMENTS

The authors want to thank Elke Beyers and Bart Mathijssen for their help in collecting and creating the stimulus material.

REFERENCES

Aaker, D. A., Stayman, D. M., & Hagerty, M. R. (1986). Warmth in advertising: Measurement, impact, and sequence effects. *Journal of Consumer Research, 12,* 365–381.

Aaker, J., & Williams, P. (1998). Empathy versus pride: The influence of emotional appeals across cultures. *Journal of Consumer Research, 25*(December), 241–261.

Axelrod, J. N. (1963). Induced moods and attitudes towards products. *Journal of Advertising Research, 3,* 19–24.

Aylesworth, A. B., & MacKenzie, S. B. (1998). Context is key: The effect of program-induced mood on thoughts about the ad. *Journal of Advertising, 27*(2), 17–27.

Baltes, P. B., & Staudinger, U. M. (1993). The search for a psychology of wisdom. *Current Directions in Psychological Science, 2*(June), 75–80.

Basseches, M. (1980). Dialectical schemata: A framework for the empirical study of the development of dialectical thinking. *Human Development, 23*(Nov–Dec), 400–421.

Bower, G. (1981). Mood and memory. *American Psychologist, 36*(2), 129–148.

Burke, M. C., & Edell, J. A. (1986). Ad reactions over time: Capturing changes in the real world. *Journal of Consumer Research, 13,* 114–118.

Cacioppo, J. T., Gardner, W. L., & Berntson, G. G. (1997). Beyond bipolar conceptualizations and measure: The case of attitudes and evaluative space. *Personality and Social Psychology Review, 1*(January), 3–25.

Cafferata, P., & Tybout, A. M. (1989). *Cognitive and affective responses to advertising.* Lexington, MA: Lexington Books.

Cantor, J. R., & Venus, P. (1980). The effects of humor on recall of a radio advertisement. *Journal of Broadcasting, 24*(1), 13–22.

Cantor, J. R., Zillman, D., & Bryant, J. (1975). Enhancement of humor appreciation by transferred excitation. *Journal of Personality and Social Psychology, 32,* 69–75.

Cronbach, L. J. (1987). Statistical tests for moderator variables: Flaws in analysis recently proposed. *Psychological Bulletin, 102*(3), 414–417.

De Pelsmacker, P., Geuens, M., & Anckaert, P. (2002). Media context and advertising effectiveness: The role of context appreciation and context/ad similarity. *Journal of Advertising, 31*(2), 49–61.

Derks, P., & Arora, S. (1993). Sex and salience in the appreciation of cartoon humor. *Humor-International Journal of Humor Research, 6*(1), 57–69.

Edell, J. A., & Burke, M. C. (1987). The power of feelings in understanding advertising effects. *Journal of Consumer Research, 14,* 421–433.

Gardner, M. P. (1985). Mood states and consumer behaviour: A critical review. *Journal of Consumer Research, 12,* 281–300.

Gardner, M. P., & Wilhelm, F. O., Jr. (1987). Consumer responses to ads with positive vs. negative appeals: Some mediating effects of content induced mood and congruency between context and ad. *Journal of Current Issues and Research in Advertising, 10*(1), 81–98.

Goldberg, M. E., & Gorn, G. J. (1987). Happy and sad TV programs: How they affect reactions to commercials. *Journal of Consumer Research, 14,* 387–403.

Goodstein, R. C. (1993). Category-based applications and extensions in advertising: Motivating more extensive ad processing. *Journal of Consumer Research, 20*(June), 87–99.

Hair, J. F., Jr., Anderson, R. E., Tatham, R. L., & Black, W. C. (1998). *Multivariate data analysis.* New Jersey: Prentice Hall Upper Saddle River.

Hasher, L., Rose, K. C., Zacks, R. T., Sanft, H., & Doren, B. (1985). Mood, recall, and selectivity effects in normal college students. *Journal of Experimental Psychology: General, 114,* 104–118.

Herr, P. M. (1989). Priming price: Prior knowledge and context effects. *Journal of Consumer Research, 16*(June), 67–75.

Holbrook, M. B., & Batra, R. (1987). Assessing the role of emotions as mediators of consumer responses to advertising. *Journal of Consumer Research, 14,* 404–420.

Irwin, J. R., & McClelland, G. H. (2001). Misleading heuristics and moderated multiple regression models. *Journal of Marketing Research, 38*(February), 100–109.

Isen, A. M., Shalker, T. E., Clark, M., & Karp, L. (1978). Affect, accessibility of material in memory, and behavior: A cognitive loop? *Journal of Personality and Social Psychology, 36,* 1–12.

Jaccard, J., Turrisi, R., & Wan, C. K. (1990). *Interaction effects in multiple regression.* Beverly Hills: Sage.

Juntunen, A. (1995). *Media context and advertising processing.* Helsinki: Helsinki School of Economics and Business Administration.

Kamins, M. A., Marks, L. J., & Skinner, D. (1991). Television commercial evaluation in the context of program induced mood: Congruency versus consistency effects. *Journal of Advertising, 20*(2), 1–14.

Klein, C. T. F., & Webster, D. M. (2000). Individual differences in argument scrutiny as motivated by need for cognitive closure. *Basic and Applied Social Psychology, 22*(2), 119–129.

Larsen, J. T., McGraw, P., & Cacioppo, J. T. (2001). Can people feel happy and sad at the same time? *Journal of Personality and Social Psychology, 81*(October), 684–696.

LaTour, M. S., Snipes, R. L., & Bliss, S. (1996). Don't be afraid of fear appeals: An experimental study. *Journal of Advertising Research, 36*(1), 59–67.

Lazarus, R. S. (1991). *Emotion and adaptation.* New York: Oxford University Press.

Lee, A., & Sternthal, B. (1999). The effects of positive mood on memory. *Journal of Consumer Research, 26,* 115–127.

Loewenstein, G., & Prelec, D. (1993). Preferences for sequences of outcomes. *Psychological Review, 100*(1), 91–108.

Lord, K. R., Burnkrant, R. E., & Unnava, H. R. (2001). The effects of program induced mood states on memory for commercial information. *Journal of Current Issues and Research in Advertising, 23,* 1–15.

McClelland, G. H. (1997). Optimal design in psychological research. *Psychological Methods, 2*(1), 3–19.

Murphy, J. H., Cunningham, I. C. M., & Wilcox, G. B. (1979). The impact of program environment on recall of humorous television commercials. *Journal of Advertising, 19,* 17–21.

Olsen, G. D., & Pracejus, J. W. (2004). Integration of positive and negative affective stimuli. *Journal of Consumer Psychology, 14*(4), 374–384.

Ortony, A., Clore, G. L., & Collins, A. (1988). *The cognitive structure of emotions.* Cambridge, CA: Cambridge University Press.

Perry, S. D., Jensowsky, S. A., King, C. M., Yi, H., Hester, J. B., & Gartenchlaeger, J. (1997). Using humorous programs as a vehicle for humorous commercials. *Journal of Communication, 47*(1), 20–39.

Plutchik, R. (1980). A general psychoevolutionary theory of emotion In: R. Plutchik & H. Kellerman (Eds), *Emotion: Theory, research, and experience: Theories of emotion* (Vol. 1, pp. 3–33). New York: Academic.

Schwarz, N. (1990). Feelings as information: Informational and motivational functions of affective states. In: R. M. Sorrentino & E. T. Higgins (Eds), *Handbook of motivation and cognition* (Vol. 2, pp. 521–561). New York: Guilford.

Schwarz, N., & Clore, G. L. (1983). Mood, misattribution, and judgments of well-being, informative and directive functions of affective states. *Journal of Personality and Social Psychology, 45,* 513–523.

Schwarz, N., & Clore, G. L. (1988). How do I feel about it? The information function of affective states. In: K. Fiedler & J. P. Forgas (Eds), *Affect, cognition and social behavior: New evidence and integrative attempts* (pp. 44–63). Toronto: C.J. Hogrefe.

Smith, S. M., Haugtvedt, C. P., Jadrich, J. M., & Anton, M. R. (1995). Understanding responses to sex appeals in advertising: An individual difference approach. In: F. Kardes & M. Sujan (Eds), *Advances in consumer research* (Vol. 22, pp. 734–739). Provo, UT: Association for Consumer Research.

Spotts, H. E., Weinberger, M. G., & Parsons, A. L. (1997). Assessing the use and impact of humor on advertising effectiveness: A contingency approach. *Journal of Advertising, 26*(3), 17–32.

Srull, T. K. (1983). Affect and memory: The impact of affective reactions in advertising on the representation of product information in memory. In: R. Bagozzi & A. Tybout (Eds), *Advances in consumer research* (Vol. 10, pp. 520–525). Ann Arbor, MI: Association for Consumer Research.

Vermeir, I. (2003). *The influence of need for closure on consumer behaviour.* Doctoral disser-
     tation, Ghent University, Belgium.
Webster, D. M., & Kruglanski, A. W. (1994). Individual differences in need for cognitive
     closure. *Journal of Personality and Social Psychology, 67*(6), 1049–1062.
Williams, P., & Aaker, J. (2002). Can mixed emotions peacefully coexist? *Journal of Consumer
     Research, 28*(4), 636–649.
Yi, Y. (1990). The effects of contextual priming in print advertisements. *Journal of Consumer
     Research, 17*, 215–222.
Yi, Y. (1993). Contextual priming effects in print advertisements: The moderating role of prior
     knowledge. *Journal of Advertising, 22*(1), 1–10.

EMOTIONAL RESPONSES: A NEW PARADIGM IN COMMUNICATION RESEARCH

Flemming Hansen, Sverre Riis Christensen, Steen Lundsteen and Larry Percy

ABSTRACT

Recent neurological research has pointed to the importance of fundamental emotional processes for most kinds of human behaviour. Measures of emotional response tendencies towards brands seem to reveal intangible aspects of brand equity, particularly in a marketing context. In this paper a procedure for estimating such emotional brand equity is presented and findings from two successive studies of more than 100 brands are reported. It demonstrates how changes that occur between two years are explainable in terms of factors identifiable in the markets, and that the measures otherwise are stable over time. Also, it is shown that the measurement procedure is extremely robust.

INTRODUCTION

As a concept under the broader heading of affect, emotions have often been used more or less synonymously with the concept of feelings. These affective

Cross-Cultural Buyer Behavior
Advances in International Marketing, Volume 18, 93–114
Copyright © 2007 by Elsevier Ltd.
ISSN: 1474-7979/doi:10.1016/S1474-7979(06)18004-7

concepts have been employed to help explain consumer choices that seemingly have had broader foundations in the psychology of the individual than sheer cognitive deliberation and evaluation. Contemporary neuroscientific research is producing new insights into how the brain works and the roles played by emotions when individuals make economic decisions. These advances have partly been made by employing brain-scanning technology to test persons who are subjected to commercial stimuli of various types. These findings are believed to be valid across different cultures. The present paper's contribution lies in integrating neuroscientific findings into the theory of consumer behaviour, and in the development of a questionnaire-based measurement methodology, which captures the emotional responses of consumers. The methodology is tested in two large-scale surveys in order to demonstrate the potential in measuring emotional responses as a prerequisite to understanding the intangible part of the so-called mental brand equity.

Affect in Consumer Behaviour Theory

Up until very recently, cognitive thinking has dominated consumer behaviour research. Bagozzi, Baumgartner, and YI (1992) have studied this by dealing with the theory of recent action. Janiszewski and Meyvis (2001) attempt to understand mere exposure (Zajonc, 1968) in terms of how it influences the processing fluency and the formation of larger chunks of information, rather than as an immediate effect of the exposure's affect. Also Barone, Miniard, and Romeo (2000), Shiv and Fedorikhin (1999), Luce (1998) and Duhachek (2005), in their concern about how to cope with conflicts between positive and negative goals, attempt to understand how consumers solve emotional problems using cognitive information processing.

Even when more affective elements are introduced they are seen in the light of cognitive choices. Pham, Cohen, Pracejus, and Hughes (2001) discuss feelings and choices in terms of judgemental properties of consciously administered feelings. Lee and Sternthal (1999) study mood as a factor influencing the stimulus object relationship in the classical cognitive response formulation. Murry, Lastovicka, and Singh (1992) attempt to understand how feelings for television programmes influence the evaluation of advertising which, in turn, influences the evaluation of brands. Finally, Adaval (2003), in his discussion of affect on brand evaluation, claims that affect influences the image of the brand and thereby is converted to a cognitive element.

Still, some authors in the last decade or two have increasingly concerned themselves with different aspects of affect. In early work, the terms feeling, emotions, moods and affect are used interchangeably. Erevelles (1998), however, emphasises a distinction between feelings/emotions, mood, affective aspects of attitudes and individual differences in affective behaviour. Here, as in most other research, feelings and emotions are used interchangeably and are seen as affective reactions of short duration to stimuli in the environment or to internal imbalances. In contrast to this, mood is seen as a longer lasting, mostly weaker affective condition of the individual.

The study of feelings/emotions has a reasonably long tradition in psychology and social psychology. Different authors (Izard, 1977; Plutchik & Kellerman, 1974; Frijda, 1986; Ekman, 1980) have proposed different listings of what they call primary, secondary and tertiary feelings – sometimes labelled emotions. Neither here nor in the consumer behaviour literature is any clear distinction between feelings and emotions found. Holbrook and Batra (1987) and Richins (1997) have reported listings of feelings/emotions of relevance for consumption behaviour. Feelings/emotions are seen by these authors as response patterns to different situations. A basic issue has, therefore, been whether such feelings/emotions are influenced by culture or if they exist in a consistent manner across different cultures. To a larger extent, the latter proposal must be regarded as inherited traits.

In dealing with different batteries of feeling questions it is always possible to distinguish between positively and negatively loaded feeling words (Ortony & Turner, 1990; Hansen, 2005). The positively loaded feelings/ emotions are seen to control approaching behaviour, whereas the negatively loaded feelings/emotions are seen to govern avoidance behaviour.

The role of emotions, as a fundamental physiological brain process guiding and influencing most individual choice behaviours, and certainly consumer choices, is becoming well documented. Here, emotions are seen as fundamentally different from feelings. Emotions are elementary, unconscious, neurological processes and sometimes labelled as somatic markers. Feelings are their cognitive counterparts. Basic research in this area has been reported by LeDoux (1998, 2002) and Damasio (1994, 2000, 2003). Using functional magnetic resonance imaging (fMRI), they have shown how, though thus far largely overlooked, elementary behaviour controlling processes in the individual play an important role in consumers' everyday lives. The impact of such processes on consumer choices has been shown by McClure, Li, Tomlin, Cypert, Montague, and Montague (2004). From an fMRI experiment, they identified how emotions associated with a brand name may pop up in consumers' evaluation process. Each of the four identical groups was asked to consume a cola drink and report upon their experience of the consumption. One group was faced with a cola brand unknown to the respondents. The second group was faced with the same unknown cola brand but with a brand name attached to it. The third group was faced with Coca Cola without knowing the brand name and finally the fourth group was given Coca Cola with the brand name attached. Only in the last group were brain responses clearly identifiable as emotional response. The ability to respond emotionally to brands in this manner relies on inherited emotional response tendencies combined with guiding mechanisms (labelled by some authors as somatic markers). These guiding mechanisms are acquired through earlier experiences with the items that eventually give rise to emotional responses. Similar findings are reported by Deppe, Sschwindt, Kugel, Plassman, and Kenning (2005).

The use of fMRI or other brain scanning devices, in consumer behaviour studies is, however, difficult. Costs per observation are extremely high and the necessary equipment is limited and, in most places, assigned to medical research. Therefore, other ways in which emotional response tendencies can be identified are needed when one wants to estimate such tendencies, as they are associated with different brands, products, company names, etc.

Building upon the work of Kroeber-Riel (1993), attempts have been made with pictorial scales, and among these is a very ingenious attempt reported by Desmet (2003). Both Kroeber-Riel and Desmet work with simplistic drawings of faces among which respondents are asked to choose. By counting what faces are chosen, and at what frequency, to describe a particular brand or product, a measure of the extent to which an underlying emotion is aroused is established. Desmet demonstrated how this measurement technique can be applied across different cultures, and how the emotions are validated on traditional verbal scales used to describe feelings and emotions. Similar work is reported by Charlton-Jones (2005) and Hollis (2005). Attempts with eye movements should also be mentioned (Hutton, Goode, & Wilson, 2006).

However, all these methodologies are cumbersome and expensive. Therefore, attempts with interview-based measures are vital for consumer behaviour research. Hansen (2005) argues that feeling words, when presented as stimuli to respondents in survey research, will tap the actual and the unconscious emotional response to the specific object in question. The argument is that, since conscious feelings are generated by unconscious emotional responses, having respondents consciously scale such feeling words will, in essence, gauge the underlying – and unconscious – emotional responses that have given rise to the feelings. The issue is further discussed below. When such data from survey research is analysed with factor analysis, Hansen (2005) demonstrates that two underlying factors result, which correspond to approach and avoidance behaviour; or to positive/negative interpretation such as joy or sorrow. These are completely in line with other research on basic emotional responses. In S–O–R terminology, with S being the stimulus, R being the response and O representing the unknown interviewing process (here emotions or somatic markers), inferences can be made about them from studying relating patterns of stimuli and responses.

Feelings and Emotions

For the last 15–20 years, most consumer behaviour research concerned with affect used the words "emotions" and "feelings" interchangeably. However, to make the concept of emotions operational in its own right, it is important to establish a distinction between emotions and feelings. This distinction is evident in the work by neurologists. For instance, Damasio (2003) and others see emotions as an underlying, inherited response controlling processes that are never conscious and that take place in the most primitive, inner parts of the brain. Feelings, on the other hand, are those cognitive counterparts associated with the underlying emotions that the individual may or may not experience consciously. This distinction will be maintained here. A thorough discussion of this distinction between feelings and emotions is found in Hansen, Christensen, and Lundsteen (forthcoming).

How Many Different Emotions?

Obviously, the feelings aroused by any state of emotion may be complex and may cover many different individual feelings. As of today, there is no general agreement among researchers as to just how many basic emotions one should expect to be able to locate; fear and happiness, however, are well documented. Different researchers think in terms of two to six basic emotions from which all others can be derived.

In medical treatment of individuals with different brain diseases, it is obviously useful to think of several different kinds of emotional distortions accounting for various mental problems. All such emotions, however, have one thing in common. They are either positive in the sense that they guide approach behaviour and are accompanied by pleasant, joyful feelings, or they are of a negative nature, accompanied by avoidance behaviour, and feelings of sadness or the like. With the present state of development in brain neurological research it seems warranted to limit the application of emotional thinking in consumer behaviour to a fundamental positive approach versus a negative avoidance view. In addition to this basic view of emotions, one may also talk about the arousal or intensity of the emotional state. One may think of this as reflected in the numeric sum of the positive and negative emotions.

In the present paper we shall, in a summary fashion, report findings from two large-scale studies where it has been attempted to quantify positive and negative emotional response tendencies aroused by brands and product categories.

THE STUDIES

The present studies rest on the assumption that systematic analysis of people's way of expressing themselves, in terms of feeling words when faced with brands or products, can be used to derive the underlying emotional response tendency associated with whatever brand or product is being studied. Basically, the idea is illustrated in Figs. 1 and 2. Fig. 1 shows how a particular brand gives rise to an emotional response which, in turn, may or may not give rise to conscious or unconscious feelings. The respondent is then able to articulate these feelings to the researcher. In Fig. 2, the opposite process is illustrated. Here, the respondent is provided with a number of relevant feeling words in connection with a particular brand or product and is asked to respond to these feeling words with a particular brand or product in mind. Based upon these responses, the underlying positive and negative emotional response tendencies aroused by the brand or product is quantified.

Fig. 1.   From Emotions to Brand Feelings to Brand Evaluation.

Fig. 2. From Brand Feelings to Emotions.

The Present Project

As indicated above, verbal scales have a distinct advantage over other methods when it comes to the measurement of emotions and of emotional responses. Namely, they lend themselves to large-scale survey research in a way that brain-scanning methodology does not. Through this advantage, the application of verbal scales of feeling words enables the researcher to produce statistically meaningful results from representative samples of normal consumers, an issue which is central to all marketers.

An opportunity arose through the active sponsorship of a research project by TNS/Gallup to measure emotional responses towards a large number of brands with the use of verbal scales as part of an ongoing research project that measures Danish consumers' lifestyles and brand affiliations.

The purpose of the project was

- to test verbal scales as a measurement device for emotional responses in a consumer behaviour context,
- to develop a measurement-based model of the standing of brands in the mental space of the consumer,
- to test a number of hypotheses concerning how intensely consumers react to various types of products and brands, and
- to provide a benchmark of brand standings for a repeat study at a later point in time.

Taking the Rossiter/Percy grid as a point of departure (Rossiter & Percy, 1998), a two-dimensional classification of types of consumer purchase situations was implemented. Here, consumer's buying motivation in two variations is juxtaposed against two variations of consumer product involvement. A number of hypotheses were developed based on interpretations of previous research's implications for assumed emotional response intensities towards product categories and individual brands.

Based upon the distinction in the Rossiter/Percy grid between low and high involvement and informational versus transformational motivation, the following hypotheses were developed.

- When involvement is low, emotional response intensity should also be low, reflecting the fact that the brand at hand is non-core to the consumer.
- When involvement is high, emotional response intensity should be high, since the brand or service at hand is closer to the personality of the consumer.
- When the buying motive is informational – meaning that the product is bought to avoid a negative situation or to remedy a negative state, such as pain relief for headache – it would seem that negative emotional reaction will be present due to the state that is to be avoided. A positive emotional response should also be present since the purchase will eventually lead to relief of the negative state. The net result of positive and negative responses will presumably be close to zero, depending on the intensity of the two responses.
- When the buying motive is transformational – meaning that the product is bought for self-gratification purposes – a strong emotional response is to be expected and of a positive nature, since the product will be associated with positive emotional memories from past experience and will, in itself, give promises of gratification.

The main purpose of the project, reported here, is to demonstrate that emotional response tendencies to brands and to product categories can be measured with the use of verbal scales. Such scales contain feeling words that are applied in a questionnaire for a piece of survey research.

Choice of Feeling Words

For the measurement task, a selection of feeling words was assembled (for a discussion of this see Hansen, 2005). Initially, a total of 24 feeling words were included in the 2003 study. Not all are equally relevant for all brands and categories, however, thus, in the analysis, 10 feeling words are chosen for each brand category. The most informative words were for the particular brand or category in question. In the second study, the basic set of feeling

	Low Involvement		High Involvement
Informational	**Shampoo:** • *Dove* • **Head &** **Shoulder** • **Sanex** **Detergents:** • *Ariel* • **BioTex** • **Neutral** • **Persil**	**Pain killers:** • *Panodil* • **Magnyl** • **Aspirin** **Gasoline:** • *Shell* • **Hydro Texaco** • **OK Benzin** • **Q8**	**Cell phone companies** *Computers* **Banks** Newspapers
Transformational		**Coffee** *Cereal* *Bread* *Cosmetics*	**Perfume** *Cars* *Airlines* *Amusement parks* *TV-Sets*

Fig. 3. Category and Brands in Rossiter/Percy Grid Included in the Study.

words was reduced to 16 by deleting the least frequently used ones. Then again, for each category, the most important ones were chosen.

Choice of Stimuli for the Studies

The first study reported was conducted in 2003 and covered approximately 800 respondents. The second study in 2004 included 4,000 respondents. Data collection was provided by TNS/Gallup in Denmark. To provide a broad coverage of different product areas, product categories were chosen to represent the four quadrants departing in the Rossiter and Percy (1998) grid. A distinction was made between more- and less-involving products and also between informational versus transformational products. A total of 64 brands were included in the first study and 100 brands in the second study (as illustrated in Fig. 3 for the first study). The choice of categories, for each quadrant, was guided by the personal counselling of Professor Larry Percy.

DATA COLLECTION

The measurements were obtained in 2003 with the questionnaire shown in Fig. 4. The main difference between the two studies follows because the first study employed a self-administered questionnaire whereas the second employed a computer-based questionnaire. Additionally, a different number of feeling words, brands and categories were used, as discussed. In the data

On the following pages, different brand names are mentioned. We are now interested in how you feel when you think of each brand name. Under each brand name there is a list of feelings that one may have when thinking of a brand. For each brand that you know, please tick the box next to the word that matches the feelings you have, when you think of the brand. There are no right or wrong answers, and you may tick a box next to many or few words – all depending on what you think is most fitting when you think of the specific brand. After this, and next to each feeling box you have ticked, please show how strong the feeling is. This is done by use of the 7-point scale, where 1 means "Not very strong feeling" and 7 means "Very strong feeling".

This question is about the mobile phone brand/mobile phone company "Sonofon". If you do not know "Sonofon", please, go to the next brand question.

Please, tick off the words that describe your feeling when you think of the brand.	Please, tick off according to how strong the feeling is.							
	Not very strong				Very strong			
271.	1	2	3	4	5	6	7	
Desire	☐	☐	☐	☐	☐	☐	☐	☐	272.
Sexy	☐	☐	☐	☐	☐	☐	☐	☐	273.
Exciting	☐	☐	☐	☐	☐	☐	☐	☐	274.
Stimulating	☐	☐	☐	☐	☐	☐	☐	☐	275.
Happy	☐	☐	☐	☐	☐	☐	☐	☐	276.
Fine	☐	☐	☐	☐	☐	☐	☐	☐	277.
Calm	☐	☐	☐	☐	☐	☐	☐	☐	278.
Fresh, healthy	☐	☐	☐	☐	☐	☐	☐	☐	279.
Pretty	☐	☐	☐	☐	☐	☐	☐	☐	280.
Expectation	☐	☐	☐	☐	☐	☐	☐	☐	281.
Pride	☐	☐	☐	☐	☐	☐	☐	☐	282.
Success	☐	☐	☐	☐	☐	☐	☐	☐	283.
Aggressive	☐	☐	☐	☐	☐	☐	☐	☐	284.
Smart	☐	☐	☐	☐	☐	☐	☐	☐	285.
Relief	☐	☐	☐	☐	☐	☐	☐	☐	286.
Critical	☐	☐	☐	☐	☐	☐	☐	☐	287.
Doubt	☐	☐	☐	☐	☐	☐	☐	☐	288.
Boring	☐	☐	☐	☐	☐	☐	☐	☐	289.
Sad	☐	☐	☐	☐	☐	☐	☐	☐	290.
Pain	☐	☐	☐	☐	☐	☐	☐	☐	291.
Loneliness	☐	☐	☐	☐	☐	☐	☐	☐	292.
Worry	☐	☐	☐	☐	☐	☐	☐	☐	293.
Irritating	☐	☐	☐	☐	☐	☐	☐	☐	294.
Fear	☐	☐	☐	☐	☐	☐	☐	☐	295.
Nothing									

Fig. 4. Questionnaire.

collection respondents were asked to pick feeling words that had any meaning for them in connection with each particular brand or product category as presented. Subsequently they were asked to rate how strongly they felt that particular feeling. The first study offered 24 feeling words while the second study offered 16. The sample sizes were 800 in 2003 and 4,000 in 2004, where each brand was evaluated by approximately every fourth respondent.

Data Analysis

In 2004, 100 brands and 26 categories were rated. From the large data matrix it is possible to select individual brands and carry out exploratory factor analysis for each using the rating on the chosen feeling words. In all 126 cases in 2004 (and 80 cases in 2003), a strong positive and a strong negative factor emerged from this procedure (Hansen et al., forthcoming). It was decided in advance that, with consumer goods, the overall positive and negative response tendency provides useful information. As such, feeling words were selected for each brand or category that were most frequently used and most clearly associated with the positive/negative dimension. In this manner, six positive and four negative feeling words were chosen for each category. The reason for choosing more positive than negative feeling words was that many more positive feeling words were used in the rating of the brands and categories. With this analysis completed for all brands and product categories it was possible to compute an overall positive and an overall negative emotional response tendency for each of these. This is illustrated in Table 1 where the computation for a single brand is illustrated.

Here, the respondent in question has rated the brand Dove with the scale values given in the second column in the table. In the first column, the 10 feeling words used for Dove (and all other shampoo brands) are listed. In the third and fifth columns, the loadings on the positive and negative evaluative dimension are respectfully given. Taking these loadings as a measure of the importance of the particular feeling words, a total positive and a total negative value can be computed for the respondent, as it is done in the fourth and the sixth columns. Here, for each respondent, the particular answer to a given question is multiplied with the corresponding factor loading from the analysis of the brand in question. This procedure was chosen since the more straightforward use of component score coefficients would have provided results less meaningful for making comparisons across categories. From this, it is possible to compute the difference between the positive and the negative score (last column). We have labelled this as the net emotional response strengths (NERS) and it is taken as the basic measure of the extent to which the respondent is drawn to or pushed away from the particular brand in question.

Before continuing with these scores, a few words are in order about the experiences gained in the course of the huge computational task handling more than 200 test items and close to 5,000 respondents over the two years.

Table 1. Example of Calculation of Net Emotional Response Strength (NERS) Score for a Respondent's Answers to the Feeling Questions for Dove (Respondent No. 283).

Emotional Statement	Answer	Factor Loading +Emotions	Positive Score (Answer × Loading)	Factor Loading −Emotion	Negative Score	NERS (Positive Score−Negative Score)
	a	b	$a \times b$	c	$a \times c$	
Desire	2	0.59	1.17	0.00	0.01	
Stimulating	3	0.74	2.21	0.02	0.06	
Happy	0	0.90	0	0.00	0	
Fine	6	0.68	4.08	−0.03	−0.02	
Fresh	4	0.75	3.01	−0.04	−0.02	
Pretty	2	0.82	1.64	0.01	0.02	
Critical	0	−0.01	0	0.75	0	
Doubt	0	−0.02	0	0.72	0	
Worry	5	0.01	0.04	0.54	2.70	
Irritating	2	−0.01	−0.03	0.90	0.18	
Total			12.12		2.93	9.20

1. Very different feeling words are used in connection with different product categories; however, all brands within the same category tend to rely upon the same feeling words. Thus, as described, a particular set of feeling words are selected for each category and used across brands and on the category.
2. For some brands, almost the same explained variance could be obtained using one or two less feeling words in the final solution. Similarly, with other brands, slight improvements in the amount of explained variance could be gained by adding one or two more feeling words in the computations. On the whole, however, for the sake of comparison across product categories, it makes sense to stay with the six positive and four negative feeling words in all cases.
3. The overall findings are not highly sensitive to minor variations in the feeling words included in the NERS computations. The same pattern, that is the rank ordering of brands, and the size of the brand's NERS scores relative to that of the category, is quite insensitive to changes in the selection of feeling words included.

FINDINGS

Each brand and each category provides its own results. An example is shown in Table 2.

In the example one may observe a negative score for the brand "Head & Shoulders." This is ascribable to the larger negative scores among non-users of the brand, probably due to the negative dandruff associations they have in connection with this brand.

It is possible to compute a NERS score for each brand and also for each category. The results for the data from the second year of analysis are shown

Table 2. Emotional Response Strength Score, Net Emotional Response Strength (NERS) for Three Shampoo Brands and Four Brands of Perfume.

Brand	Valid Respondents N	+Emotion	−Emotion	Difference (NERS-Score)
Dove	40	4.981	1.604	3.377
Head & Shoulders	29	2.376	2.996	−0.620
Sanex	42	6.833	1.284	5.552
Category		4.730	1.961	2.770

Table 3.   Average NERS Scores by Rossiter & Percy Grid Category,
2003 and 2004 Study.

	Informational		Transformational	
	2003	2004	2003	2004
Low involvement	3.36	−0.36	6.14	1.86
High involvement	4.89	0.66	6.21	3.42

in the appendix. Here, the scores are grouped depending on high/low involvement and on informational versus transformational buying motives.
The average scores for products and brands in the different categories are
provided in Table 3. Here, the scores suggest increased NERS with more
involving and more transformational kinds of products. In a sense, one will
also expect the numeric sum of the feeling scores to reflect the extent to which
the individual is involved in the issue; with more involvement, there is more
emotional response. Table 3 also demonstrates this notion, where the numeric
sum of the positive and negative emotional response scores is computed.

The Stability of the NERS Scores

Forty-one brands and product categories were included both in the 2003
and the 2004 data collection. A comparison of the NERS scores for these
brands between the two study years is shown in Fig. 5. Two observations
can be made from the diagram and the corresponding regression analyses.
   First, the scores in 2004 are significantly lower than the corresponding
scores in 2003. In fact, the scores practically correspond to the value of the
constant in the straight-line equation. This phenomenon may be accounted
for by the differences in methodology in the data collection in the two years.
Whereas in the first year self-administered written questionnaires were
mailed out and returned, in the second year members of an internet panel
were approached. For one thing, the latter reduces the sample population to
people aged between 15 and 65. Also, the interviewing procedure feasible
on a computer screen makes the whole rating procedure fundamentally
different from what is going on when respondents are working with a self-
administered printed questionnaire. Differences of this nature are not uncommon in the research industry.
   Second, when tested for the significance of the difference between the
scores in the two years, 16 out of the 41 possible cases represent significant

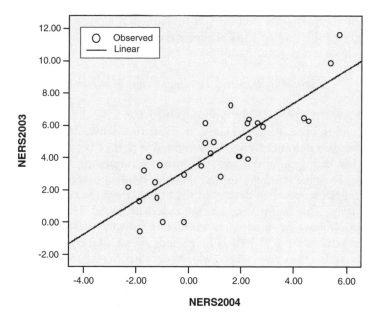

Fig. 5. NERS Scores in 2003 and 2004 for Brands Included in the Studies in Both Years ($NERS_{2003} = 0.914 NERS_{2004} + 3.692$; $R^2 = 0.619$, $p < 0.000$ (0.95 Confidence Interval)).

differences. It is important to ask what causes these 16 changes from the one year to the other. In analysing the data it is possible, in all but one case, to find very meaningful explanations for the changes that have occurred. We cannot cover all 16 cases here but rather offer two examples.

For the cereal brands, NERS decreases for the category as such. Kellogg's, in particular, experienced decreases of the NERS scale over the two-year frame. In the year 2003–2004 the obesity debate became very hot in Denmark, and Kellogg's was much criticised for its sugar-covered cereals. In addition to this, in the same year, Kellogg's withdrew from the Coop stores because of disagreements on trade conditions and thereby lost one-third of its distribution. Undoubtedly, these two factors explain the development in the NERS scores for the product category and of Kellogg's in particular.

A very different case appears in the bank industry. On the whole, banks give rise to quite low NERS scores, with the major banks scoring lower than the smaller ones. In this market, between 2003 and 2004, the BG Bank improved significantly from one year to the other. This may be seen as the effect of large advertising spending, sponsoring and personal education efforts of the personnel, following a fundamental strategy change for this subsidiary of the leading bank, Danske Bank.

Emotional Response Tendencies and Brand Equity

The findings reported in the appendix provide a wealth of information about leading brands in the Danish market. In a sense, one may interpret the scores as a quantification of the intangible part of the different brands' equity. Looked upon in this way, a number of interesting observations can be made. In some markets we find that the product category gives rise to higher NERS scores than do any of the brands from the category included in the study. This is, for instance, the case with bread. Here it seems that what people have in mind when evaluating bread is freshly baked bread from the baker's store as well as homemade bread, and not the pre-packed bread available in supermarkets, which was rated in the study.

Conversely, in other areas such as real estate agents, we find the category having very low NERS scores. However, some of the major operators, even though they also give rise to low NERS scores, are being judged slightly more positive than the category in general. Still, another observation relates to outstanding brands. In some areas, the majority of brands score lower than the category; however, one or two brands deviate from this pattern and yield a higher score. This is the case with Tivoli, Bang, and Olufsen (in the 2003 data) and Tide detergent. Here, the brands have managed to acquire a unique standing among its consumers that result in very high NERS scores.

CONCLUSIONS

The studies reported here demonstrate that it is possible to quantify, in a meaningful manner, intangible brand equity in terms of the emotional response tendencies associated with brands and with products. To the extent that many brand choices are made very quickly in front of the shelves in a supermarket, these emotional response tendencies are likely to play an important role in guiding consumer behaviour. Moreover, emotions activated by brand names may, in turn, influence the cognitive processes activated when further evaluation of the brands take place. It has been demonstrated that, although such emotional response tendencies are relatively stable over time, they also undergo changes when changing market conditions occur. Also they are likely to reveal cross-cultural differences when applied internationally.

Much advertising evaluation is based upon cognitive thinking, not least on measures such as advertising recall, and advertising liking. To the extent that emotional response tendencies become modified when respondents are exposed to advertising, the NERS measure lends itself as an instrument in advertising tracking and advertising pre-testing. The sensitivity of these measures has yet to be thoroughly documented. Tentative findings from a commercial research institute using feeling words similar to those used in the NERS have, however, suggested that such sensitivity is there (Du Plessis, 2005; Charlton-Jones, 2005).

In terms of future research two directions are particularly promising. First, it would be useful to study how NERS relate to emotions measured with eye scanning, pictorial tests and fMRI scanning. Second, it is important to shed light on how sensitive NERS scores are to specific marketing communication provided by advertising, displays, packaging design, etc. Both topics are in focus in ongoing projects at Center for Marketing Communication.

ACKNOWLEDGMENTS

The authors are grateful for the contributions made to this project by Research Director Rolf Randrup, Gallup-TNS, Copenhagen.

REFERENCES

Adaval, R. (2003). How good gets better and bad gets worse: Understanding the impact of affect on evaluations of known brands. *Journal of Consumer Research, 30*(3), 352–367.

Bagozzi, R. P., Baumgartner, H., & YI, Y. (1992). State versus action orientation and the theory of reasoned action: An application to coupon usage. *Journal of Consumer Research, 18*(4), 505–518.

Barone, M. J., Miniard, P. W., & Romeo, J. B. (2000). The influence of positive mood on brand extension evaluations. *Journal of Consumer Research, 26*(4), 386–400.

Charlton-Jones, J. (2005). Capturing emotions in advertising and benefiting from the knowledge. *Proceedings of the 2005 European advertising effectiveness symposium*, Budapest, June.

Damasio, A. (1994). *Descarte's error: Emotion, reason, and the human brain*. New York: Grosset/Putnam.

Damasio, A. (2000). *The feeling of what happens*. London: Vintage.

Damasio, A. (2003). *Looking for Spinoza: Joy, sorrow, and the feeling brain*. New York: Harcourt.

Deppe, M., Sschwindt, W., Kugel, H., Plassman, H., & Kenning, P. (2005). Nonlinear responses within the medial prefrontal cortex reveal when specific implicit information influences economic decision making. *Journal of Neuroimaging, 15,* 171–182.

Desmet, P. M. A. (2003). Measuring emotions. In: M. A. Blythe, A. F. Monk, K. Overbeeke & P. C. Wright (Eds), *Funology: From usability to enjoyment* (pp. 111–123). Dordrecht: Kluwer Academic Publishers.

Du Plessis, E. (2005). *The advertised mind.* London: Kogan Page.

Duhachek, A. (2005). Coping: A multidimensional, hierarchical framework of responses to stressful consumption episodes. *Journal of Consumer Research, 32*(1), 41–53.

Ekman, P. (1980). Biological and cultural contributions to body and facial movement in the expression of emotions. In: A. O. Rorty (Ed.), *Explaining emotions.* Berkeley: University of California Press.

Erevelles, S. (1998). The role of affect in marketing. *Journal of Business Research, 42,* 199–215.

Frijda (1986). *The emotions.* Cambridge, England: Cambridge University Press.

Hansen, F. (2005). Distinguishing between feelings and emotions in understanding communication effects. *Journal of Business Research, 58,* 1426–1436.

Hansen, F., Christensen, S. R., & Lundsteen, S. (Forthcoming). Emotions, advertising and consumer choice. Copenhagen: CBS Press.

Holbrook, M. B., & Batra, R. (1987). Assessing the role of emotions as mediators of consumer responses to advertising. *The Journal of Consumer Research, 14*(3), 404–420.

Hollis, N. (2005). Measuring the power of emotions. *Proceedings from the 2005 European advertising effectiveness symposium,* Budapest, Hungary, June.

Hutton, S. B., Goode, A., & Wilson, P. (2006). Using eye tracking to measure consumer engagement during television commercial viewing. *Proceedings from ICORIA 2006,* Bath, England.

Izard, C. E. (1977). *Human emotions.* New York: Plenum Press.

Janiszewski, C., & Meyvis, T. (2001). Effects of brand logo complexity, repetition, and spacing on processing fluency and judgment, 28, June.

Kroeber-Riel, W. (1993). *Bildkommunikation (pictorial communication).* Munich: Vahlen. English summary provided by LANGNER, T., Justus-Liebig-University, Giessen, August.

LeDoux, J. (1998). *The emotional brain.* London: Phoenix.

LeDoux, J. (2002). *Synaptic self: How our brains become who we are.* New York: Viking.

Lee, A. Y., & Sternthal, B. (1999). The effects of positive mood on memory. *Journal of Consumer Research, 26*(2), 115–127.

Luce, M. F. (1998). Choosing to avoid: Coping with negatively emotion-laden consumer decisions. *Journal of Consumer Research, 24*(4), 409–433.

McClure, S., Li, J., Tomilin, D., Cypert, K. S., Montague, L. M., & Montague, P. R. (2004). Neural correlates of behavioural preference for culturally familiar drinks. *Neuron, 44,* 379–387.

Murry, J. P., Lastovicka, J. L., & Singh, S. N. (1992). Feeling and liking responses to television programs: An examination of two explanations for media-context effects. *Journal of Consumer Research, 18*(4), 441–451.

Ortony, A., & Turner, T. J. (1990). What's basic about basic emotions? *Psychological Review, 97,* 313.

Pham, M. T., Cohen, J. B., Pracejus, J. W., & Hughes, G. D. (2001). Affect monitoring and the primacy of feelings in judgment. *Journal of Consumer Research, 28*(September), 167–188.

Plutchik, R., & Kellerman, H. (1974). *Emotions profile index – manual.* Los Angeles: Western Psychological Services.

Richins, M. L. (1997). Measuring emotions in the consumption experience. *Journal of Consumer Research*, 24(September), 127–142.

Rossiter, J. R., & Percy, L. (1998). *Advertising communication and promotion management.* New York: McGraw-Hill.

Shiv, B., & Fedorikhin, A. (1999). Heart and mind in conflict: The interplay of affect and cognition in consumer decision making. *Journal of Consumer Research, 26*(3), 224–238.

Zajonc, R. B. (1968). Attitudinal effects of mere exposure. *Journal of Personality and Social Psychology, 9*(2), 1–27.

APPENDIX

Rank	Brand	NERS
1	Tivoli	5.71
2	Legoland	5.40
3	Lego	4.86
4	Bakken	4.56
5	BonBon-land	4.37
6	Brio	3.82
7	Spies Rejser	3.36
8	Tjæreborg Rejser	3.35
9	Fisher Price	3.19
10	Star Tour	3.12
11	My Travel	2.95
12	After Eight	2.86
13	Schulstad	2.82
14	Toms	2.81
15	DR 2	2.73
16	Kohberg	2.62
17	Rynkeby	2.52
18	Faxe Kondi	2.46
19	Stimorol	2.45
20	Ota	2.41
21	Merrild	2.30
22	Gevalia	2.30
23	Haribo	2.29
24	Karat	2.25
25	Sanex	2.23
26	SorBits	2.20

APPENDIX (*Continued*)

Rank	Brand	NERS
27	Coca Cola	2.20
28	Zulu	2.17
29	Nokia	2.08
30	Matas	1.98
31	Dove	1.94
32	BKI	1.90
33	TV2	1.87
34	Malaco	1.83
35	Rød Ålborg	1.83
36	BonBon	1.78
37	Gammel Dansk	1.73
38	Sony Ericsson	1.72
39	Urban	1.69
40	MetroXpress	1.63
41	Bacardi	1.63
42	Kellogg's	1.63
43	Hatting	1.59
44	Lurpak	1.59
45	Samsung	1.42
46	DR 1	1.36
47	Martini	1.30
48	Thiele	1.28
49	OK	1.21
50	Kærgården	1.13
51	Telmore	1.13
52	Engholm	1.12
53	Politiken	0.95
54	Garnier Fructis	0.89
55	Kims	0.89
56	Synoptik	0.86
57	Femina	0.85
58	Q8	0.83
59	Statoli	0.68
60	Bakkedal	0.66
61	Siemens	0.65
62	Estrella	0.64
63	Hydro	0.62

APPENDIX (*Continued*)

Rank	Brand	NERS
64	Berlingske Tide	0.61
65	Alt for Damern	−0.53
66	Jyllands-Poster	0.48
67	3+	0.46
68	Jyske	0.46
69	TV3	0.45
70	CBB Mobil	0.15
71	Nykredit	0.07
72	Fun Saftevand	−0.13
73	Realkredit Dann	−0.13
74	Head & Should	−0.17
75	Shell	−0.19
76	BRF Kredit	−0.50
77	EDC	−0.57
78	Danbolig	−0.59
79	Home	−0.61
80	Nybolig	−0.69
81	Tryg	−0.70
82	BG	−0.98
83	Mobil 3	−0.99
84	Topdanmark	−1.01
85	Nordea	−1.11
86	Codan	−1.15
87	TDC Mobil	−1.21
88	Danske	−1.28
89	BT	−1.52
90	Billed Bladet	−1.56
91	Fair forsikring	−1.65
92	Sonofon	−1.71
93	Telia	−1.85
94	Orange	−1.87
95	Alm. Brand	−1.90
96	Her og nu	−2.05
97	Debitel	−2.08
98	Ekstra-bladet	−2.30
99	Kig ind	−2.38
100	Se & Hør	−2.60

APPENDIX (*Continued*)

Rank	Category	NERS
1	Amusement parks	5.04
2	Coffee	4.26
3	Toys	3.95
4	Bread	3.64
5	Charter companies	3.41
6	Beverages	2.40
7	Shampoo	2.26
8	News papers	2.22
9	Cereals	2.17
10	Candy	2.15
11	Spirits	1.32
12	Glasses	1.26
13	TV stations	0.77
14	Mobile phones	0.46
15	Chips	0.28
16	Butter	0.27
17	Weekly magazines	−0.44
18	Mortgage companies	−0.56
19	Banks	−0.65
20	Gasoline	−0.94
21	Real estate dealers	−2.06
22	Mobile companies	−2.28
23	Insurance	−2.63

"TRADING UP": A CONSUMPTION VALUE APPROACH

Eunju Ko and Heewon Sung

ABSTRACT

"Trading up" is the phenomenon that describes consumers' willingness to pay premiums on goods that are emotionally meaningful to them. The meaning of a good is reliant on an individual's consumption values. The purpose of this study was to examine the phenomenon of trading up among Korean university students. A total of 223 usable surveys were analyzed. Fifty-one product categories were reported for trading up, and divided into four classifications: clothes, fashion accessories, small electronics, and other appliances. These four classifications were significantly associated with brand types, retailing formats, and information sources. Finally, respondents were classified into three groups according to consumption values and each group exhibited different relationships with the marketing mix variables.

INTRODUCTION

In the 21st century, changes in the lifestyles and the values of individuals have greatly affected not only the worldwide consumer market, but the entire field of marketing. Consumers have become more sophisticated and

Cross-Cultural Buyer Behavior
Advances in International Marketing, Volume 18, 115–137
Copyright © 2007 by Elsevier Ltd.
All rights of reproduction in any form reserved
ISSN: 1474-7979/doi:10.1016/S1474-7979(06)18005-9

refined in their tastes than ever before. They have more discretionary money and more product knowledge and they are exposed to a wide variety of product choices in the global marketplace. As a result, their consumption behaviors have polarized since they make a purchase depending on their subjective, emotional values rather than on standardized product attributes. Consumers tend to demand either a high-ended product or a low-cost product to meet their needs in every category of goods (Silverstein & Fiske, 2003). This describes the phenomena of "trading up" and "trading down." That is, if an individual is valued on fashion items, but not on well-being foods, this person will tend to buy designer label t-shirts at boutiques (trading up) and generic foods at the supermarket (trading down).

The trading up phenomenon originated from America's middle market, but has evolved into a worldwide trend in Europe and Japan (Silverstein & Fiske, 2004). Very little research has investigated the consumption values and the adoption of new-luxury goods of Korean consumers, however, who are considered a target for testing new products in the global market.

Korea is the one of the leading countries in the area of information infra. About 72.8% of the whole population over the age of 6, and 98% of the population under the age of 30 have used the internet (National Internet Development Agency of Korea, 2006). The speed of the internet, as well as the possession rate of the mobile phone, is the highest in the world. The exchange rate of the mobile phone is the world's shortest at less than 2 years. Thus, the rates of information acquisition and diffusion have accelerated in Korea. Further, word of mouth through the online network also boosts the formation of a new trend. As such, Korean consumers have built up their refined tastes through informational technology advantages.

The change in family structure of Korea is another reason why the country is a good test market. There are three primary changes to note. First, Korea recorded the lowest birthrate (1.17) among OECD countries in 2002. The Korean current report indicates a birth rate 1.08 in 2005. The major reason for the low birthrate is the increase in workingwomen and the late marriage trend. Second, a change has been noted in women. Women, especially those in younger generations, have begun to weigh self-development, or self-satisfaction, against their sacrifice for family-related duties (Park, 2006; Yoo, 2005). These factors have contributed to an increase in disposable income as well as an interest in new fashion trends. Finally, the younger generations who have buying power are continuously exposed to state-of-the-art goods and have thus become one of the largest consumer segments of luxury brands. Although some of the goods may be priced beyond their discretionary cash limits, this segment sacrifices money, which may have been initially allocated for personal expenses, in order to afford such luxury goods.

The purpose of this study is to examine the "trading up" behaviors of young Korean consumers in order to identify market opportunities. While previous studies have focused on a limited number of product categories, this study's purpose was broad in scope. The aim of this research was to discover what types of goods consumers considered meaningful. Fundamental information would be provided regarding which product categories consumers trade up as well as the reasons behind their actions. Further, it is necessary for each product category to specify the brand types, the retailing formats, and the information sources in order to suggest detailed marketing strategies. Lastly, identifying difference of consumer groups based upon consumption values would be helpful in understanding consumption behaviors. Understanding such differences of consumer groups in regards to lifestyle factors and to demographic characteristics would be useful in segmenting the potential market for brand development strategies.

LITERATURE REVIEW

Trading Up Phenomenon

Trading up is the phenomenon in which consumers, especially those in the middle class, tend to pay a premium for products or services with high levels of quality, taste, and aspiration because they are emotionally meaningful to them (Silverstein & Fiske, 2004). Sometimes, the prices of goods are disproportionate to the consumer's monthly income levels; however, they are still willing to pay due to self-satisfaction purposes. On the other hand, individuals are also trading down. This is illustrated "when consumers choose the low-cost alternative in categories of little important to them" (Silverstein & Fiske, 2004, p. 5). Trading down occurs when a consumer decides to spend less on certain product categories that they do not value. This is the critical and the opposite side of trading up since low-cost alternatives allow consumers to have some discretionary money with which to trade up. Trading up and trading down phenomena are manifest in the example of an individual driving a BMW while shopping at Wal-mart, or of an individual carrying a Louis Vuitton bag while coordinating from Gap. For this study, we focused only on the trading up phenomenon.

Trading up consumption is usually associated with new-luxury goods. New-luxury goods are defined as

> goods [that] evoke and engage consumers' emotions while feeding their aspirations for a better life ... Unlike old-luxury goods, they can generate high volumes despite their relatively high prices. (Silverstein & Fiske, 2003, p. 48)

New-luxury products and services can include apparel and fashion accessories, home furnishings, electronics, automobiles, and even personal care items. Among these, there are three types of new-luxury goods: accessible super-premium products, line extensions of old-luxury brands, and masstige products (Silverstein & Fiske, 2003, 2005). Accessible super-premium products possess higher levels of quality and taste than others in the same category, but are affordable enough to the middle market consumers (i.e. Starbucks, Belvedre Vodka).

Traditional old-luxury brands extend their brand lines by offering less expensive versions of products. Old luxury goods are defined as well-designed goods possessing the extraordinary quality and craftsmanship of traditional luxury brands such as *Louis Vuitton, Chanel,* or *Tiffany.* Old-luxury brands convey premiums for prestige, image, and rarity value, and, as such, offer premium prices for small quantities. As new-luxury goods, old-luxury brands provided lower-priced versions of goods which maintained the traditional old-luxury image and were easily accessible to middle market consumers. *Tiffany, Zegna, Burberry,* and *Mercedes-Benz* are examples of old-luxury companies extending their brand lines.

Lastly, masstige products are positioned between conventional mass markets and premium old-luxury brands. 'Masstige' is a compound word of 'mass' and 'prestige,' so masstige products deliver a premium with higher level of quality and of taste than conventional goods, and are in higher quantity volumes than traditional luxury brands. They are priced higher than mass market products, but lower than old-luxury brands. *Coach, Miu Miu,* and *Armani Exchange* are the examples of masstige brands.

New-luxury goods appeal to the consumer's emotional benefits, such as prestige, self-fulfillment, or group membership. They are offered at high yet accessible prices to middle market consumers. As a result, the trading up phenomenon creates new market opportunities by stimulating a positively related price–demand curve. That is, the higher the price, the higher the demand.

Trading up phenomenon has been observed in Korea. The Samsung Fashion Institute (2002) reported that the consumption of new-luxury goods and the incidence of value shopping were increasing in popularity, especially among young generations. These behaviors are similar to those of trading up and trading down. This report indicated the importance of consumers in their 20s as a salient market for luxury goods. In particular, this market prefers to purchase fashion accessories, including purses, sunglasses, or shoes, as they are less expensive than other categories. Thus, singles in these age groups were labeled as a potentially significant consumer market (Son, 2006; Yoo, 2005). They show a higher propensity to consume an expensive product than married people if it reflects their personalities or satisfies their emotional needs.

Consumption Values

Values reflect a consumer's beliefs about life. Values guide decisions, evaluations, and actions that an individual makes in a variety of situations. Although consumers may use the same product, each could provide different benefits. This is a result of consumption values, which explain the reasons and motivations for an individual's purchase and for their use of a certain product (Sheth, Newman, & Gross, 1991). Accordingly, the concept of consumption values is applicable to understand the trading up phenomena among Korean consumers.

The five consumption values in this study were based on the studies conducted by Sheth et al. (1991) and Kim and Lim (2001). The consumption values identified were emotional values, functional values, situational values, epistemic values, expressive values, and self-expressive values. Emotional values refer to the positive or negative feeling associated with product ownership. Functional values are defined as a product's capacity for practical and physical performances, including product quality, function, price, and utilitarian service. The attributes of functional benefits are relatively more tangible and concrete than the other values (Lai, 1995). Situational values refer to the benefits acquired from a product's appropriateness in relating to a personal circumstance (i.e. age, gender, or social group) or to a condition (i.e. an event, a meeting, the weather, or a season). Epistemic values refer to the benefits associated with exploratory, novelty- and variety-seeking behaviors to satisfy desires for curiosity, uniqueness, and new knowledge. Self-expressive values are defined as the benefits acquired from satisfying desires for the expression of an individual's self-image or personality, or for the pursuit of current fashion trends in the incidence that consumers purchase or use fashion products.

RESEARCH METHODOLOGY

Purpose of Study

The purpose of this study is twofold: (1) to examine the phenomenon of "trading up" among Korean university students and (2) to identify the relationship between the product categories selected to be traded up and the individual's consumption values. This study's purposes were fulfilled through the following four objectives.

Objective 1. To identify the valuable products that consumers owned and that consumers are willing to trade up.

Objective 2. To identify the reasons why the reported products are meaningful to them.

Objective 3. To examine the potential brands, the retailers, and the information sources that consumers are willing to trade up.

Objective 4. To classify consumers according to consumption values and to examine the demographics, the lifestyles, and the marketing mix variables (i.e. product, price, retailing format, information source) relating to these groups.

Research Method and Sampling

Data was collected from university students employing a convenience sampling method between the last week of November and the second week of December 2005. A 66-item questionnaire was administered. The first section included items regarding the most valuable goods respondents owned (reason, brand name, and price), and the three product types, listed in order, that they wished to purchase by sparing personal expenses. Respondents were also asked to write brand name, price, retailing format, and information source, as well as reasons to trade up for each product. Questions regarding product type, reason, brand name, and price were asked using an open-ended format.

The second section included items relating to consumption values and general lifestyles as measured by a five-point Likert scale ranging from "strongly disagree" (1) to "strongly agree" (5). The demographic questions included gender, age, residential district, monthly income of the family, total personal expenses per month, and clothing expenses per month. The measurement instrument used was modified from previous studies (Han & Kim, 2002; Lee, 2003; Lim, 2005). The SPSS WIN 10.0 program was used for all data analyses, descriptive statistics, frequency analysis, crosstab and χ^2 analysis, factor analysis, ANOVA with Duncan test, and K-means cluster analysis.

FINDINGS AND DISCUSSION

Description of Respondents

A total of 223 questionnaires were analyzed. Approximately 79% of those surveyed were female university students. Age ranged from 19 to 29, with a mean age of 22 years. One hundred and thirty five respondents (60.5%) have lived in the city of Seoul. About 51.1% ($N = 114$) had a monthly household income of more than 4,000,000 Korean won (US$4,000, US$1 is approximately 1,000 Korean won). It appears as though these respondents believe that they are above the middle class. In terms of monthly spending, about 74% ($N = 165$) spent 200–500,000 Korean won for total personal expenses and 58% of respondents spent 50,000–200,000 Korean won on clothing alone.

An exploratory factor analysis using the principal component with varimax rotation generated five lifestyle dimensions, which explained 64.21% of the variance (Table 1). The first factor identified was computer orientation. A higher mean indicated greater consumer involvement with computers or the internet. Communication in the form of chatting, through the internet presented the lowest mean score ($M = 2.57$) among the 17 lifestyle items. The second factor, achievement orientation, presented the highest mean score (factor $M = 3.82$) of the five factors. The mean for the statement, trying to achieve one's resolution, was especially high ($M = 4.07$). This indicates that respondents, university students, show a high level of achievement.

The third factor, social activity, indicated that respondents were relatively active and sociable in the social setting. Respondents showed more than an average level of material orientation (the fourth factor). The last factor identified was the tendency to be frugal. Respondents reported that they did spare money, but did not save it. They agreed that they purchased only products that they needed.

Owned/Potential Products and Reasons for Trading Up

Fifty-one categories were classified into four groups based on the similar characteristics. The first group was clothing, which included coats, jackets, suits, jeans, dress, and underwear. The second group was fashion accessories, which included purses, shoes, jewelry, sunglasses, watches, and cosmetics/perfume. The third category was small electronics, such as mobile

Table 1. Means and Factor Loading for Lifestyle Variables.

Items	(Mean)[a] Mean	Factor Loading	Eigen Value	% of Variance
Factor 1: Computer orientation ($\alpha = 0.75$)	(3.14)		2.426	14.268
I spend my leisure time in front of the computer	3.35	0.842		
I surf the internet without clear purpose	3.35	0.794		
I have sit up all night in front of the computer	3.28	0.756		
I enjoy chatting through the internet	2.57	0.606		
Factor 2: Achievement orientation ($\alpha = 0.72$)	(3.82)		2.375	13.970
I have a continuous desire to achieve something	3.97	0.805		
I try to achieve my resolution	4.07	0.746		
I have confidence in my future	3.57	0.698		
I express my opinion clearly at the meeting	3.67	0.676		
Factor 3: Social activity ($\alpha = 0.80$)	(3.46)		2.228	13.107
I like to get along with people because of my sociable character	3.75	0.866		
I actively participate in my peer group	3.47	0.815		
I take the central role in a gathering	3.17	0.768		
Factor 4: Material orientation ($\alpha = 0.81$)	(3.21)		2.199	12.934
A person who earn lots of money is called as succeed	2.92	0.905		
I think it is better to have high salary than any other conditions	3.25	0.853		
I prefer a successful businessman to successful scholar	3.44	0.779		
Factor 5: Frugality ($\alpha = 0.55$)	(3.07)		1.688	9.928
I save a sum out of my pocket money	2.86	0.813		
Sometimes, I spare money by not eating junk foods	3.25	0.713		
I rarely spend my money if it is not necessary	3.13	0.608		

(Mean)[a] = Mean of total items in one factor.

phones, MP3 players, cameras, PDA, PSP, electronic dictionary, and office equipment (CD, DVD, USB, books, etc.). The final group included other appliances such as furniture, computers, household appliances, musical instruments, automobiles and motorcycles, and flight tickets.

A χ^2 test indicated a significant difference between the observed values and the expected values ($\chi^2 = 69.081$, $p = 0.000$), indicating that two variables, product category and order to be purchased, were related. Clothing and fashion accessories recorded a high proportion of the total frequencies (Table 2). A large discrepancy was shown in the small electronics of the owned products category. In the first order to trade up, the other appliances category, specifically computer and automobile categories, presented large discrepancies from their expected values. Clothing in the second order, and fashion accessories in the third order, also showed large discrepancies. Respondents first seem to purchase the appliances they require for daily life, and then to purchase fashion accessories with their remaining disposable money.

The reasons that respondents named as to why they owned certain products was mostly because they were expensive (16.6%) and provided high satisfaction. 16.1% responded that they were just favorites without specific reasons for ownership. The other reasons reported, in order, were that products were gifted or absorbed in memories (13.3%), were pure necessity of the life (9.5%), and were frequently used (9.5%).

The reasons for trading up to premium products were categorized into six groups based on consumption values of previous studies (Kim & Lim, 2001; Ryou, 2002; Sheth et al., 1991). The six consumption values are emotional

Table 2. Crosstabulation between Product Categories and Order to be Purchased for Trading Up.

Product Categories	Orders				
	Owned Products	Order to be Purchased for Trading Up			Total (%)[b]
		1st	2nd	3rd	
Clothing (E)[a]	51 (56.1)	51 (58.2)	72 (57.2)	52 (54.5)	226 (26.5)
Fashion accessories (E)	67 (78.9)	72 (81.9)	74 (80.4)	105 (76.7)	318 (37.2)
Small electronics (E)	59 (42.7)	32 (44.3)	47 (43.5)	34 (41.5)	172 (20.1)
Other appliances (E)	35 (34.3)	65 (35.6)	23 (34.9)	15 (33.3)	138 (16.2)
Total (%)[b]	212 (24.8)	220 (25.8)	216 (25.3)	206 (24.1)	854 (100)

(E)[a] = Expected count; (%)[b] = Percentage of total.

values (satisfaction, self-confidences, pleasure, delight, superiority, pride, refreshing feeling, envy), functional values (price, brand, quality, design, color, fitness, durability, function, convenience, economic efficiency, utility, and versatility), situational values (appropriateness to personal situation such as age, gender, or social group or condition such as specific event, place, and season), epistemic values (novelty, curiosity, variety, uniqueness, boredom), expressive values (desires to express personality, conspicuousness, fashion leadership, attractive appearance, and positive image), and the necessity of product values (basic necessities, out of order or lost). Necessity of product values indicates the essentials that are need for day-to-day life.

Emotional values were most frequently mentioned as the reason for trading up (27%), followed by necessity (24%), functional values (20%), epistemic values, situational values, and expressive values (Table 3). The total number of cases was obtained by summing the reasons for each product that respondents reported in the three orders.

A χ^2 test indicated that there were significant differences associated between the reasons to trade up and the product categories ($\chi^2 = 81.347$, $p = 0.000$). Situational values presented a large discrepancy in the expected values of fashion clothing. Respondents seem to trade up in the clothing category due to personal appropriateness. Emotional, epistemic and expressive benefits were highly associated with fashion accessories. Respondents, the university students, seem to prefer to trade up fashion accessories, rather than fashion clothing, for self-satisfaction, for self-expressiveness, or for differentiation. Small electronics and other appliances were selected only

Table 3. Crosstabulation between Product Categories and Reasons to Trade Up.

Reasons	Product Categories				
	Clothing	Fashion Accessories	Small Electronics	Other Appliances	Total (%)[b]
Emotional values (E)[a]	42 (45.2)	68 (62.5)	28 (27.9)	24 (26.5)	162 (27.0)
Functional values (E)	35 (33.2)	39 (45.9)	17 (20.5)	28 (19.5)	119 (19.9)
Situational values (E)	36 (17.8)	24 (24.7)	1 (11.0)	3 (10.5)	64 (10.7)
Epistemic values (E)	17 (19.8)	33 (27.4)	14 (12.2)	7 (11.6)	71 (11.9)
Expressive values (E)	12 (10.9)	24 (15.0)	3 (6.7)	0 (6.4)	39 (6.5)
Necessity values (E)	25 (40.1)	43 (55.5)	40 (24.8)	36 (23.6)	144 (24.0)
Total (%)[b]	167 (27.9)	231 (38.6)	103 (17.2)	98 (16.4)	599 (100)

(E)[a] = Expected count; (%)[b] = Percentage of total.

out of necessity. Functional values presented a large discrepancy in the category of other appliances. Peculiar or particular features of products might be especially important in the purchase of appliances such as computers or automobiles.

Brands, Places, and Information Sources for Trading Up

Up to 114 different brands were listed by respondents as products that they owned. For fashion clothing and accessories, Levi's (6 times), Louis Vuitton (5), and Prada (5) were most frequently cited. Dolce & Gabbana, Bulgari, Ferragamo, Guess, MCM (3); Christian Dior, Lloyd, Mine, Bally, Chanel, System, Egoist, Coach (2) were also mentioned. The other fashion brands listed varied from Giordano to Armani, and from a Keun Hwa Fur to a Chaumet watch. Findings indicate that respondents valued not only prestige brand products, but also mass-market products as long as they convey significant meanings to consumers. As for the brands of electronics and appliances owned, Samsung (21) was most frequently appeared. iPod (9), Nikon (7), Hyundai automobile, LG, Sky mobile phone, and Sony (4) were also mentioned. Prices ranged from 7,000 Korean won for a Parker sharp pencil, to 30,000,000 Korean won for a KIA automobile ($M = 1,215,010$ Korean won).

With respect to products to potentially trade up to, a total of 191 were mentioned; among these products, 149 were fashion brands and 42 were electronics and other appliances. The most frequently reported fashion brands were Gucci (24), Louis Vuitton (18), Christian Dior (15), Diesel (14), Chanel, Guess (10), Time (including Time Homme) (8), Mark Jacobs (7), System, Levi's, Armani, MCM, and Seven Jeans (6). For electronics and other appliances, Samsung once again had the highest frequency (53). It was followed by Sony (30), iPod (18), Sky, Cannon (9), Nikon, Macintosh, Motorola (7), and LG (6). Product prices ranged from 6,000 Won for Missha cosmetics to 230,000,000 Korean won for an apartment, with a mean of 2,106,062 Korean won.

One hundred and ninety one brands were divided into domestic brands and foreign brands. These two groups were then sorted again by the price and the brand image position. This classification system resulted in four distinct brand categories. Domestic brands were divided into moderate- and better-priced brands. Domestic-moderate-priced brands included national, casual, or sportswear brands which sell at a low-to-moderate price zone. Examples include Roem, Mcginn Knightsbridge, On & On, System, Pro-specs, and

Sambo. Domestic-better-priced brands included national brands which sell at an above moderate to high price zone. Examples of these brands include Time, Beanpole, Obzee, Samsung Sense, Anycall, and Hyundai. Foreign brands were divided into better and masstige brands and old-luxury brands. Foreign better and masstige brands included products following a moderate pricing strategy, which are aimed toward the mass consumer market. This category included moderate-priced products (i.e. Sisley, Guess, Mango, Estee Lauder, Tommy Hilfiger), premium jeans (i.e. Hudson Jean, Diesel, Seven Jean), masstige fashion brands (i.e. MCM, Coach, Miu Miu), and other international brands (i.e. Nikon, Sony, Honda). Foreign old-luxury brands included designer brands and other similarly priced products like *Gucci, Chanel, TAG Heuer, Apple iPod, Cannon, Bang & Olfsen, BMW,* and *Ferrari.*

A χ^2 test presented a significant difference ($\chi^2 = 167.111$, $p = 0.000$), indicating that the two variables, product category and brand category, were associated. Table 4 shows that respondents were more likely to trade up to foreign brands, particularly for fashion accessories and for clothing. More specifically, respondents preferred to purchase fashion accessories of foreign old-luxury brands. University students also seem to consider clothing in the foreign brand better and masstige category as prestigious.

Table 5 shows the possible retailing formats respondents visit in order to trade up to premium products. A χ^2 test indicated that there were significant differences among retailers according to product category ($\chi^2 = 234.575$, $p = 0.000$). Respondents who intended to buy fashion clothing and

Table 4. Crosstabulation between Product Categories and Brand Groups.

Brand Groups	Product Categories				
	Clothing	Fashion Accessories	Small Electronics	Other Appliances	Total (%)[b]
Domestic-moderate price (E)[a]	41 (21.7)	16 (29.6)	16 (13.4)	5 (13.3)	78 (14.1)
Domestic-better price (E)	28 (27.0)	7 (36.8)	21 (16.7)	41 (16.5)	97 (17.5)
Foreign-better and masstige (E)	67 (53.2)	62 (72.5)	31 (32.8)	31 (32.5)	191 (34.5)
Foreign-old-luxury (E)	18 (52.1)	125 (71.0)	27 (32.1)	17 (31.8)	187 (33.8)
Total (%)[b]	154 (27.8)	210 (38.0)	95 (17.2)	94 (17.0)	553 (100)

(E)[a] = Expected count; (%)[b] = Percentage of total.

Table 5. Crosstabulation between Product Categories and Retailing Formats.

Retail Types	Product Categories				
	Clothes	Fashion Accessories	Small Electronics	Other Appliances	Total (%)[b]
Department Store (E)[a]	114 (72.8)	146 (102.9)	11 (52.6)	3 (45.6)	274 (47.0)
Specialty/ Sales Agency (E)	21 (53.2)	39 (75.1)	69 (38.4)	71 (33.3)	200 (34.3)
Off-Price Store (E)	9 (11.4)	8 (16.2)	14 (8.3)	12 (7.2)	43 (7.4)
Internet/ Home shopping (E)	11 (17.5)	26 (24.8)	18 (12.7)	11 (11.0)	66 (11.3)
Total (%)[b]	155 (26.6)	219 (37.6)	112 (19.2)	97 (16.6)	583 (100)

(E)[a] = Expected count; (%)[b] = Percentage of total.

accessories mostly visited department stores. This is probably due to the fact that clothing products are premium products that are likely to be sold at these establishments. Small electronics and household appliances were more likely to be purchased at either a specialty store or at an off-price store (discount stores, outlet mall, and conventional stores). These differences seem to be closely related to product attributes.

With respect to information sources for products to potentially trade up to, a χ^2 test indicated significant differences between the observed values and the expected values ($\chi^2 = 44.410$, $p = 0.000$). Information sources were associated with product categories statistically (Table 6). Respondents tended to depend on print media the most, especially for the fashion accessory category. Information gathered from family or friends was relied upon when purchasing fashion clothing. When respondents were purchasing electronics and appliances, they were more likely to count on broadcast media and on the internet to gather information.

Lifestyles, Demographics, and Marketing Mix Variables Compared by Consumption Value Groups

Since consumption values guide consumers' product choices (Sheth et al., 1991) and since consumers assign different weights to each value, it is necessary to identify groups of similar respondents. To classify the respondents according to consumption values, a factor analysis was performed using five

Table 6. Crosstabulation between Product Categories and Information Sources.

Information Sources	Product Categories				
	Clothing	Fashion Accessories	Small Electronics	Other Appliances	Total (%)[b]
Family/friends (E)[a]	42 (35.4)	39 (50.0)	25 (22.1)	22 (20.4)	128 (21.3)
Sales persons (E)	33 (30.1)	40 (42.6)	14 (18.9)	22 (17.4)	109 (18.1)
Print media (E)	72 (70.2)	124 (99.3)	30 (44.0)	28 (40.6)	254 (42.3)
TV/radio/internet (E)	19 (30.4)	32 (43.0)	35 (19.0)	24 (17.6)	110 (18.3)
Total (%)[b]	166 (27.6)	235 (39.1)	104 (17.3)	96 (16.0)	601 (100)

(E)[a] = Expected count; (%)[b] = Percentage of total.

factors (expressive, epistemic, functional, emotional, and social values). These five factors explained 64% of the variance. Of the 21 items, one item listed in the social value factor was deleted due to a low-inter-item correlation. Table 7 notes that respondents consider emotional values to be very important (factor mean = 4.46), particularly the self-satisfaction item which weighed heavily in their consumption choices (item mean = 4.70, when 5 = strongly agree). Expressive values, however, are shown to have a lower than average factor mean (2.89).

According to these five consumption value factors, respondents were classified using K-means cluster analysis. Three statistically significant groups were identified. Table 8 presents the factor loading means of the consumption values for each group, while Table 9 employed ANOVA tests in order to identify the different characteristics among three consumer groups.

Group 1: The conspicuous group. The first group represents a high level of expressive, epistemic, and social values, when compared to the other groups. People in this group are conflicted with the need to conform to their social group while still maintaining aspirations to be conspicuous and unique. As conformity is emphasized by this group, members are more likely to be active in social gatherings and to value money. To satisfy their conflicted nature, people of this group tend to use clothing as the means of self-expression and of self-prominence, and therefore tend to pursue materialism. This description is comparable with consumers who purchase masstige products (Suh & Cho, 2004).

Group 2: The innovator group. The second group identified considers epistemic values and emotional values to be meaningful. Members of this

Table 7. Means and Factor Loading for Consumption Value Variables.

Items	(Mean)[a] Mean	Factor Loading	Eigen Value	% of Variance
Factor 1: Expressive values ($\alpha = 0.87$)	(2.89)		3.634	18.169
I consider whether it makes me look wealthy	2.79	0.906		
I consider whether it is a well-known brand	2.99	0.841		
I consider whether it makes me look successful	2.67	0.825		
I consider whether it makes me conspicuous	2.97	0.737		
I consider whether it expresses my social status	3.06	0.697		
Factor 2: Epistemic values ($\alpha = 0.74$)	(3.83)		2.924	14.618
I consider whether it is unique	3.97	0.757		
I consider whether it is a new style	3.84	0.746		
I consider whether it is distinguishable from others	4.07	0.737		
I consider whether it provokes my curiosity	4.00	0.587		
I consider whether it leads the new fashion	3.27	0.503		
Factor 3: Functional values ($\alpha = 0.76$)	(3.88)		2.456	12.280
I consider the durability and quality of material of the goods	4.02	0.853		
I consider the comfortableness of the goods	3.86	0.834		
I consider the practicality of the goods	4.06	0.827		
I consider the versatility of the goods	3.57	0.413		
Factor 4: Emotional values ($\alpha = 0.73$)	(4.46)		2.143	10.716
I consider whether it fulfill my satisfaction	4.70	0.762		
I consider the design or color of the goods	4.63	0.708		

Table 7. (*Continued*)

Items	(Mean)[a] Mean	Factor Loading	Eigen Value	% of Variance
I consider whether I am happy when I have this	4.35	0.619		
I consider whether it expresses my personality	4.17	0.587		
Factor 5: Social value ($\alpha = 0.70$)	(3.20)		1.652	8.261
I consider whether it is suitable for my age, sex, and social status	3.38	0.814		
I consider whether it is appropriate for my social groups (colleagues and/or university)	3.03	0.741		

(Mean)[a] = Mean of total items in one factor.

Table 8. Differences of Classified Consumer Groups by Consumption Value Factors.

Factors	Groups			
	Conspicuous Group ($N = 107$)	Innovator Group ($N = 69$)	Practical Group ($N = 37$)	F
Expressive values	0.465 A	−0.405 B	−0.559 B	88.076*
Epistemic values	0.252 A	0.370 A	−1.380 B	220.905*
Functional values	−0.020 B	−0.250 C	0.568 A	26.722*
Emotional values	−0.190 B	0.287 A	0.195 A	21.639*
Social values	0.520 A	−0.932 C	0.228 B	234.882*

Note: A, B, C = Significant mean differences by Duncan test.
*$p < 0.001$.

group pursue uniqueness, newness, and variety for fun, pleasure, or for satisfaction. They are neither concerned with social pressure nor the functional features of products. This group was also more willing to pay a premium for the products that they wanted. Members of this group show a higher level of achievement than the other two groups, suggesting that respondents classified in this group tend to have leadership abilities. The characteristics described about of the members in Group 2 are similar with the qualities of innovators as described by Rogers (1995). Rogers (1995) describes the innovators as

Table 9. Differences of Classified Consumer Groups in Lifestyles and Demographics.

Variables	Groups			
	Conspicuous Group (N = 103)	Innovator Group (N = 65)	Practical Group (N = 36)	F
Lifestyles				
Computer oriented	0.008	−0.012	0.138	0.88
Achievement oriented	−0.068 B	0.216 A	−0.244 B	8.94***
Social activity	0.102 A	−0.040 AB	−0.172 B	3.44*
Material oriented	0.254 A	−0.250 B	−0.179 B	19.26***
Frugality	−0.016	0.028	0.016	0.13
Demographics				
Age	22.25 A	22.48 A	21.84 B	4.21*
Monthly income	4.54	4.41	4.30	1.02
Personal expense	3.62 A	3.61 A	2.95 B	11.49***
Clothing expense	3.30 A	2.94 B	2.46 C	19.06***

Note: A, B, C = Significant mean differences by Duncan test.
*$p<0.05$.
***$p<0.001$.

those who are highly interested in new ideas, venturesomeness, and risk-taking. They have a higher level of income, are better educated, have more self-confidence, and are less dependent on group norms.

Group 3: The practical group. The third group identified cares the most about functional values and self-satisfaction. Members of this group value feasibility and practicality. They consider the physical and practical features of product to be important to their satisfaction. This group is the least likely to pay a premium for goods, as they spend the least amount of money on clothing and personal expenses.

Trading Up Tendencies of the Conspicuous, Innovator, and Practical Groups

When examining the demographic data, the monthly income level of the family was not significant. This finding supports that the trading up phenomenon is not limited to one social-economic class, but is evident in every class. Trading up was also found to be present in each of the three groups. A χ^2 test was used to examine the associations between the three consumer groups and the product categories to be traded up. The total number of cases examined in the χ^2 tests was larger than the sample sizes since the total number of cases was obtained from the sum of each product in the three ranks.

As shown in Table 10, three consumer groups were associated with product categories to trade up ($\chi^2 = 20.797, p = 0.002$). The Conspicuous group and the Innovator group presented large discrepancies from the expected values for fashion accessories. In fitting with their description, the Conspicuous group is willing to trade up to fashion accessories in order to satisfy their desire to be noticed and also to maintain their belongingness to their social group. Innovators, however, are willing to trade up this category for a different reason. They consume fashion accessories for differentiation and novelty purposes. The Practical group was more involved with the other three product categories to trade up than with fashion accessories. This also fits their description as members of the Practical group prefer to purchase feasible and practical products.

Table 11 depicts the brands, the retailing formats, and the information sources used to trade up by the three consumer groups. A χ^2 test indicated that significant differences were found between domestic–foreign brands ($\chi^2 = 27.345, p = 0.000$), retailing formats ($\chi^2 = 18.925, p = 0.004$), and information sources ($\chi^2 = 25.646, p = 0.000$) corresponding to the consumer groups.

In terms of brands selected in the trading up process, both the Conspicuous group and the Innovator group preferred foreign old-luxury brands, while the Practical group favored domestic brands. The selection of these brands corresponds with the consumption values outlined in the description

Table 10. Crosstabulation between Product Categories and Information Sources.

Product Categories	Groups			
	Conspicuous Group	Innovator Group	Practical Group	Total (%)[b]
Clothing (E)[a]	81 (84.0)	53 (53.7)	33 ((29.3)	167 (27.1)
Fashion accessories (E)	136 (121.8)	83 (77.8)	23 (42.4)	242 (39.3)
Small electronics (E)	51 (54.4)	29 (34.7)	28 (18.9)	108 (17.5)
Housing appliances (E)	42 (49.8)	33 (31.8)	24 (17.4)	99 (16.1)
Total (%)[b]	310 (50.3)	198 (32.1)	108 (17.5)	616 (100)

(E)[a] = Expected count; (%)[b] = Percentage of total.

Table 11. Crosstabulation between Product Categories and Information Sources.

Variables	Groups			
	Conspicuous Group	Innovator Group	Practical Group	Total (%)[b]
Brand types				
Domestic-moderate price (E)[a]	35 (37.8)	21 (23.8)	19 (13.4)	75 (14.1)
Domestic-better price (E)	42 (47.4)	24 (29.9)	28 (16.8)	94 (17.7)
Foreign-better and masstige (E)	94 (92.2)	54 (58.1)	35 (32.7)	183 (34.4)
Foreign-old-luxury (E)	97 (90.7)	70 (57.2)	13 (32.1)	180 (33.8)
Total (%)[b]	268 (50.4)	169 (31.8)	95 (17.9)	532 (100)
Retailing formats				
Department stores (E)[a]	160 (138.0)	71 (76.6)	31 (47.4)	262 (46.5)
Specialty stores (E)	89 (102.7)	61 (57.0)	45 (35.3)	195 (34.6)
Off-price stores (E)	18 (22.1)	15 (12.3)	9 (7.6)	42 (7.4)
Internet/home shopping (E)	30 (34.2)	18 (19.0)	17 (11.8)	65 (11.5)
Total (%)[b]	297 (52.7)	165 (29.3)	102 (18.1)	564 (100)
Information sources				
Family/friends (E)[a]	55 (62.6)	37 (39.0)	30 (20.4)	122 (21.1)
Sales persons (E)	66 (55.9)	24 (34.8)	19 (18.3)	109 (18.8)
Print media (E)	126 (124.6)	94 (77.6)	23 (40.7)	243 (42.0)
Broadcast media/internet (E)	50 (53.9)	30 (33.5)	25 (17.6)	105 (18.1)
Total (%)[b]	297 (51.3)	185 (32.0)	97 (16.8)	579 (100)

(E)[a] = Expected count; (%)[b] = Percentage of total.

of each group. Foreign old-luxury brands simultaneously fulfill the need to be noticed of the Conspicuous group and the need to be novel of the Innovators. Domestic brands are the more sensible option to satisfy the practical nature of Practical group.

Each group preferred to shop at a different retailing location. The Conspicuous group was more likely to shop at department stores. Department stores may be preferred by this group as a retailing format because they are more likely to carry the fashion accessory products they trade up for and because their location is accepted by their social group. Innovators did not insist on department stores, but rather preferred shopping at specialty stores. It was also interesting to note that Innovators were willing to shop in off-price stores as long as the products offered there satisfied their needs. These two retailing locations fit with the personality of Innovator group, as they tend to look for unique, novel, and extraordinary goods regardless of price or of other member's views. The Practical group preferred to shop at either specialty stores or on the internet/home shopping mall rather than at department stores. For this group, it is much more practical to go directly to a store that sells the product that they wish to trade up rather than search through a department store. Additionally, this group tends to trade up in categories that are only available at specialty stores or on the internet.

As mentioned before, members of the Conspicuous group are extremely social people who seek conformity with their peers. Therefore, it is logical that the information source most readily used by this group would be sales people. A sales person not only satisfies this group's need for social inter-action, they also provide a certain degree of approval from the group. Innovators, on the other hand, were more reliant on print media. Innovators have no need for the possible approval from sales people that the Conspic-uous group desires. Print media is a more suitable information source for this group, as many times the newest products and innovations are first found in print. The Practical group is, however, more dependent on family and friends and on broadcast media as information sources than the other consumer groups. It seems that members of the Practical group know whom to ask and where to go in order to gain the information that they desire, and can then evaluate the product's features technically and professionally.

CONCLUSIONS AND IMPLICATIONS

As the consumption of new-luxury goods is a growing trend, this study investigated the phenomenon of trading up to these new-luxury goods among young Korean consumers. Trading up is a consumption behavior by which consumers, typically in the middle class, will pay a premium to ac-quire new-luxury brands that they find "emotionally meaningful" rather than choosing to pay a more proportionate amount to their social-economic status for a good. Findings showed that respondents already owned old-luxury or masstige fashion products to some extent, most of which were foreign brands. Respondents considered these products to be valuable as they were expensive, satisfying, memorable, or were necessities. Findings support the previous report that consumers in their 20s are the major po-tential target for luxury brands in Korea (Samsung Fashion Institute, 2002).

Consumption values explain the reasons and motivations for an individ-ual's purchase of certain product. These values played an important role in the decision to trade up to new-luxury goods. Six consumption values were identified, while five were used in the factor analysis. In the comparison with reasons to trade up, emotional, functional, epistemic, expressive values were found to be important to respondents. While social values, such as consumption values, were not mentioned by respondents, they did, however, point out situational values that were related to specific occasions or to personal characteristics rather than social groups. Respondents seem to consider social values either as unimportant or as too natural. Necessity is another significant reason respondents needed to trade up although it is not measured by consumption values. Necessity could be a fundamental need or a motivation of consumption values. Future research could analyze the relationship between the meaning of necessity and the consumption values in a qualitative method.

Respondents provided a wide variety of product categories, brands, and price ranges with which they were willing to trade up. More than 66% of items mentioned involved fashion, including clothing and accessories. This might be because the majority of respondents were women, or because the young generation is highly involved with fashion items in order to express individuality (i.e. the metrosexual trend). Respondents seem to prefer foreign brands to domestic brands if they are positioned at similar price zone. For fashion accessories, respondents definitely demand foreign luxury brands. Consumers might believe that foreign brands deliver more visible and concrete benefits than domestic brands do. Domestic brands need to create certain benefits to appeal to consumers' emotional values and to properly communicate distinct meanings. Emphasizing consumption values according to consumer characteristics would be effective since each consumer group demands different values from a typical product.

Consumers today seek goods that are both astonishing and exclusive, yet still utilitarian. Brands need to respond to the market's needs, and build a strong brand identity that is distinctive and persuasive enough to remain in the consumers' minds. Brand extensions, either upward or downward, is another way to attract the middle market consumers if the business has already built strong brand image in the market. For fashion products specifically, utilizing department stores, family/friends, and print media are suitable for marketing mix strategies. For the other appliances, it would be appropriate to focus on specialty stores and internet/home shopping mall as retail formats.

Three consumer groups were identified and described by analyzing the respondent's consumption values. Conspicuous group members tend to consume products in order to be unique yet do not want to deviate from their social groups. Innovator group members are searching for newness and uniqueness, and try to stimulate his/her curiosity. These two groups want to trade up to similar products, but for very different reasons. One desires to be conspicuous, while the other wants to be innovative. The former wants to belong to its social boundary while the latter does not care for belonging-ness. Thus, the Innovator group could be a target market for new products. Based on the innovators' feedback and word of mouth effects, influential marketing could be used to attract followers. The Practical group, however, emphasizes functional values, such as how the products are convenient, durable, comfortable, and practical. If those features satisfy these demands, they will buy it. The Practical group is associated with small electronics or complex appliances. This group might have a more complicated decision making and evaluation process than the other two groups.

Additional research is necessary to confirm these findings to an extended sample size. This study was preliminary research on trading up consumption among university students and the sample was not balanced in gender and/or monthly income levels, both of which might influence the results. Although what the respondent's currently own is known, no measure of purchase intention was taken. Respondents might report products that they wish to trade up to, but do not intend to purchase in actuality. However, markets for new-luxury goods still would have great potential. Consumers would trade up at every level of product category if the product creates consumption values and conveys a super-premium as they see appropriate.

REFERENCES

Han, H. J., & Kim, M. S. (2002). Relating consumption values to prepurchase decision making of apparels. *Journal of the Korean Society of Clothing and Textiles, 26*(6), 853–864.

Kim, S., & Lim, S. (2001). A study on clothing consumption value: A qualitative approach. *Journal of the Korean Society of Clothing and Textiles, 25*(9), 1621–1632.

Lai, A. W. (1995). Consumer values, product benefits and customer value: A consumption behavior approach. *Advances in Consumer Research, 22*, 381–388.

Lee, M. (2003). A study of appearance behavior and lifestyle of adolescents. *Journal of the Korean Society of Clothing and Textiles, 27*(9/10), 1101–1111.

Lim, K. B. (2005). A study on the women consumers' clothing consumption value and in-volvement: Comparative analysis of large and small city. *Journal of the Korean Society of Clothing and Textiles, 29*(1), 68–78.

National Internet Development Agency of Korea (2006). *Research on the internet usage during the second half of 2005.* Seoul, Korea.

Park, I. K. (2006). *Difference of 'fair-ents' from 'parents': X-generation aged from 26 to 35 shows different parents styles.* Retrieved on January 17, 2006, from Hankooki.com Web site: http://news.hankooki.com/lpage/economy/200601/h2006011520422521500.htm

Rogers, E. M. (1995). *Diffusion of innovations* (4th ed.). New York, NY: Thee Free Press.

Ryou, E. (2002). A study on the effect of clothing consumption value on service quality of internet apparel shopping mall. *Journal of the Korean Society of Costume, 52*(3), 161–169.

Samsung Fashion Institute (2002). *Consumer trend and luxury in fashion market.* Retrieved on December 29, 2005, from http://www.samsungdesign.net

Sheth, J. N., Newman, B. I., & Gross, B. L. (1991). Why we buy what we buy: A theory of consumption values. *Journal of Business Research, 22*(2), 159–170.

Silverstein, M. J., & Fiske, N. (2003). Luxury for the masses. *Harvard Business Review, 81*(4), 48–57.

Silverstein, M. J., & Fiske, N. (2004). *Trading up: Trends, brands, and practices 2004 research update.* Retrieved on December 29, 2005, from http://www.bcg.com/publications/files/TradingUp2004ResUpdate51104.pdf

Silverstein, M. J., & Fiske, N. (2005). *Trading up* (Boston Consulting Group Trans.). Seoul: Sejong Books, Inc. (Original work published 2003).

Son, S. T. (2006). *Stingy at ordinary times, but generous in buying luxury goods.* Retrieved on January 17, 2006, from http://news.naver.com/news/read.php?mode = LSD&office_id = 015&article_id = 0000863364&section_id = 0&menu_id = 0

Suh, J., & Cho, H. (2004). *The new consumer group, masstige. Samsung Fashion Institute.* Retrieved on December 29, 2005, from http://www.samsungdesign.net

Yoo, J. Y. (2005). *The most interests of 2635 are money.* Retrieved on December 29, 2005, from http://news.naver.com/news/read.php?mode = LSD&office_id = 009&article_id = 0000467743&section_id = 101&menu_id = 101

PART III:
CULTURAL FACTORS IN
BUYER BEHAVIOR

THE "WE-ME" CULTURE: MARKETING TO KOREAN CONSUMERS

Dae Ryun Chang

ABSTRACT

This paper is a focused examination of the parallel collectivistic and individualistic tendencies of South Korean consumers. The "We-Me" concept argues that the two seemingly countervailing tendencies can actually co-exist. The paper discusses the phenomenon, its underlying causes, and the strategic implications of how to market to such consumers.

RAMYUN: THE "MODEL T" OF KOREAN MARKETING

Ramyun (instant noodles): the "Model T" of Korean marketing. Not exactly the vanguard of modern manufacturing but at least from a marketing standpoint it holds the same lofty position as Henry Ford's revolutionary product. In the early 1960s, this product was imported in from Japan and localized with the Samyang brand name. Korea in this period of time had a per capita annual income of a few hundred dollars and even then that was

Cross-Cultural Buyer Behavior
Advances in International Marketing, Volume 18, 141–157
ISSN: 1474-7979/doi:10.1016/S1474-7979(06)18006-0

not enough to buy rice for the hungry masses. But then this magical product arrived that was not only affordable to everyone but also fast! It essentially became a staple of Korean life, both for the rich and poor. Samyang would enjoy a 20-year ride of prosperity until the early 1980s when it came up against, ironically, the General Motors of Korean instant noodles, Nongshim. Nongshim was a spin-off of Lotte, the giant Korean Japanese confectionary company. Like GM, Nongshim offered a variety of Ramyun brands, Nuguri (thick noodles), Ansungtangmyun (milder soup), and most notably, Shin Ramyun (spicy soup). Nongshim divided, conquered, and reunited Koreans on a single brand, Shin Ramyun, which is the undisputed Ramyun champion of Korea with annual sales of about $300 million. More important than that, it is "The Ramyun" to most Koreans. People ask for Shin Ramyun as any American would ask for a "Band Aid." Even though there are more than 100 other Ramyun brands in Korea, they are mere dwarfs in the presence of the colossal Shin Ramyun. A popular inexpensive dish among Koreans is "Budae chigae" (army soup) that is made from kimchi, cheap army style sausage (hence the name), and of course Ramyun. Even among foreigners old Korean hands swear by it. The key ingredient is Shin Ramyun. In any part of any city in Korea one can easily find Korean food diners called "Bunshikjum." Again a key menu item is Shin Ramyun. In supermarkets all over Korea, there is a big Ramyun section that will have rows of shelves with just one brand, yes Shin Ramyun. Before the Seoul Olympics, consumers did not have much choice of brands. But now, there is choice aplenty in Korea. But even with the freedom to choose, seemingly the only choice for Koreans is Shin Ramyun. Competitors have come and competitors have gone. They tried milder noodles. They tried thinner noodles. They tried spicier soup. They tried smaller packages – all to no avail. Even the parent company has been unsuccessful in launching new types of Ramyun. Getting people to stop eating Shin Ramyun is almost as difficult as asking them to go without rice. While the example of Shin Ramyun is extreme, it is not unique. Hite beer, Saempyo soy sauce, Daeil bandages are just few of the many generic-like brands that represent a whole category. Foreign brands are not immune. Prada, Rolex, Ballentine, Mercedes Benz, Chanel, Ferragamo, Montblanc, and Taylor Made are perhaps better known in Korea than they are in their home countries. Nowadays it is a rare sight indeed to see a Korean woman not carrying a Prada bag. Brands are important everywhere. What makes Korea more interesting is that everyone knows and wants these products and brands. In short, individual choice is driven by the collective will.

THE "WE-ME" PHENOMENON

Shin Ramyun is the ultimate example of what I call the "We-Me" Syndrome of Korean marketing (allowing for the grammatical misuse). Most Asian countries have strong collectivistic cultures. In comparison many western countries are highly individualistic. Korea is both. It does not neatly fall into either category but instead seems to be both, simultaneously. This framework can help to further explain the value paradoxes that Asian countries have (deMooij, 1999).

A common example of "We-Me" is how a group of people will order the same menu item in a restaurant. Young and old, rich and poor, male and female, it makes no difference. It is a Korean thing. There is still a communal aspect to eating in Korea. We still share food such as eating soup from just one bowl. We pass around alcohol in cups that we drank from as a sign of bonding. But at the same time Koreans are not afraid to show their personal side. We love to sing and dance, even when sober. Almost as a rule everyone must have a "number 18" song. This number represents one's personal favorite song. Also people are usually asked what their personal talents are such as in singing, doing impersonations, and so on. But often these individual "number 18 songs" and "talents" turn out to be pretty similar such as everyone singing Kim Kunmo's latest hit or everyone doing the same impression of a famous local baseball manager. Again they are individual choices determined by the collective will. It is "We-Me."

What exactly is the "We-Me Syndrome?" The "We" refers to a culture's collectivistic tendencies. In the case of Korea, there are so many to speak of. Holidays are a good example when during the major ones such as the Lunar New Year or Korean Thanksgiving called Chusok, literally tens of millions of Koreans will take "trains, planes, and automobiles" to trek their way back to their ancestral hometowns to pay respect to their parents, eat the traditional meals, and then endure the long arduous trip back. It is like Thanksgiving or Labor Day weekend in the U.S., but magnified perhaps about ten times over. Since about 40% of the Korean population lives in and around Seoul, the logistical nightmare of these annual rites can easily be imagined.

The "Me" refers to a culture's individualistic tendencies. In recent years, the word "individualism" (called "kaesung" in Korean) has become a buzzword in Korea. Until not too long ago, if you told someone that he had "strong individualism" he might have smacked you in the face. This is because there was a very thin line between the Korean meaning of "individualism" and "selfishness." But nowadays it is meant as a compliment and implies someone with creativity and initiative. An interesting albeit extreme example of "Me" in Korea is the popularity of Ha Risoo, a self-confessed transgender (a sex changed person). Perhaps as truly a world-first, a cosmetics company in Korea used Ha as their model in their advertising campaign. Since then Ha has become a major sought-after celebrity in Korea and is mentioned sometimes as one criterion of Korean beauty. Her face and hairstyle, for example, is displayed in many salons for other people to emulate.

THE FALSE CONSENSUS EFFECT

The "We-Me" phenomenon can be traced to what sociologists call "the false consensus" effect (Ross, Greene, & House, 1977). It is the notion that we assume that others think and act like we do. This assumption may conform to reality but then again often it does not. For example, a person may assume that most people do not obey traffic laws and therefore that person could become laxer in policing himself when driving. If in reality most people are actually law-abiding, then that individual's assumption of false consensus ends up affecting him in a negative way. Of course, it could work positively as well where the assumption and behavior are reversed, i.e. someone being more morally upright to conform to his perception of others even though this perception is false. Immigrant populations have a tendency to hold on to cultural norms prevailing when they left and pass them on their children only to find that they have radically changed thereafter. The false consensus in Korea was perhaps best exemplified by the results of an annual survey that asked if the respondent felt they belonged to the middle class. For a long time, about 70% of the respondents answered that indeed they belonged to the middle class. The actual economic data would tell you otherwise and it took something drastic in the order of a national financial crisis in 1997 to shatter this long-held collective belief. The false consensus that so many Koreans were economically well-off could be attributed by efforts made by previous governments to instill pride among the populace that their hard work was making a difference. Also in the late 1980s, the shrinking export markets were offset by an expanding domestic market sparked by the propaganda of the illusive "per capita income of $10,000." Even after the economic crisis, access to credit cards was expanded; passersby were paid on the streets to sign up, and Koreans of all walks of life were encouraged to shop until they dropped. Not surprisingly, millions of

Koreans soon after declared personal bankruptcy. Now the consensus, real or false, is that we are economically depressed despite annual growth of about 5%. Of course, when everyone, including those well-off, stop buying, then the economy really does become bad. Another false consensus is that all the spoils of Korea's economic prosperity have been enjoyed by a limited few. The whipping boys for everything from high real estate prices to excessive spending for children's education are people living in Kang-Nam (south of the Han River). When Koreans talk about the "South–North Problem," it is usually about the great sociological divide between the upper and lower neighborhoods of the Han River. On a national scale, the false consensus that the system favors only some privileged people has created significant social ill will.

"WE-ME" AS A DISTRIBUTION CONCEPT

The "We-Me" concept essentially argues that collective and individual tendencies can co-exist. There is a lovely Korean word "Jae-Ban Tae-Ban" which means "Half-Me" and "Half-We." When someone is asked why he or she did something, a common refrain is this word and is used to signify these two forces at work. We can use a distribution to illustrate our point. As shown below (Fig. 1) a distribution maps out both the location and frequency of individual points in some population. The individual points represent the "Me" in any culture. The wider the distribution, the greater is the individualism of that culture. The "We" is captured in two ways. When a

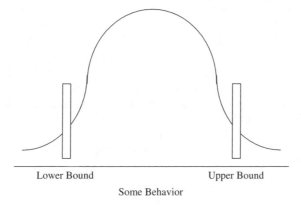

Lower Bound   Upper Bound

Some Behavior

Fig. 1.   Culture as a Distribution.

distribution is not spread out it indicates that there is greater conformity to collective norms. Also, a distribution that is bounded on either indicates a strong "We" tendency. That means if individuals are not free or regulate themselves from transgressing beyond a certain point, then this implies a collective "We" constraint.

With the distribution analogy we can thus easily see how the "We" and the "Me" can concurrently exist. It requires the "We" conditions that there are bounds and going "out of bounds" means becoming a social outcast. The upper bound constrains people from being too conspicuous such as flaunting an overly expensive foreign brand. The lower bound pulls people in for fear that they might be left behind. People deem that they have to belong to a group to have an identity. The need to be part of a group in Korea is very strong. Also, the "Me" need is satisfied by people manifesting their individualism by approaching but not exceeding the far reaches of the cultural bounds. In cosmetics, for example, the demand for brands may be very similar (the "We" part), but people may set themselves apart from others by using a slightly different style of point makeup. For example, many young Korean women will ask for an acceptable brand like Chanel lipstick but then use a different shade of red that is to their personal liking.

A distribution can be used to compare the makeup of different cultures. Many western cultures, especially those comprised of heavy immigration from other cultures will naturally exhibit a wide distribution. Moreover, given the greater emphasis on diversity and individualism in these cultures, the cultural bounds noted above will be less pronounced. Being an individual, a "maverick" in these societies has positive connotations such as that of creativity and nonconformity.

Let us begin then looking at Korea from a "We" perspective. Korea is perhaps the "Ivory Soap" of ethnic groups. The advertising slogan says this brand is 99% pure and the same can be said of Korea. She may be the most homogeneous culture in the world. For a long time Korea was called the "Hermit Kingdom" because it closed itself from outside influences. Despite numerous invasions and meddling from its larger neighboring countries throughout its history Korea has been able to maintain its ethnic and cultural identity. The cultural homogeneity of Korea is an inescapable facet of marketing in Korea. Moreover, many factors help compound the already high homogeneity of the Korean market. It is well known that there is a concentration of people with the common surnames of Kim, Lee, and Park. The famous Korean joke about this is that if you threw a rock from atop Namsan (the highest mountain inside Seoul), there is a high probability that you will hit someone with one of the three main surnames. Also as mentioned above, almost 40% of the population lives in and around Seoul. Combining these two factors alone would suggest that just targeting Kims living in Seoul would represent about a tenth of the whole market! But most of all, the key underlying factor that promotes cultural homogeneity is Korea's prevailing Confucian heritage. Confucianism preaches harmony through individual conformance to its doctrines. Even if some of these doctrines were well intended when they were first conceived many have become anachronistic such as the rule about marriage. Confucian ideology states that couples with the same surname and surname origin (called 'Bon' in Korean) cannot marry. While this custom is no longer legally binding (repealed a few years ago) most families still follow it nonetheless. This can be a problem with surnames such as Chang, the tenth most common name in Korea but one that essentially has only one surname origin (Indong). Even more surprising to western observers might be that people do not mind and sometimes actually enjoy being conformist. This is a common trait found in collective societies and certainly will not be unique just to Korea. Westerners may be amused as to how Asians will often order the same food as a group but what they fail to understand is that we enjoy eating the same food, or wearing the same clothes, and belonging to the same groups. This is collectivism at its best and at its worst. One of the virtues most valued in Confucian societies is group harmony. Group harmony is a common corporate slogan in Korea such as in the LG Group. The biggest box office movies in Korea in recent years were "Shilmido" (a real life story about a hit squad of convicts mobilized to go to North Korea), "Taekugki: The Brotherhood," and "The King's Jester" (a movie about homosexuality in ancient Korean court). All three movies were seen by over 12 million adults or roughly half the national adult population. What makes their success even more astounding is that these numbers were achieved in just over a month.

Of course, there is a downside to conformity because people who are different (those who go out of the upper or lower bounds as diagrammed above) can be severely ostracized. A word that has become part of modern Korean parlance is "Wang Ta" and is an abbreviated term for "King of the Outcasts." Since someone who is tagged as a "Wang Ta" not only does not belong to a group but also can be subjected to public abuse and humiliation, the pressure to conform to group norms becomes intense. A notable example happened during the IMF crisis when well-to-do Koreans were urged not to buy foreign cars or other luxury goods.

Some examples of "We" tendencies are fashion, housing, marriage, and in general, brand choices. The general concept of being fashionable is of course to be trendy and also somewhat individualistic. Unlike the west, however, there is a much greater emphasis on the trendy aspect. Whereas no two women in the west would want to be caught dead wearing the same outfit, that would not be cause for any significant alarm in Korea as long as what they were wearing was acceptable. In the case of men, of course, the social embarrassment is even less so and in fact wearing the same clothes may be a cause for celebration. Indeed it is not an uncommon sight to see many men wearing the same popular fashion trend. Part of the similarity of fashion stems from the bounding that is either implicit, or sometimes, even institutionalized within companies. When many Korean companies adopted a "no tie" policy, perhaps fearing the worst, employees were issued a dress code (with pictures) whereby they could choose between two or three types of "casual" wear.

Housing is also another example of "We"-like behavior in Korea. For many years a key status symbol for Koreans has been to own an apartment in the Apgujung neighborhood. Despite the fact that prices in one of the apartment complexes such as Hyundai will vary as much as six or seven times between the cheapest and the most expensive, from the outside the rows of a multitude of buildings almost look identical and are differentiated only by the building number. In fact even the most expensive units that might cost millions of dollars will look for the most part quite drab on the outside. The prices of these apartments, therefore, are not determined by any ostentatious aspect, but rather by their size and location within the complex. The appearance of uniformity is maintained, but the actual diversity that exists is known only to the residents living inside these complexes. The mammoth high rises that have sprouted up in neighborhoods of Seoul such as Dogok and in Bundang are exhibiting some signs of creative life. But we still have a far way to go in terms of having truly striking building architecture.

In any culture one of the most important institutions is that of marriage. Korea is experiencing upheaval in a relative sense because less people are getting married and when they do the incidence of divorce is on the rise. These factors notwithstanding, the cultural norms or false consensus regarding marriage have not changed much. Regardless of social standing marriage is still the union not of two people but of two families. Often young people will date someone for years only to marry someone else that they have known briefly but through a proper inter-family introduction. After marriage the family life cycle is remarkably similar across people. Couples have children (ideally two) within the first few years and then spend most of their time worrying about educating them. Education is without a doubt a national obsession and will be discussed later. The pressure to get married is still very strong in Korea. For women it is strong when they are of a certain age but diminishes (people around them give up) when they are past it. Ironically, the pressure on men is more persistent because they are expected to pass on the family name. Also since single men can marry at any age people around them do not give up pressuring them.

An interesting phenomenon in Korea of late is the burgeoning market for pets. It was not long ago that dogs and cats were raised only by a small segment of the Korean population. In recent years, however, many apartment households in Korea have begun to have a pet (one estimate is that there are over 800 thousand pets in Seoul alone). Many ancillary markets have been derived from this trend such as pet shops, pet grooming centers, pet cafes, and veterinary hospitals. The "We" aspect of raising pets is not only that many families and even single people will have a pet, but also that certain breeds (e.g. at the time of this writing, the Maltese) will be in fashion for a certain period of time.

"WE-ME" AND MARKETING PRACTICE

The epitome of the "We" culture in Korea is their brand choice behavior. Korea is a very brand-conscious country and just one visit to any major department store in Seoul would prove it. Many countries in Asia are quite similar at least in this respect. The number of stores for luxury brands like Hermes and Ferragamo in Korea is remarkable when considering the density of the local population. I recall an experience about 12 years ago when I bought a Callaway driver abroad thinking I would be one of the first Koreans to use it at home. I discovered that not only did everyone in my foursome have the same club but so did most people in the next two foursomes as well. This example points to a "flavor of the month" aspect for brands in Korea, i.e. only a limited number of brands are popular at any given time. Of course this duration can be sometimes lengthy as in the case of Shin Ramyun and thus offers an interesting research question as to what promotes such a long brand life. Some other long-living brands are Hite Beer and Maxwell House Coffee. At a glance, it seems food items are less prone to change as consumers tend to have "sticky" taste buds. We should not forget, however, that both Hite and Shin Ramyun replaced, almost overnight, the once seemingly "irreplaceable" cultural icons OB Beer and Samyang Ramyun. Thus with one false move any brand in any category can be potentially vulnerable to sudden and rapid change in consumer preferences.

One of the key roles that brands play is they can symbolize status and in group conscious societies brands provide social identity. In western countries, the social strata being wide lead to a wide variety of brands being demanded. In Asian countries and perhaps especially in Korea, the homogeneity and group conformity pressure lead to the acceptance of a fewer number of brands. This has been coupled at least in the past with a supply situation where virtual monopolies existed with domestic brands and legal restrictions allowed only a few foreign brands to be sold. As a result people are used to choosing from just a few brands. Some notable albeit extreme examples of this phenomenon are the demand for luxurious brands in many categories that take on almost a generic nature. Ballentine scotch (17 year old of course), Prada or Gucci handbags, Taylor Made drivers, Chanel makeup, and Armani suits are some examples. Foreign companies that are established elsewhere but not in Korea will be hard pressed not only overcoming local competition, but more significantly their better-known foreign rivals.

The singularity of demand for products and brands has important implications for marketing in Korea. First and foremost it obviates one of the most fundamental principles of marketing, namely the need for market segmentation. Market segmentation is generally considered a vital marketing strategy in most countries. When demand is diverse it is only logical that different needs and wants have to be catered to in different ways. But using the same logic, when demand is not diverse then the opposite strategy, namely no segmentation should apply. From a company's perspective, market segmentation allows it to stake out a portion of the market for its own, one where not only can it maximize its so-called core competence but where competition will not be as severe. But again this famous strategy known as avoiding the "majority fallacy" still requires a distribution of demand that is fairly wide. If the distribution is concentrated as illustrated above, then specialization on non-mainstream segments may not be profitable enough to warrant special treatment. Looking at the beer market, as an example, there is a huge mainstream segment and the few other segments that exist (premium, foreign, light) are too minor to be of any significance. The same can be said of the Soju category, which is a potent local alcohol, and also the Ramyun category as explained above. In each of these categories not only is there a dominant segment but also there is a dominant brand that has over 50% market share of the total market. The presence of these colossal brands presents a dual challenge to late entrants coming into the market. The primary challenge is to appeal to consumers in a manner that is different from other brands. What makes Korea a difficult market, however, is that the secondary challenge is not being too different from what consumers are used to especially with the dominant brand. In a nutshell this seemingly paradoxical strategy is to be "familiarly different." Advertising strategy should follow a similar path. Television rating is measured by something called a "share." It measures how many households watching television are tuned in to a particular program. In October 2004, the top U.S. show C.S.I had a share of 26 whereas during the same in Korea the top show was a drama called "Condition for Love" with a share of 70 for women and 52 for men. In Korea, it seems, Oscar telecast-like numbers are a common occurrence. Blame it on lack of channels. That was true 10 years ago but not anymore. We have cable, Korea has the highest broadband internet penetration in the world, and we now have satellite TV. But 10 years from now we will still have Superbowl like ratings for certain shows. With all the media to choose from advertisers still must spend huge sums of money on broadcast TV to get exposure. Creative strategy for advertising in Korea also manifests similar aspects. To the untrained eye, there does not appear to be much creativity in Korean advertising. For example, some actors and actresses like Bae Yongjun and Lee Young Ae appear as spokespersons in a multitude of ads for a wide range of brands even though they are hired to "exclusive" contracts. Also, there are some executional formats that do not go away such as the end use of English voiceovers of the brand name. Distribution is the same story. Everyone and we mean everyone shops at big department stores like Lotte. The downtown Lotte might be the biggest department store in Asia. There is no segmentation here. It is not Nieman Marcus. It is not Macy's. It is not Wal-Mart. It is perhaps all of them combined. It is a middle-of-the-road store to everybody in Korea. Whether you buy an expensive watch or just a pair of inexpensive socks you get the same drab shopping bag. Since everyone shops in department stores companies need to get into these shops. Recently, the top three department store chains have bought up independent stores in the provinces. What was mostly a Seoul phenomenon has now become a national phenomenon. Brand and "We-Me" rules, it seems, in distribution as well.

"WE-ME" GOES DIGITAL

How has the "We-Me Syndrome" impacted the digital scene in Korea? The whole digital explosion is a prime example of "We-Me" run amok. About 25 million Koreans have cell phones. That is practically every Korean man, woman, and child between the ages of 12 and 60. Korea is wired and it is wireless. About 15 million Koreans have some type of internet connection at home and about the same number use wireless internet. We are connected. A common sight is to see a young man and woman walking while holding hands but also talking separately on their cell phones to someone else. The need to be part of connected masses stirred the cell phone sales. The need to be computer literate pushed the penetration of internet and broadband. Korea has the highest installed base of ADSL and VDSL in the world. At the height of the venture boom in Korea, there were over 4,000 startups in the country. Most had some connection with the internet. But in the truest "We-Me" tradition, most Korean users of the internet access just a few Korean sites. Even a late-comer grandiose portal site called Korea.com, despite spending millions of dollars on advertising, failed to lure users away from the first popular sites such as Daum. This is "We-Me" combined with a key internet characteristic, community. People cannot leave Daum because they would be out of the loop. They would just be "Me" without being "We." The internet was made for Koreans. No wonder it is such a huge success. As of September 2005, a mini homepage and blog site called Cyworld (http://www.cyworld.com) that is operated by Nate, a portal and affiliate of SK Telecom, reported its 12 millionth subscriber (Businessweek, 2005). Here is yet another amazing statistic: the internet research firm Korea Click cites that over 91% of internet users aged 19–24 regularly visit Cyworld (ZDnet Korea, 2004). So what explains its popularity? In a nutshell a whole bunch of good "We" and "Me" mechanics. The most prominent "We" feature is the "wave ride" that disseminates blogs to "first kin." In this pyramid like network, each "first kin" will then pass on that blog to their "first kin," and anyway, you probably get the picture. In no time, tens of thousands of people can receive that blog. Koreans like to say that there are only three degrees of separation between any two persons and this is proved time and time again in Cyworld. The mini homepages effectively become a popularity contest of who has the most visitors and so on. The "Me" features are equally creative. Users create idealized self-caricatures called "Avatars" that have been sub-branded as "Mini Me" at Cyworld. In the safe haven of the internet users can virtually cross over beyond the bounds that in real life would not be possible. These visual alter egos allow repressed Koreans to let their hair down. The mini homepages are venues for other self-expression not only through blogs but also with the use of music and uploaded pictures. Maintenance of these sites becomes a full time activity. The end result is that nowadays Korea can be divided simply into two classes of people: those who "Cy" and those who (still) do not.

"WE-ME" AND WOMEN

So far we have not differentiated the "We-Me" concept among men and women. It is common knowledge that women, regardless of national origin, will by nature have a higher We-orientation than men. This is evident by one simple look at women-oriented cable channels like the aptly named WE (short for Women's Entertainment) in the U.S. and On Style in Korea. So to talk about how we should emphasize the collectivistic tendency of women may sound like yesterday's news. Many aspects, however, point to a much stronger We-dynamic for Korean women. A big part of this equation is the Confucian dogma that pits Korean women as being subservient to Korean men. Ironically, Korean women unlike many western cultures keep their surnames even after they marry. This belies the fact that they do not use or are asked about their names thereafter. Instead they are referred to as someone's wife or someone's mother. Thus the individuality of Korean women has long been suppressed and in its place they are identified as being members of larger entities such as their families, companies, or even age brackets. As for the latter there are four large segments: (1) students, (2) young unmarried women ("Agassi"), (3) married women ("Ajuma"), and (4) grandmothers ("Halmony"). In terms of marketing significance, the important segments are the middle two. What separate these two middle types are not only age but also the institution of marriage. One is tempted to speculate that among the four groups young unmarried women (let's call them the YUM) will have the highest "Me" proclivity. After all, YUM do not have husbands or children to look after nor are they bound to a desk like the millions of students who cram for years vying for placements at prestigious universities. Hence the YUM on paper are free. Some cosmetic brands and their extensions such as Laneige and Laneige Girl have successfully stimulated the need to be different among the YUM using their noted tagline "Everyday New Face." Even with the YUM, however, upon closer inspection the picture is not all that clear. In many respects, they manifest the highest symptoms of certain We-like behavior. For instance, the YUM's consciousness of luxury brands is undoubtedly the highest and this can be easily verified by a trip to any luxury mall in Seoul. Among the YUM that work many spend a large portion of their paychecks to buy acceptable luxury brands not necessarily to show off but to make sure that they are not "left behind." Also, the YUM drive the demand for community-based websites like Cyworld. These sites enable Korean women to keep tabs not only on what their friends are up to but also what the latest is on fashion, music, movies, and nightclub scene. One newspaper recently reported that only about 12% of the YUM watch broadcast television and it is shrinking even further. Perhaps this is one result of the movement en masse of the YUM to another medium. The scoop on the YUM is that their behavior is more "We-Me" than just "Me" since their individualities are defined within the tight boundaries of their inner circle. As for married women, they represent perhaps the most critical target for Korean marketing. This is "We" marketing pure and simple. Korean married women are the captains of their households. They make purchase decisions for their husbands, children, sometimes parents-in-law, and of course themselves. It is therefore hard to be a Me-type of buyer when your decision affects so many other people. A few years ago LG's high-end refrigerator called Dios created a mini stir when the woman in the ad boasted, "I am happy to be a woman." Some feminists claimed that this campaign reinforced the cultural stereotyping of women as belonging to the kitchen and enjoying that domesticated role in society. Many other Korean advertising campaigns have played up this notion of the married woman's centrality in their family. This tradition is becoming even stronger because of the "well-being" craze that has taken, recently, Korea by storm. Housewives now have to worry about half-submerged hot baths for their husbands and organic foods for their children. In one survey, over 90% of married women measured their success in life in terms of their children's success in school and in life. This seemingly innocent statistic reveals the enormous pressure that married women face regarding their children's education. Many married Korean women will undertake low-paying manual labor jobs to earn extra money to pay for expensive extra-curricular schooling for their children. The number of placements to the top schools in Korea is so limited and there is so much disenchantment with the rigid style of secondary education that many families have resorted to sending their children abroad. In the more affluent Kang-Nam (south of the Han river) section of Seoul, this mini-exodus of mothers and children to English-speaking countries such as the U.S., Canada, and Australia has created a legion of men called "Kirugi" (Korean for goose) to signify fathers living alone. Children's education is without a doubt the rawest nerve for Korean married women.

STRATEGY IMPLICATIONS

So the million dollar question is "what must marketing managers do to be more effective in the face of the "We-Me" phenomenon?" The first step is to accept that the unit of analysis must be converted away from the "individual" to the "individual as a member of a group." For instance, research methods that survey only individual responses may mask group tendencies. Triangulation of these results with focus group findings will put companies on safer ground. A useful analogy is to think in terms of a "buying center" as is commonly done in industrial marketing.

The second step is to categorize products into three classes: (1) predominantly "We" product markets, (2) predominantly "Me" product markets, and (3) a combination of "We" and "Me" product markets. This can complement the "product use condition" approach (Zhang & Gelb, 1996) especially for collectivistic countries like Korea. The basis for this classification will come from experience and other knowledge of the Korean marketplace. The predominantly "We" products would be things that we like to traditionally consume in groups or those that have "social" value. The Korean alcohol mentioned earlier, Soju, falls under this category. There is an old ritual of how Koreans drink Soju that is usually followed faithfully including drinking it in small cups that is passed around. Other "We" products, also mentioned earlier, are movies and DVD rentals whose demands are influenced significantly by word-of-mouth and top 10 lists. The predominantly "Me" products would be things that reflect a foreign influence or those that can be consumed alone. Starbucks has introduced Koreans to different types of coffee (for a long time people asked for a generic "Blend" brew that tasted quite "Bland") and its "coffee of the day" that is sold at a discount only adds to changing the variety-seeking in this market. Beer is a product that has become more "Me" and despite Hite's stranglehold on the mass market, young drinkers flaunt their individualism with their choice of Corona, Stella Artois, and even Guinness. We see therefore that even within the same alcohol category, products will vary in their "We" and "Me" tendencies. Of course, the most difficult classification is the "We-and-Me" product markets. This is where marketing managers have to almost straddle the two dynamics and be agile enough to mobilize resources when major shifts occur to either end. The best examples of "We-Me" products are Japanese brands. Koreans have a love–hate relationship with anything Japanese. The false consensus is that all Koreans are patriotic and will choose Korean over Japanese brands. The reality is that with the liberalization of the Korean market to all Japanese products, more and more Koreans are choosing Japanese brands like Sony and Lexus. Neither of the two brands emphasizes its Japanese origin and this subtle approach suits the "We-Me" ambivalent situation perfectly.

The third step is to make sure that the subcomponents of the marketing strategy, commonly called the 4 P's (product, price, place, promotion),

match the chosen "We-Me" segment. Let's first look at the predominantly
"We" market. The appropriate product strategy here would be to adopt the
well-known undifferentiated marketing philosophy where trivial differences
between segments are de-emphasized in favor of their commonalities. Pricing reflects the undifferentiated nature of the product and can be uniformly
high such as for quality products or low such as for mass appeal products.
The emphasis for place strategy is to use distribution that has the highest
pull. An obvious choice is department stores but other options should be
explored such as hyperstores and chains such as E-Mart. The promotion
strategy could be a two-pronged approach that first targets mass audiences
using mass media vehicles such as the Chosun daily or prime time television
shows, and second uses a creative message that overtly or discreetly cele-
brates communal values. Some ads stir up the herd mentality such as that
for Woongjin's water purifier brand Coway where noted spokeswoman Kim
Jungeun coos, "Are you still not using Coway?" As for the predominantly
"Me" markets, we can apply the prototypical individual-centered strategies
practiced elsewhere such as in the U.S. Product strategy here needs to be
more customized and there is a premium on being able to offer more variety.
Mobile handsets are becoming increasingly personalized and therefore,
consumers demand more model choices. The keyword for pricing under a
mostly "Me" regime is flexibility. Unlike the previous market, the price
structure must be able to accommodate different product and service combinations. Companies should unbundle their product's various components
as much as possible to increase customization and the number of price
points. Distribution can be a major challenge for "Me" product markets.
This is because Korean distribution has traditionally been designed more
from a "We" standpoint. The savior for "Me" markets has been parcel
delivery services and so-called "Quick" (motorcycle courier) services. For a
very low price, people can receive within-one-hour or same day delivery of a
myriad of products (even Chinese food) to their offices, homes, or thanks to
cell phones outside locations. Promotion is becoming personalized with new
media such as cable and satellite TV channels making some inroads, and
especially for young Koreans websites and cell phones are emerging as
promising channels. For Korean women there are hundreds of magazines
that are becoming more specialized by interest areas. As for the difficult
"We-Me" market, the strategy should be to use the subcomponents in an
integrated manner so that the "We" or "Me" aspects are best satisfied by a
specific element. In short, managers should not feel pressed to reflect both
"We" and "Me" in every facet of their subcomponents. This is analogous to
the global-local debate that has raged on in international marketing for

ages. Even though people generally assume that global marketers such as Coca Cola and McDonalds pursue a standardized global marketing strategy, the truth is that many of their subcomponents such as pricing and advertising are localized. That same philosophy should hold for "We-Me" products. For instance, newly built apartment complexes should use a "We" product and advertising approach that appeals and satisfies some common aspirations of what Koreans desire as acceptable housing in terms of branding, design, and layout. For these same markets, however, the pricing and distribution can be more "Me" in substance since people will differ in their ability to afford and to access these apartments or the showrooms.

SUMMARY

Any culture can be likened to a house. Any culture will have many facades and depending on which side one sees the impression one gets may not be the complete picture. The danger of this happening in Korea is somewhat greater since in many respects Korea is a young country. Despite its thousands of years of recorded history, Korea is relatively new to capitalism and it is especially new to marketing. At the same time, Confucianism and even some shaman traditions still prevail. Therefore, there are various forces at play that are sorting themselves out even in how Koreans behave as consumers. So if we accept the "culture as a house" analogy, our ultimate path toward understanding that culture is to enter and really live in that house and experience all that it has to offer.

REFERENCES

Businessweek (2005). *E-Society: My world is Cyworld.* http://www.businessweek.com/Vmagazine/content/05_39/b3952405.htm

deMooij, M. (1999). *Global marketing and advertising: Understanding cultural paradoxes.* Thousand Oaks, CA: Sage.

Ross, L. D., Greene, D., & House, P. (1977). The false consensus effect: An egocentric bias in social perception and attribution processes. *Journal of Experimental Social Psychology, 13*, 279–301.

Zdnet Korea (2004). http://www.zdnet.co.kr/news/internet/0,39031211,39130634,00.htm

Zhang, Y., & Gelb, B. (1996). Matching advertising appeals to culture: The influence of products' use conditions. *Journal of Advertising, 25*(3), 29–46.

DO THE LITTLE EMPERORS RULE? COMPARING INFORMATIVENESS AND APPEAL TYPES IN CHINESE, AMERICAN, AND FRENCH MAGAZINE ADVERTISING

Lu Zheng, Joseph E. Phelps, Yorgo Pasadeos and Shuhua Zhou

ABSTRACT

This study compares the informativeness and the appeals used in magazine advertising in China with those used in France and in the United States. It provides international marketers with a snapshot of current magazine advertising tactics and provides scholars with an assessment of how consistently expectations based on seminal cross-cultural research predict the informativeness and the appeals used in magazine advertising in each country. Surprisingly, the expectations based on the literature were most often inconsistent with the observations. These findings should serve as a reminder to international marketing scholars that the seminal cross-cultural works, as useful as they are in providing cultural insights, were never intended to apply equally to all subgroups (e.g., the Little Emperors) within a culture.

Cross-Cultural Buyer Behavior
Advances in International Marketing, Volume 18, 159–177
Copyright © 2007 by Elsevier Ltd.
ISSN: 1474-7979/doi:10.1016/S1474-7979(06)18007-2

INTRODUCTION

Marketing scholars are well aware that buying behavior is influenced by the various components of a given culture (e.g., De Mooij, 2001, 2004; Gunaratne & Rahman, 2005; Weber, 2002). Indeed, De Mooij's (2001, p. 31) analysis of cross-cultural consumer behavior indicates that "while for some products [consumption] differences between countries worldwide can be explained by differences in national income, in more economically homogeneous Europe most [consumption] differences can only be explained by culture."

Furthermore, people in different cultures respond to different types of advertising appeals (e.g., Chiou, 2002; Pae, Samiee, & Tai, 2002; Zhang & Neelankavil, 1997). For some marketers this has been a lesson learned the hard way. According to De Mooij (2001), running standardized advertising campaigns, that were developed in London or New York and that reflected Anglo-American values, in cultures with different values resulted in sub-optimization of sales. Clearly, advertising is heavily influenced by the distinctive cultural history, the values, and the beliefs of its creators, and of its audience (Rotzoll & Haefner, 1990; Taylor, Hoy, & Haley, 1996).

Thus, advertising appeals that are culturally congruent should have more impact on buyer behavior in a given culture (Gunaratne & Rahman, 2005; Zhang & Neelankavil, 1997). Mueller (1987, p. 52) claims that "advertising tends to reflect the prevalent values of a culture in which it exists, insofar as those values can be used to shape consumption ethic." Thus, examining the use of advertising appeals across cultures should provide insights into those important prevalent values that marketers believe are driving buyer behavior.

Purpose of Paper

In the current paper we are particularly interested in comparing the informativeness and advertising appeals used in magazine advertising in China, France, and the United States. This interest is driven by the belief that the prevalent values of an important segment of the Chinese market, and therefore the appeals used to influence this segment, may fall more in line with Western culture than with traditional Chinese culture. If this is the case, then the general cultural descriptions provided in the literature may be misleading at times and an update of our knowledge in this area could prove useful.

We believe that the emergence of Western values is the result of socio-cultural and economic environments uniquely experienced by the current generation of Chinese consumers. The dramatic growth in the Chinese economy over the past few decades has certainly impacted the affluence of this segment. Still, we agree with De Mooij (2001) that a new economy does not necessarily create new values as the seemingly old values become manifest in consumption and in consumption behavior. There have been other important changes taking place in China over the past few decades. Perhaps, the most important of these is the so-called "Little Emperor Syndrome" which grew out of China's strict family planning policy. The Chinese government launched its one child policy in the late 1970s to alleviate the country's population burden. It has been said that this policy forced parents and grandparents to place all their hopes and to heap all of their love on this only child, thereby creating a generation of indulgent and self-centered children (Janeway, 1987; Ji & McNeal, 2001).

Those Little Emperors represent a large portion of the Chinese X-Generation (18–35-year olds with high education and high income) (Zhang & Sharon, 2003), which some marketers perceive as the most dominant consumer segment in China (Dou, Wang, & Zhou, 2006; Li, 1998). This generation grew up as China opened itself to the outside world and transitioned to a market economy (Ji & McNeal, 2001). During this period Chinese youth embraced private consumerism to a greater extent than their parents (Zhou, Zhang, & Vertinsky, 2002). It was also during this time that Western values such as individualism were adopted to a greater extent among the Little Emperors.

If marketing practitioners have recognized this "westernization" and if Mueller is correct and their advertising uses the prevalent values to drive buyer behavior, then the advertising appeals should reflect those Western values. Mueller (1987) identified sets of traditional Eastern appeals and modern Western appeals. If the advertising targeting the Little Emperors is using more Western appeals (e.g., individual, hard-sell, and product merit) than would be expected, given the scholarly literature, it may be time to reexamine current scholarly thinking in this area. To more fully gauge the relative utilization of Western and Eastern appeals, it would be useful to compare appeal usage in China with that of a Western country. It should be even more insightful to compare the appeal usage in China with two Western countries (France and the United States) that vary on important cultural characteristics. In sum, the findings of the current study will provide international marketers with a snapshot of current magazine advertising tactics in China, France, and the United States. Most importantly, this study will provide scholars with an assessment of how consistently expectations based on seminal cross-cultural research predict the informativeness and appeals used in magazine advertising in each country.

RELEVANT LITERATURE AND RESEARCH QUESTIONS

Over the years, few scholars have contributed as much to our understanding of cultural influence as Hofstede and Hall. Hofstede's work provides a seminal examination of cultural influence on values in the workplace. After years of extensive analysis he crafted a model to differentiate cultures. The five dimensions in his model are power distance, individualism, masculinity, uncertainty avoidance, and long-term orientation. Scores for those dimensions are now available for at least 74 countries and regions (Hofstede, 2003). The scores for the three countries of interest in this study – China, France, and the United States – vary dramatically. Table 1 shows that although the scores for the three countries vary by dimension, the distinction (highest, middle, and lowest) in each case is clear. Owing to their relative scores on these cultural dimensions, one may assume that the advertising of the three countries would accordingly exhibit distinctive characteristics.

Hall (1976) emphasized the strong linkage between a culture's context level and the characteristics of communication in that culture. In high-context cultures, the message tends to be less important than the context where the communication occurs. To effectively interpret the message, the recipient is supposed to detect all the nuances and grasp the subtle, unuttered and implicit contextual factors where the communication takes place. In low-context cultures, the message is usually delivered in a very explicit and straightforward manner. The mass of information is clearly coded and the context plays a limited role in interpreting the message. To effectively

Table 1. Hofstede's Cultural Dimensions.

	China	France	United States	World Average
Power distance index	80	68	40	55
Individualism	20	71	91	43
Masculinity	66	43	62	50
Uncertainty avoidance index	30	86	46	64
Long-term orientation	118	N/A	29	45

persuade the receiver, the speaker seeks to avoid any ambiguity by providing enough information. According to Hall (1976), American culture is located toward the lower end of the context scale, with French culture being a mixture of high and low context, and Chinese culture situated at the high-context end of the scale. Because of their relative positions along the cultural context continuum, one may assume that the advertising of the three countries would accordingly exhibit distinctive characteristics. Thus, the different positions that France and the United States hold on the cultural context continuum as well as their relative ranking on Hofstede's cultural dimensions make them well suited to serve as distinct and separate benchmarks of Western culture.

Advertising Appeals

As noted earlier, the appeal types were selected because they represented modern Western appeals and traditional Eastern appeals (Mueller, 1987). The expectations for appeal type usage are based on the work of Hofstede or Hall.

Western Appeals

Hofstede listed the United States as the most individualistic country in the world. France also receives a high score on individualism. China, on the other hand, is a collectivist society and it ranks the lowest on individualism among all Asian countries. The expectation based on Hofstede's work is clearly that an *individual appeal*, with its emphasis on standing out in the crowd, is least likely to show up in Chinese advertising, is more likely to show up in French advertising, and is most likely to be used in U.S. advertising. Lin's (2001) finding that Chinese TV commercials utilized fewer individual appeals than American TV commercials is consistent with these expectations. However, Zhang and Sharon (2003) reported that *individual appeals* were more frequently presented in Chinese magazine advertisements than in Chinese TV commercials. Understanding differences in appeal usage across media is interesting. The current study, however, examines magazine advertising from China, France, and the United States so that the relative use of individual appeals can be assessed across cultures.

Mueller (1987) characterized *hard-sell* advertising appeals as the stressing of product advantages and performance by explicit comparisons, whereas product merit appeals are characterized by an in-depth description of some feature of the product with the benefit to the consumer being secondary or implied. Based on Hall's work one would predict that Chinese advertisements would feature the fewest such appeals. China, as a high-context culture, relies more on implicit understanding of product reputation and tradition. The United States, on the other hand, is a low-context culture that depends on explicit information to ensure successful communication. As such, it is reasonable to predict that the United States would rely most, among the three countries, on the *hard-sell appeal*, whereas France, being a country whose context level ranks in the middle, would feature a moderate amount of such appeals. Additional research indicates a close relationship between cultural context level and usage of the *hard-sell* and *product merit appeals*. Compared with American advertisements, French advertisements have been found to use a more symbolic and indirect approach (Cutler & Javalgi, 1992; Taylor et al., 1996). In addition, French advertisements are less likely to use comparative advertising, an important hard-sell technique (Cutler & Javalgi, 1992). In contrast to French advertisements, American advertisements have been more likely to stress brand names and to use testimonials of celebrities or other credible sources, two salient features of a *hard-sell appeal*. American advertisements have also been found to demonstrate much higher product visibility and focus more frequently on specific product characteristics than their French counterparts (Zandpour, Chang, & Catalano, 1992). Researchers have additionally found that, compared with U.S. advertisements, Chinese advertisements were less likely to use the comparative technique (Cheng & Schweitzer, 1996), the hard-sell, and the product merit appeals Lin (2001).

Eastern Appeals

According to Mueller (1987), *status appeals* suggest that the use of a particular product will improve users' position/rank within their reference group. Hofstede classified the United States as a low-power-distance society whereas France and China were classified as high-power-distance societies. A high ranking suggests an uneven distribution of power and wealth in a society as well as the presence of a caste system that impedes upward social mobility. In contrast, a low power distance ranking indicates more equal access to opportunities and a wider distribution of power and wealth. Hall and Hall (1989) contended that people demonstrate great sensitivity to hierarchy and status in a highly stratified society. Since Hofstede classified China and France as two high-power-distance countries, the expectation is that the *status appeal* will be more frequently used in China and France than in the United States.

Group consensus appeals are characterized by the portrayal of individuals as an integral part of a group and by an emphasis on the conformity to the group will (Mueller, 1987). According to Hofstede's rankings, China is considered much more collectivist than France and the United States. As the United States is ranked as the most individualistic culture, one would expect that *group consensus appeals* would appear the least frequently in magazine advertising in the United States and that Chinese advertisements would make more frequent use of this appeal type. Accordingly, previous research indicates that *group consensus* constitutes an effective advertising appeal among Chinese consumers (Cheng, 1994). Moreover, *group consensus* appeals were presented more frequently in Chinese TV commercials than in their American counterparts (Lin, 2001). Whether this finding will hold for current magazine advertising in the United States and China is not yet known and we could not locate any research that has assessed the usage frequency of *group consensus* appeals in French magazine advertising.

The *oneness with nature appeal* stresses a harmonious relationship between man and nature, with a focus on the back-to-nature themes (Mueller, 1987). Unlike the other appeals, a clear expectation concerning the relative usage of oneness with nature appeals does not immediately emerge from Hall or Hofstede's work. However, in their summary of the major cultural differences between China and the United States, Pan, Chaffee, Chu, and Ju (1994) report that "U.S. culture emphasizes active mastery in the person-nature relationship, whereas traditional Chinese-culture emphasizes passive acceptance of fate by seeking harmony with nature" (Lin, 2001, p. 84). The expectation flowing from this difference is that *oneness with nature appeals* would be used more frequently in Chinese advertising. Lin's (2001) research comparing Chinese and U.S. television commercials supports this expectation. To our knowledge, no research has investigated the usage of *oneness with nature appeals* in French advertisements; however, according to Engel, Blackwell, and Miniard (1990), both American and French cultures believe that people can master the earth. Therefore, it is also expected that French and U.S. advertisements will use the *oneness with nature appeal* with roughly the same frequency.

Research Question 1. How well do the predictions based on Hofstede's and Hall's work fit with the observed appeal usage in each country and what is the relative usage of Western and Eastern appeals in Chinese magazine advertising?

Table 2 provides a summary of the appeal usage and informativeness expectations for each country.

Table 2. Expectations of Usage Frequency of Appeals and Information Cues.

	China	France	United States
Individualism	3	2	1
Hard sell	3	2	1
Product merit	3	2	1
Status	1	2	3
Group consensus	1	2	3
Oneness with nature	1	–	2
Informativeness	3	2	1

Note: The frequency of the ad appeals and information cues presented is ranked in a scale of 1–3, with 1 indicating the highest frequency of occurrence and 3 the lowest. "–" indicates uncertainty about the ranking due to absence of relevant research finding.

Informativeness

The type and number of information cues explicitly expressed in the magazine advertisements should vary dramatically by country according to their relative positions along the cultural context continuum. According to Hall and Hall (1989), people in high-context cultures are more skilled in grasping the subtle and implicit contextual factors when interpreting a message. As such, fewer explicit cues are included in the message. People in a low-context culture, however, such as the United States, are more tuned to receiving messages with the information delivered in a more explicit fashion. Therefore, based on Hall's work, one would expect the magazine advertisements from the United States to contain the most information cues, followed by the French advertisements, with the Chinese advertisements presenting the fewest information cues (see Table 2). There is reason to question this expectation as Rice and Lu (1988) reported finding more information cues in Chinese magazine advertising than in U.S. magazine advertising.

Research Question 2. How well do the predictions based on Hall's work fit with the observed number of explicit information cues in the Chinese, French, and U.S. magazine advertisements?

METHOD

Content analysis was used in the present study. Data were obtained from advertisements in Chinese, French and U.S. magazines. Some of these

Table 3. Selected Magazines.

	China	France	United States
News magazine	*Sanlian*	*Le Point*	*Time*
Men's magazine	*Shishang Xiansheng*	*Maximal*	*Gentlemen's Quarterly*
Women's magazine	*Shishang Cosmo*	*Marie Claire*	*Glamour*
Business magazine	*Caijing*	*Capital*	*Fortune*

magazines have domestic and international versions, which address distinctive target audiences and feature different advertisements, so it is important to note that the sampled magazines in the current study were all domestic editions, purchased in China, France, and the U.S., respectively.

To cover a wide range of product categories in the advertisements, four types of magazines were selected from each country of interest: one news magazine, one men's magazine, one women's magazine, and one business magazine. The magazines were selected based on a number of criteria: paid circulation, type of audience, advertising revenue, magazine content, and number of advertisements in each issue. Table 3 shows the list of selected magazines.

Product Categories

The advertisements were classified into 27 product categories: watch/sunglass/jewelry, automotive, bank/financial, alcohol and tobacco, airlines and transport, computer/software/hardware, women's clothes, men's clothes, children's products, electronics, cosmetics, office appliance, real estate, hotel/restaurant, recreation/entertainment, medicine and personal hygiene products, laundry products, food and beverage, DVD/CD/Videogames, service, household appliances, PR, cell phone, furniture, leather, and miscellaneous. An examination of the product categories showed that they are fairly evenly distributed among the three countries. Personal items, such as watches, jewelry, and clothes (China = 35.0%, USA = 20.5%, and France = 24.7% of all advertisements) and health-related products, such as medicine, cosmetics, and skincare (China = 25.3%, USA = 26.0%, and France = 25.6% of all advertisements) made up the largest percentage of advertisements.

Coding Scheme for Measuring General Message Appeals

Mueller's (1987) coding scheme was adopted to examine advertising appeals. Mueller's instrument has been widely utilized to evaluate advertising appeals in various cultures. The presence of a certain appeal was coded as "1" and its absence was coded as "0."

Coding Scheme for Measuring Information Cues

The coding scheme developed by Taylor, Miracle, and Wilson (1997) was adopted in the current study. Their scheme utilized the work of Stewart and Furse (1986) to update and to expand the classic Resnik and Stern (1977) scale. Whereas the Resnik and Stern (1977) scale included 14 information cues, Taylor et al.'s (1997) scale can assess 30 information cues. During a pretest of the coding scheme, in which 10 advertisements from each type of magazine from each of the three countries were coded, it became obvious that "website" was a frequently employed cue. Therefore, a 31st cue, *website*, was added. Definitions of the information cues are listed in the appendix. The presence of each cue was coded as "1" and its absence was coded as "0." The total number of information cues used in each advertisement was also summed. In addition to the primary variables of interest discussed above, the following variables were also coded in the present study: (a) country of publication; (b) magazine type; and (c) month of publication.

Unit of Analysis and Data Collection

The unit of analysis is the magazine advertisement (half-page or larger) of a specific brand in the 12 selected magazines (four from each country of interest). For weekly and biweekly magazines, we randomly picked an issue from each month. Any duplicated advertisements for the same brand in the same language were excluded from the sample to eliminate redundancies that may skew the results (Stern & Resnik, 1991). All the half-page or larger advertisements in the November 2005, December 2005, and January 2006 issues of the selected magazines constitute the database of the current research. The reader will note that this sampling took place during a holiday period in all three countries. Although Christmas may not be celebrated to the same extent in all three countries, a large number of young, affluent, Chinese celebrate a consumerist version of Christmas (Fowler & Qin, 2005). Furthermore, Spring Festival, a major holiday in China also fell in January 2006. Thus, although the sampling took place over a holiday season, it included important holidays in all of the countries studied. A total of 1,901 magazine advertisements were coded: 558 Chinese, 590 French, and 753 American advertisements.

Coders and Inter-Coder Agreement

Two trilingual graduate students worked as coders. They received extensive training and were tested on a pilot exercise of 15 magazine advertisements from each country. Following this training, 40 advertisements from each type of magazine in each country were coded by both coders. Thus, 480 or 25.2% of the sample of 1,901 advertisements were coded by both coders and inter-coder reliability tests were performed according to Holsti's (1969) formula. For informativeness level, the inter-coder agreement was 93%. For advertising appeals, the inter-coder agreement was 92%. Both figures exceed the minimum inter-coder reliability of 85% specified by Kassarjian (1977).

FINDINGS

Advertising Appeals

The first research question asked how well the seminal cross-cultural research works would predict advertising appeal usage. Six of Mueller's (1987) appeal types, including three Western and three Eastern appeals, were examined. Two tables list the relevant results. Table 4 shows the usage of each appeal type by country and Table 5 lists the predicted outcomes based on the literature as well as the observed outcome.

Western Appeals

Based on Hofstede's work, it was predicted that the U.S. magazine advertisements would utilize the most *individual appeals*, followed by France, and that the Chinese advertisements would utilize the fewest such appeals. There was, overall, a statistically significant difference in terms of the use of *individual appeals* among the magazine advertisements of the three countries.

Table 4. Presence of Specific Appeals by Country.

Appeal	China (%)	France (%)	United States (%)	χ^2 $(df = 2)$	p
Individual	51.6	40.3	35.5	35.07	<0.001
Hard sell	17.9	26.3	48.2	149.16	<0.001
Product merit	66.3	48.6	55.2	37.13	<0.001
Status	89.1	18.0	12.0	949.01	<0.001
Group consensus	14.3	15.3	17.7	2.95	n.s.
Oneness with nature	17.7	15.3	6.9	39.13	<0.001

Table 5. Usage Frequency of Advertising Appeals and Information
Cues Predictions vs. Results.

		China	France	United States
Individual	Prediction	3	2	1
	Result	1	2*	3*
Hard sell	Prediction	3	2	1
	Result	3	2	1
Products merits	Prediction	3	2	1
	Result	1	3	2
Status	Prediction	1	2	3
	Result	1	2	3
Group consensus	Prediction	1	2	3
	Result	3*	2*	1*
Oneness with nature	Prediction	1	–	2
	Result	1*	2*	3
Informativeness	Prediction	3	2	1
	Result	1*	3	2*

Note: The frequency of the ad appeals and information cues presented is ranked in a scale of
1–3, with 1 indicating the highest frequency of occurrence and 3 the lowest.
*Indicates a lack of a statistically significant difference between countries.

($\chi^2 = 35.07$, $df = 2$, $p < 0.001$). Additional logistic regression tests showed that
Chinese magazine advertisements were 1.58 times as likely to portray *individual
appeals* as the French advertisements and 1.94 times as likely as the U.S.
advertisements ($p < 0.01$). No significant difference was found between the
French and the American advertisements ($p > 0.05$). That is, Chinese magazine
advertisements used *individual appeals* the most frequently among the three
national samples. This finding runs counter to the prediction based on
Hofstede's work.

It was predicted that U.S. advertisements would feature the most *hard-sell
appeals*, with French advertisements second, and with Chinese advertisements using the fewest. There was a statistically significant overall difference
in terms of the use of *hard-sell appeals* among magazine advertisements from
the three countries ($\chi^2 = 149.16$, $df = 2$, $p < 0.001$). Logistic regression tests
showed that American magazine advertisements did, in fact, use the most
hard-sell appeals whereas the Chinese advertisements used the fewest. Specifically, American magazine advertisements were 4.26 times as likely to use
hard-sell appeals as their Chinese counterparts, and 2.61 times as likely to
use *hard-sell appeals* as French advertisements ($p < 0.001$). Moreover,
French advertisements were 1.63 times as likely to use *hard-sell appeals* as

Chinese advertisements ($p = 0.01$). These findings are in line with expectations based on the literature.

The use of the *product merit appeal* was predicted to vary according to cultural context level, with the most being found in the U.S. advertisements, followed by the French advertisements, and with the Chinese advertisements using the fewest. There was a statistically significant overall difference in terms of the use of *product merit appeals* among magazine advertisements from the three countries ($\chi^2 = 37.13$, $df = 2$, $p < 0.001$). Additional logistic regression tests showed that Chinese magazine advertisements were 1.59 times as likely to portray *product merit appeals* as American advertisements ($p < 0.001$). American magazine advertisements were 1.3 times as likely to use *product merit appeals* as the French advertisements ($p < 0.05$). In other words, Chinese advertisements used the most *product merit appeals*, followed by U.S. advertisements, with French advertisements utilizing the fewest. This finding runs contrary to the prediction based on Hall's work.

Eastern Appeals

It was predicted that *status appeals* would be more frequent in Chinese and French advertisements than in U.S. advertisements. There was a statistically significant difference in the presence of *status appeals* among magazine advertisements from the three countries ($\chi^2 = 949.01$, $df = 2$, $p < 0.001$). Further tests showed that Chinese advertisements were 37 and 60 times, respectively, as likely as their French and American counterparts to use *status appeals* ($p < 0.001$). In addition, French advertisements were 1.61 times as likely as American advertisements to employ *status appeals* ($p < 0.01$). With *status appeals*, the observations match the expectations based on the literature.

Based on the literature, the expectation was that Chinese advertisements would use *group consensus appeals* more frequently than French and American advertisements. However, no statistically significant difference in the use of the *group consensus appeals* was found among the magazine advertisements from China, France and the United States ($\chi^2 = 2.95$, $df = 2$, $p > 0.05$). This Eastern appeal was used infrequently in all three countries. The only other appeal to be used so sparingly was the *oneness with nature appeal* (see Table 4).

As with the other Eastern appeals, it was predicted that Chinese magazine advertisements would utilize *oneness with nature* appeals more than their French and their American counterparts. There was a statistically significant difference in the presence of the *oneness with nature* appeal employed in the magazine advertisements of the three nations ($\chi^2 = 39.13$, $df = 2$, $p < 0.01$). Both Chinese and French magazine advertisements were more likely to use this appeal than their American counterparts. Specifically, Chinese magazine advertisements were 2.91 times as likely, and French advertisements were 2.43 times as likely, to use *oneness with nature* appeal as American magazine advertisements. However, the findings only partially support the expectations as binary logistic regression tests indicated that there was not a statistically significant difference in the use of this appeal between advertisements from China and France ($p > 0.05$).

Informativeness

The second research question focused on the informativeness of the three countries' magazine advertisements and on how closely literature based expectations would reflect direct observations of informativeness. It was predicted that the American advertisements would feature the most information cues whereas the Chinese advertisements would employ the fewest information cues. An ANOVA test indicated that there was an overall statistically significant difference ($F_{(2, 1,898)} = 83.94$, $p < 0.001$) in terms of the average number of information cues used in magazine advertisements from China, France and the United States. As shown in Table 6, the simple mean scores indicate that the Chinese advertisements contained the most information cues. This finding contradicts the prediction, based on Hall's cultural context theory, that the Chinese advertisements would feature the fewest cues. The subsequent post hoc tests revealed that the difference between the Chinese and the U.S. advertisements was not significant ($p > 0.05$), and that both Chinese and American magazine advertisements employed more information cues than their French counterparts ($p < 0.001$). Specifically, the Chinese and the American advertisements utilized 2.34 and 2.02 more cues than the French advertisements, respectively ($p < 0.001$).

Table 6. Informativeness by Country.

Country	Mean	% of Advertisements with at least 1 Cue	% of Advertisements with 5 + Cues
China	6.31	98.6	63.8
United States	5.99	97.9	59.1
France	3.97	96.6	36.1

DISCUSSION AND SUGGESTIONS FOR
FUTURE RESEARCH

The expectations based on the literature were consistent with the observations for only two (i.e., *status and hard-sell*) of the six appeals examined. The observations were inconsistent with expectations for four of the appeals and were also inconsistent with regard to expectations of the informativeness of the advertisements. *Status* was by far the most frequently used appeal in the Chinese advertisements. Chinese magazine advertisements were a staggering 60 times as likely as their American counterparts to use *status appeals* and were 37 times as likely to do so as the French advertisements. However, this was the only finding for the Eastern appeals that was consistent with expectations. Although the findings relating to *oneness with nature*, another Eastern appeal, fell in the expected direction, there was not a significant difference in usage between the Chinese and the French advertisements. Perhaps even more interesting is that the Chinese advertisements used the Western *hard-sell appeals* just as frequently as they used *oneness with nature appeals* and even more than *group consensus appeals*. None of these three appeals were used extensively in the Chinese advertisements. Still, finding the least used (in the Chinese advertisements) Western appeal to be just as frequently used as two (*oneness with nature and group consensus*) of the three Eastern appeals is an indication of what marketers may believe resonates with the Little Emperors. Marketers do not seem to believe that *group consensus appeals* reflect prevalent values among the Little Emperors any more than it does among magazine readers in the U.S. and France as there were no differences in usage frequency by country for this appeal.

As noted above, *hard-sell* was the only Western appeal for which the observations were consistent with the expectations. The relatively limited use of *hard-sell appeals* in Chinese and French advertisements conforms to the norms of the advertising profession (Zandpour et al., 1994) and cultural values in these two countries. First, direct comparative advertising, a key feature in a *hard-sell* approach, is deemed unethical in China and France. In contrast, the use of direct comparative advertising is encouraged in the United States by the Federal Trade Commission (FTC). Second, the relatively infrequent occurrence of *hard-sell appeals* in Chinese advertisements may reflect the implicit adherence to the country's traditional cultural values, such as modesty, love for harmony, and avoidance of direct confrontation.

The findings were inconsistent with expectations with regard to the *individual* and *product-merit appeals*. In fact, the Chinese advertisements used these Western appeals more frequently than did the advertisements from France and the United States. The heavy use of *individual appeals* in Chinese magazine advertisements represents a polar opposite to the expectations based on Hofstede's rankings for Chinese culture. However, the current study is not the first to note a relatively high usage of *individual appeals* in Chinese magazine advertisements. Zhang and Sharon (2003) found the *individual appeal* used significantly more in Chinese magazine advertisements than in Chinese TV commercials. They attributed this to the distinctive target audiences of the two media. While Chinese TV is targeted toward the general public, the X-Generation constitutes the primary target audience of Chinese magazine advertisements (China: The "X" Generation Study, 1996; Zhang & Sharon, 2003). Such a comparison between Chinese magazine advertisements and Chinese TV commercials cannot, however, provide a sense of how Chinese usage of *individual appeals* compares with that of highly individualistic societies such as the United States and France. The current study addressed this void with unexpected results.

Chinese magazine advertisements were also found to use *product merit appeals* the most frequently among the three countries. This, too, is the opposite of what was expected and is yet another indication that marketers believe that Western appeals will resonate with the Little Emperors. Of course, there are alternative explanations. The heavy usage of that appeal in Chinese advertisements may be explained by China's advertising regulations and the perceived function of Chinese advertisements. Per Article 9 of Advertising Law of People's Republic of China (1995), "Statements in advertisements of the performance, origin of production, use, quality, price, producer and manufacturer, valid term and promise, and service's items, manner, quality, price and promise of the goods advertised shall be clear and explicit." Our finding is also in line with previous research on the function of Chinese advertisements. Zhou et al. (2002) found that for Chinese consumers, advertisements constituted a very important medium of product- and service-related information and helped them make better purchase decisions.

Overall, the appeal usage found in the current study suggests that the advertisements created for this young, affluent, Chinese audience reflect both Western and Eastern values but that more Western appeals dominate. These findings should serve as a reminder to marketing researchers that the seminal cross-cultural works, as useful as they are in providing cultural insights, should not be assumed to apply equally to all subgroups within a culture. In other words, while the Little Emperors may not rule, they, along with the other members of China's Generation X, should be treated as a special audience for whom the traditional Eastern approaches may not lead to the most effective communication.

Informativeness

As was the case for many of the appeal types, the informativeness findings are not consistent with the expectations. Indeed, the findings contradict the expectations that the advertisements in the lowest context culture, the United States, would contain more information than their Chinese counterparts. In fact, Chinese advertisements were the most informative. One explanation is simply that the specific audience that these Chinese magazines target is substantially different from the typical Chinese consumer. However, Rice and Lu (1988) also found Chinese magazine advertisements to be more informative than advertisements in American magazines and it appears that the target audience for their magazines was a bit more general than that of the current study.

There are other plausible explanations. The findings can be understood from a function-oriented perspective. In fact, the distinctive functions of advertisements in different nations, along with the cultural context levels, appear to play a decisive role in determining the level of informativeness in advertisements. In particular, advertisements from China and France, two high-context countries, have different functions and satisfy distinctive needs. In China, people turn to advertisements for more detailed product information to help them make purchase decisions (Zhou et al., 2002). The French are more likely to derive product information by themselves from in-store comparisons of the products (Green & Langeard, 1975). Furthermore, there are additional factors, such as government regulations and forces within the advertising industry (Zandpour et al., 1994), which are known to influence advertising messages. In sum, there are a number of reasons why the cultural context level may not be a perfect predictor of informativeness.

As is always the case, an understanding of what is happening must be in place before an understanding of why it is happening can develop. The findings of the current study provide international marketers with a snapshot of what is happening in magazine advertising in the United States, France, and China. This study also provides marketing scholars with evidence that the advertising appeals were often inconsistent with expectations derived from Hall's and Hofstede's work. As discussed above, these findings bring forth a number of questions. We hope that the current work will stimulate more in-depth research to address these issues.

REFERENCES

Advertising Law of People's Republic of China (1995). Retrieved on September 16, 2005, from http://us.tom.com/english/434.htm

Cheng, H. (1994). Reflection of cultural values: A content analysis of Chinese magazine advertisements from 1982 and 1992. *International Journal of Advertising, 13*(2), 167–183.

Cheng, H., & Schweitzer, J. C. (1996). Cultural values reflected in Chinese and U.S. television commercials. *Journal of Advertising Research, 36*(3), 27–45.

China: The "X" Generation Study (1996). *China: The "X" generation study.* Shanghai: MBL Taiwan and J. Walter Thomson.

Chiou, J. S. (2002). The effectiveness of different advertising message appeals in the Eastern emerging society: Using Taiwanese TV commercials as an example. *International Journal of Advertising, 20*, 297–317.

Cutler, B. D., & Javalgi, R. G. (1992). A cross-cultural analysis of the visual components of print advertising: The United States and the European community. *Journal of Advertising Research, 32*(1), 71–80.

De Mooij, M. (2001). Convergence and divergence in consumer behavior. *World Advertising Research Center*, October, 30–33.

De Mooij, M. (2004). *Consumer behavior and culture: Consequences for global marketing and advertising.* Thousand Oaks, CA: Sage Publications.

Dou, W., Wang, G., & Zhou, N. (2006). Generational and regional differences in media consumption patterns of Chinese generation X consumers. *Journal of Advertising, 35*(2), 101–110.

Engel, J. F., Blackwell, R. D., & Miniard, P. W. (1990). *Consumer behavior* (6th ed.). Chicago: Dryden Press.

Fowler, G., & Qin, J. (2005). China's Yuletide Revolution; Nation's Yuppies Embracing Christmas as Time for Love; Ms. Ji, Romance, and KFC embrace. *The Wall Street Journal*, December 22, B1.

Green, R. T., & Langeard, E. (1975). A cross-national comparison of consumer habits and innovator characteristics: What makes French and U.S. consumer different? *Journal of Marketing, 39*, 34–41.

Gunaratne, A., & Rahman, K. (2005). Embodying the cultural syndrome and product characteristics in advertising strategy. *ANZMAC 2005 Conference: Advertising/Marketing Communication Issues.*

Hall, E. T. (1976). *Beyond culture.* Garden City, NY: Anchor Books, Doubleday.

Hall, E. T., & Hall, M. R. (1989). *Understanding cultural differences: Germans, French and Americans.* Yarmouth, ME: Intercultural Press, Inc.

Hofstede, G. (2003). *Geert Hofstede*TM *cultural dimensions* [Online]. Retrieved on September 6, 2006, from http://www.geert-hofstede.com

Holsti, O. (1969). *Content analysis for the social sciences and humanities.* Reading, MA: Addison-Wesley.

Janeway, E. (1987). China's only child: This strict policy is controlling China's population problem. But will only children make unwilling socialists? *Psychology Today, 21*, 44–49.

Ji, M. F., & McNeal, J. U. (2001). How Chinese children's commercials differ from those of the United States: A content analysis. *Journal of Advertising, 30*(3), 79–92.

Kassarjian, H. H. (1977). Content analysis in consumer research. *Journal of Consumer Research, 26*(4), 8–18.

Li, C. (1998). *China: The consumer revolution.* Singapore: Wiley.

Lin, C. (2001). Cultural values reflected in Chinese and American television advertising. *Journal of Advertising, 30*(4), 83–94.

Mueller, B. (1987). Reflections of culture: An analysis of Japanese and American advertising appeals. *Journal of Advertising Research, 27*(3), 51–59.

Pae, J. H., Samiee, S., & Tai, S. (2002). Global advertising strategy: The moderating role of brand familiarity and execution style. *International Marketing Review, 19,* 176–189.

Pan, Z., Chaffee, S. H., Chu, G. C., & Ju, Y. (1994). *To see ourselves: Comparing traditional Chinese and American cultural values.* Boulder, CO: Westview Press.

Resnik, A., & Stern, B. L. (1977). An analysis of information content in television advertising. *Journal of Marketing, 41*(1), 50–53.

Rice, M. D., & Lu, Z. (1988). A content analysis of Chinese magazine advertisements. *Journal of Advertising, 17*(4), 43–48.

Rotzoll, K. B., & Haefner, J. E. (1990). *Advertising in contemporary society.* Cincinnati: South-Western Publishing Co.

Stern, B. L., & Resnik, A. J. (1991). Information content in television advertising: A replication and extension. *Journal of Advertising Research, 31*(3), 36–47.

Stewart, D. W., & Furse, D. H. (1986). *Effective television advertising.* Lexington, MA: Lexington Books.

Taylor, C. R., Miracle, G. E., & Wilson, D. R. (1997). The impact of information level on the effectiveness of U.S. and Korean television commercials. *Journal of Advertising, 26*(1), 1–18.

Taylor, R. E., Hoy, M. G., & Haley, E. (1996). How French advertising professionals develop creative strategy. *Journal of Advertising, 25*(1), 1–14.

Weber, J. M. (2002). Differences in purchase behavior between France and the USA: The cosmetic industry. *Journal of Fashion Marketing and Management, 6*(4), 396–407.

Zandpour, F., Campos, V., Catalano, J., Chang, C., Cho, Y. D., Hoobyar, R., Jiang, S. F., Lin, M. C., Madrid, S., Scheideler, H., & Osborn, S. T. (1994). Global reach and local touch: Achieving cultural fitness in TV advertising. *Journal of Advertising Research, 34*(5), 35–63.

Zandpour, F., Chang, C., & Catalano, J. (1992). Stories, symbols and straight talk: A comparative analysis of French, Taiwanese and American TV commercials. *Journal of Advertising Research, 32*(1), 25–37.

Zhang, J., & Sharon, S. (2003). Cultural values in advertisements to the Chinese X generation: Promoting modernity and individualism. *Journal of Advertising, 32*(1), 23–33.

Zhang, Y., & Neelankavil, J. P. (1997). The influence of culture on advertising effectiveness in China and the USA: A cross-cultural study. *Journal of European Marketing, 31,* 134–149.

Zhou, D., Zhang, W., & Vertinsky, I. (2002). Advertising trends in China. *Journal of Advertising Research, 42*(3), 73–81.

THE DRIVERS OF CUSTOMER SATISFACTION WITH INDUSTRIAL GOODS: AN INTERNATIONAL STUDY

Fabian Festge and Manfred Schwaiger

ABSTRACT

The importance of customer satisfaction as a critical success factor has been recognized by practitioners and academics for several years now. Although customer satisfaction plays an important role in industrial markets due to their special characteristics, most researchers focus on consumer goods or services, leaving industrial goods fairly uncovered. In order to give manufacturers of industrial goods well-founded recommendations on how to reach a high level of satisfaction, the main drivers of customer satisfaction have to be revealed. The identification of these drivers is the primary goal of this study. Taking into account that there has been a change of paradigms in scale development we created a state-of-the-art questionnaire consisting of 15 constructs to be measured with 52 items, which was administered to respondents in 12 countries worldwide. The drivers' analysis using Partial-Least-Squares (PLS) reveals a lot of penalty-services, whereas only the quality of machines and the quality of quotations offer a significant chance on increasing customer satisfaction, therefore disagreeing with previous results.

Cross-Cultural Buyer Behavior
Advances in International Marketing, Volume 18, 179–207
ISSN: 1474-7979/doi:10.1016/S1474-7979(06)18008-4

MOTIVATION FOR THE STUDY

Increasing competition in a globalized economy forces companies to permanently search for key success factors, in tangible as well as intangible areas. Owing to the technical improvements achieved in the field of information and communication technology the possibilities of creating sustainable advantages based on tangible assets are mostly utilized. For this reason many academics and practitioners have focused their work on developing and exploiting competitive advantages based on intangible assets such as customer loyalty (e.g. Reichheld, 1996), brand strength (e.g. Aaker & Joachimsthaler, 2000) and corporate reputation (e.g. Schwaiger, 2004; Schwaiger & Cannon, 2004).

In this context, customer satisfaction has been a central topic in marketing over the last decade. The reason therefore is the numerous advantages for a company resulting from a high level of customer satisfaction, among them positive influence on customer loyalty (Anderson & Sullivan, 1993; Biong, 1993; Fornell, Johnson, Anderson, Cha, & Bryant, 1996; Halstead & Page, 1992; LaBarbera & Mazursky, 1983; Mittal & Kamakura, 2001; Rust, Inman, Jia, & Zahorik, 1999), customer retention (Garbarino & Johnson, 1999; Reynolds & Beatty, 1999), willingness to pay (Homburg, Koschate, & Hoyer, 2004), price tolerance (Anderson, 1996), price sensitivity (Stock, 2005) and word-of-mouth recommendation (Albrecht & Zemke, 1985; Hart, Heskett, & Sasser, 1990; TARP, 1979, 1986). In order to draw benefits from the advantages mentioned companies have to know, which drivers show high impact on customer satisfaction.

Despite the multitude of publications in this field, a new study is able to give additional scientific insights on customer satisfaction, apart from company specific information. First, existing studies on customer satisfaction primarily focus on the effects of single influencing variables such as product quality (Churchill & Surprenant, 1982; Swan & Combs, 1976) or service quality (Taylor & Baker, 1994; Woodside, Frey, & Daly, 1989), thereby mostly concentrating on consumer goods and services (see Oliver, 1997 for a further overview). Owing to this, until today capital goods are in lack of scientific care (Homburg & Rudolph, 2001). This is somewhat surprising considering the characteristics of industrial markets. Compared to consumer goods and services, there are mostly only few potential customers, who in addition are not anonymous and between whom a high level of interaction exists (Bingham & Raffield, 1990). Hence, the possible consequences of customer satisfaction, especially a positive or negative word-of-mouth recommendation can have a much larger impact on the success of industrial goods manufacturers than on consumer goods manufacturers or service providers. The negligence of customer satisfaction in industrial markets is often explained by the methodological problems resulting from the above mentioned market characteristics (McQuiston, 1989).

An exception in this context is the work of Homburg and Rudolph (2001), in which the authors analyze the effects of different influencing variables on customer satisfaction with industrial goods. But a transference of their results on the custom designed machinery and systems examined in this paper is impossible, because the authors focus on product businesses, which are very similar to consumer goods. In addition, Homburg and Rudolph use a covariance-based structural equation model to identify drivers, implicitly assuming a reflective construct specification of customer satisfaction. The faultiness of this assumption will be shown in the course of this paper, and we will point out which methodological and content-related problems prevent us from using the INDSAT (INDustrial SATisfaction) scale (Homburg & Rudolph, 2001).

Summarizing, the goals of this paper are to develop a measurement tool and to identify the main drivers of customer satisfaction in the field of custom designed machinery and systems using data from an international survey. We picked out this type of industrial goods because it accurately reflects the main characteristics of industrial markets (among others: few potential customers, not anonymous, high level of interaction).

In the first section, we briefly describe the scale development procedure still dominating today's marketing. Subsequently, we demonstrate that the construct 'customer satisfaction' does not fulfill the main assumptions underlying reflective construct specification (Blalock, 1969). In order to develop a reliable and valid measurement tool for customer satisfaction with custom made machinery and systems we conducted a first empirical study (third section) mixing qualitative and quantitative approaches described in the second section. The fourth section is then devoted to the second goal, i.e. identifying the main drivers of customer satisfaction. Finally, we discuss managerial implications and limitations.

BACKGROUND: SCALE DEVELOPMENT AND CONSTRUCT SPECIFICATION OF CUSTOMER SATISFACTION

Only a few widely accepted measurement tools for customer satisfaction exist. The most prevalent one is SERVQUAL (Parasuraman, Zeithaml, &

Berry, 1988, 1991, 1994), which focuses on marketing services and is there-fore unsuitable for our purpose. The only published tool for measuring customer satisfaction with industrial products and services is the INDSAT scale developed by Homburg and Rudolph (2001). It was designed for product businesses or multipurpose equipments (Rudolph, 1998), which are very similar to consumer goods (Meffert, 1998). Moreover, all INDSAT constructs are to be specified according to Churchill's (1979) domain-sampling paradigm, thus purifying an original item pool using different techniques (like exploratory and confirmatory factor analysis) to verify the reliability and validity of the entire measurement model, e.g. by calculating coefficient alpha (Cronbach, 1951; Churchill, 1979).

Although this approach is consistent with numerous other scale devel-opment approaches in marketing (see e.g. Kohli & Jaworski, 1990; Kohli, Jaworski, & Kumar, 1993), it is only valid if one can assume a causal relationship from the construct (latent variable) to the measurement items (Bollen, 1989; Bollen & Lennox, 1991; Edwards & Bagozzi, 2000; Rossiter, 2002), that is, if we are dealing with reflective indicators, which – due to the correlation based purifying process – are exchangeable (Jarvis, Mackenzie, & Podsakoff, 2003).

As opposed to reflective indicators, formative indicators are not caused by, but constitute the construct (Bollen, 1989; Bollen & Lennox, 1991; Edwards & Bagozzi, 2000; Rossiter, 2002). In this study, the researchers decided that the correct specification of customer satisfaction has to be formative. To justify this we look at typical items. We can easily imagine that a customer's specific satisfaction with a supplier is increased because of better reachability of employees in manufacturing sites, whereas the reaction to requests made by telephone and the reaction to written requests remain unaffected. This would become obvious by low correlations between these three indicators, so that a scale development process based on Cronbach's alpha could winnow out important items and lower the validity of the scale (Fig. 1). In other

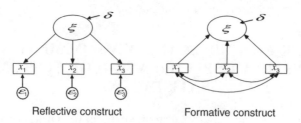

Reflective construct   Formative construct

Fig. 1.   Reflective vs. Formative Construct.

words, "omitting an indicator is omitting a part of the construct" (Bollen & Lennox, 1991, p. 308).

We developed our questionnaire in accordance with Rossiter's (2002) C-OAR-SE procedure using the help of experts and a sample of target raters combined with a reasonable cutoff for inclusion (Rossiter, 2002, p. 314). C-OAR-SE denotes (C)onstruct definition, (O)bject classification, (A)ttribute classification, (R)ater identification, (S)cale formation, and (E)numeration and describes the steps of the process we have undergone (see third section). Decisive for evaluating the quality of a formative measurement model developed according to C-OAR-SE is exclusively its validity, which only experts can decide on.

DEVELOPMENT OF MEASUREMENT TOOL

The Conceptual Phase

The objects under investigation are the actual and potential (former customers and customers of the competition) customers of a strategic business unit of a leading German based, worldwide manufacturer of custom made machinery and systems. Because companies usually do not compete on the corporate level, but rather on the business unit level, we concentrated on the business unit showing the highest sales. Customers are defined as the single plant using the machines and systems, since (1) also industrial markets are characterized by an increasing consolidation and therefore consist of numerous corporate groups, so that purchasing decisions are partly centralized and decentralized; (2) the plants are the beneficiaries of the machines and systems and therefore most experienced with different suppliers; and (3) even if purchasing decisions in some cases are centralized on the corporate level, the plant at least still has an influence through positive or negative word-to-mouth recommendation.

The investigated machines include packing machines for powdery bulk materials, in this case cement. A system is defined as a combination of multiple single machines as, for example, a bag applicator, a packing machine, and a palletizer.

Owing to the comparatively small number of (potential) customers in industrial markets, a complete population survey in 18 European countries was attempted. The plants and the informants were identified via the sales force of the targeted company, since they dispose of the most formal and informal market information (Anderson, Chu, & Weitz, 1987) and therefore guaranty an unambiguous identification of the buying-center members involved in the purchasing processes. The subsidiaries or sales representatives in each country were asked to provide a complete list of all actual and potential customers active in their representation area. The importance of identifying potential customers in order to prevent a potential bias resulting from predominant consideration of actual customers was clearly pointed out.

This method led to the situation that in some instances only one informant per plant was identified, which complies with the single informant technique. This technique is often criticized for apparently not leading to valid data (Phillips, 1981), since the key informants do not necessarily have a relation to the area under investigation. But referring to this technique, John and Reve (1982, p. 522) show that "careful selection of informants in conjunction with the use of internally consistent multi-item scales can provide reliable and valid data in a variety of channel settings." Identifying the informants via the sales force guarantees a relation of the informants to the suppliers, so that the use of the single informant technique is unproblematic in this case. A standardized online-questionnaire was used for data collection. It consisted of six parts of questions regarding (A) the plant, (B) investment decisions, (C) overall satisfaction and customer retention, (D) the importance of and the customer's satisfaction with the relevant items, (E) the company's reputation (see Schwaiger, 2004), and (F) future customer demands. Since only the questions included in parts C and D are relevant for scale development, we only describe their identification and operationalization.

Given our definition of customer satisfaction, there are generally tow ways of measuring it. One alternative is using a double scale as done by Parasuraman et al. (1988): one scale measuring the customer's expectation regarding the performance feature and another one capturing the customer's perceived market service performance. Our decision against this and for the other alternative, a single scale directly assessing a customer's satisfaction, grounds on the fact that the question concerning the nature and role of expectations in the comparison process have yet not been completely settled (see, e.g. Babakus & Boller, 1992; Cronin & Taylor, 1992; Oliver, 1993; Yoon & Ekinci, 2003 for a more recent publication).

In addition, business deals concerning industrial goods are processes during which a customer's experience can influence his/her expectations. Separately measured expectations thus do not necessarily reflect the customer's actual expectations used in the comparison process (Grönroos, 1993).

While overall satisfaction was measured using a single item ("All in all, how satisfied are you with …?"), multiple steps were undertaken to identify the supplier's performance features (items) relevant for a customer's satisfaction. First, a detailed literature review was performed aiming at identifying performance features repeatedly included in customer satisfaction studies. An analysis of specific measurement tools, as for example INDSAT, was limited since the original item pools are often not published (see, e.g. Homburg & Rudolph, 2001). This step led to the identification of 53 items.

To assure the integrity, unambiguousness and comprehensibility of the items we then discussed the performance feature pool with executives of the manufacturer. The participants of this group discussion were selected in a way that all functional areas were represented. Thus, the discussion group included at least one executive from general management, R&D, sales, production, and after-sales service. In order to cover the process aspect of business deals regarding industrial goods the items were assigned to different phases of the supplier–customer relationship. We used the concept of Backhaus and Günter (1976) which distinguishes between the phases pre-inquiry, negotiation, delivery/commissioning, and warranty. The group discussion led to the identification of six additional items.

In order to prevent a supplier specific view of customer satisfaction, a pretest was performed, in which a total of seven customers were interviewed either by telephone or face-to-face. Again, the goal of this pretest was the verification of the item's integrity, unambiguousness and comprehensibility. The customers were chosen, so that they represented different west and east European countries and also potential customers of the targeted manufacturer. These interviews revealed that another 11 items were still missing, leading to a performance feature pool consisting of 70 performance features.

Data Collection

A total of 239 informants in 165 plants were identified by the sales force. Given the consideration of west and east European plants a translation of the questionnaire into a universal language (English) was necessary. We did this using the translation-/back translation method (Douglas & Craig, 1983; Malholtra, Agarwal, & Peterson, 1996) supported by translators from the subsidiaries and representatives of the manufacturer. Before collecting data, the informants were contacted by telephone and asked for their participation in the study. Additionally the email addresses provided by the sales force were verified and each customer was asked if he or she preferred a German or English version of the questionnaire. A total of 145 informants (60.6%) assured their participation.

Data collection was performed using the online-tool formgen. A few days after the telephonic acquisition, the informants received a personalized email including a link to their individual questionnaire. This method gives each informant the possibility of interrupting his answering process, if necessary, without loosing answers already given. Two weeks later, the informants who had not yet answered were reminded of participating.

The respondents were asked to evaluate their overall satisfaction and the customer's satisfaction with the performance features for their key supplier and, if possible, for a backup supplier. Overall satisfaction and the customer's satisfaction with the performance features were measured using a seven-point scale ranging from "I am very satisfied" (7) to "I am very unsatisfied" (1), with no verbal labels for scale points 2 through 6. In addition, a response possibility "cannot evaluate" was included, since some respondents may have been well experienced with a supplier regarding some performance features, but rather inexperienced with others.

The informants were also asked to indicate the performance feature's importance for their investment decision using a seven-point scale ranging from "That is very important to me" (7) to "That is very unimportant to me" (1), with no verbal labels for scale points 2 through 6. A "cannot evaluate" response alternative was not given since the importance of a performance feature for the investment decision is independent from a customer's experience with a supplier. This data was surveyed in order to identify so-called penalty-services. Penalty-services are dissatisfiers (in terms of Herzberg, Mausner, & Snyderman, 1959), i.e. aspects that cause dissatisfaction if not fulfilled, but do not cause satisfaction even if fulfilled. Dissatisfiers are easy to identify, because respondents say these aspects are important to them, but there is only a small correlation between the satisfaction with these aspects and the overall satisfaction with a certain supplier.

A total of 81 informants reacted to the email, of which 57 questionnaires could be analyzed. Relating to the addressed informants this corresponds to a response rate of 39.31%. To evaluate the sample's quality the informants were asked to state if they are actively involved in investment decisions or not. Of the 57 respondents 52 or 92.29% were actively involved, so that actually those people were reached, who are experienced with different suppliers and to whom it is important to induce customer satisfaction.

Data Analysis and Results

The database used for analysis contains the 65 satisfaction evaluations of the plant's with their key and backup suppliers. The number of satisfaction evaluations is larger than the number of respondents, as respondents were allowed to evaluate more than one supplier. Missing values appearing due to the questionnaire's length were substituted using simple imputation methods[1] (Little & Rubin, 2002). In contrast to Rossiter (2002) who explicitly disapproves of using statistical methods for scale development, we statistically evaluated the items identified by means of an exploratory factor analysis. But in this case, the results of the exploratory factor analysis were not used to eliminate items due to their factor loadings; instead, the only purpose of our factor analysis was to utilize correlations between the indicators and thus identify information redundancies. This prevented us from getting troubles due to multicollinearity while parameterizing our SEM later on, and ensured maximum care when treating our respondents who would be more reluctant to fill out a questionnaire with all items for time reasons.

The number of extracted factors was determined using the Kaiser-criterion (Kaiser, 1974), and a varimax rotation was performed to facilitate interpretation.

All together 16 factors were extracted explaining 84.1% of variance. Since none of the factor loadings regarding the 16th factor exceeds the critical threshold of 0.5, this factor forms a kind of "residual factor" which is not considered for factor interpretation.

Starting from this factor solution, the second step of data analysis aimed at reducing the measurement model's complexity by eliminating information redundancies. For this each factor was separately looked at, and the pertinent items – if necessary and if content-related reasonable – were combined, rephrased, or eliminated. This may need further explanation: Selecting the pertinent items, which was necessary in case there were different formulation suggestions, was done with assistance of branch experts. Combination and elimination was carried out according to the following rules: If items showing high factor loadings on a specific factor obviously did measure different aspects (e.g. "company's flexibility regarding project partners" and "product compatibility with machines of different make"), despite high correlation we did not combine or eliminate items but formed a separate construct instead, which is the proper way in formative scale development. However, if items showed high correlation *and* were closely related from a content point of view (e.g. language skills of sales personnel, language skills of technicians, and so on) we decided to combine these items in order to reduce length of the questionnaire. In the latter case, we (e.g. selected only one item "language skills of personnel") knowing that we have to accept a certain loss of precision. If changes were necessary, we thoroughly paid attention not to neglect important aspects of customer satisfaction with custom made machinery and systems. Moreover, we ensured a one-dimensional verbalization of the items.

These changes reduced the performance feature pool from 70 items to 52 (see Table 1 for the final item list). The changes were then discussed and approved by executives on the supplier's side.

DRIVER IDENTIFICATION

Research Method

In most cases, covariance-based structural equation models (CBSEM) are used to analyze causal relationships between latent variables (Bagozzi & Baumgartner, 1994; Fornell & Bookstein, 1982). CBSEM typically assume a reflective construct specification (Chin & Newsted, 1999), even if handling (very) few formative constructs would be possible. Variance-based methods (VBSEM) like Partial Least Squares (PLS, cf. Wold, 1975, 1982) analysis should be preferred, if the researcher's focus is placed on the explanation of an endogenous construct, as it is the case in our study with customer satisfaction. As PLS has no problems in handling formative as well as reflective constructs, another good reason exists to prefer this approach.

Contrary to CBSEM, which attempt to reproduce the observed covariance matrix using a maximum-likelihood function, PLS understands the latent variables as weighted sums of their respective indicators (Chin & Newsted, 1999; Fornell & Cha, 1994) and attempts to predict values for the latent variables (component scores) using multiple regressions (Chin, 1998; Chin & Newsted, 1999; Fornell & Bookstein, 1982; Fornell & Cha, 1994). PLS not only has the decisive advantage of being suitable for analyzing causal relationships between formative constructs, it also provides the possibility of simultaneously analyzing categorical and ratio-level indicators in one model, making no specific assumptions about the variable's distributions and having less restrictive requirements concerning the sample size (Chin, 1998; Chin & Newsted, 1999; Fornell & Bookstein, 1982). According to Chin (1998) the necessary sample size for successfully estimating a PLS

Table 1. The Final Measurement Model.

Factor	Performance Features
Satisfaction with the machines and systems (factor 1)	1. Reliability of the machines and systems 2. Life-time of the machines and systems 3. Machine's/system's first-line-maintenance capabilities 4. Technological advancement of the machines and systems compared to "state-of-the-art" 5. Capacity of the machines and systems 6. Functionality/user friendliness operation of the machines and systems 7. Appearance (design) of the machines and systems 8. Quality of the provided operating instructions 9. Cleanliness of the machine's/system's filling process 10. Weight accuracy of the machines and systems
Satisfaction with the services (factor 2)	11. Delivery time of machines and systems 12. Reliability of given target dates 13. Reliability of given statements 14. Quality of installation and commissioning services 15. Duration of installation and commissioning services 16. Timely availability of the after-sales services 17. Local availability of the after-sales services 18. Fast processing of complaints/problems 19. Price of after-sales services 20. Availability/delivery time of spare parts
Satisfaction with the representation (factor 3)	21. Corporate representation by means of sales literature 22. Corporate representation by means of print media (i.e. periodical, professional journals) 23. Corporate representation by means of the internet (i.e. Web site) 24. Corporate representation by means of events (i.e. trade shows, conferences/symposiums) 25. Possibility to utilize services via e-business 26. Broadness of the product line
Satisfaction with the quotations (factor 4)	27. Composition of quotations 28. Transparency of quotations
Satisfaction with the company's flexibility (factor 5)	29. Company's flexibility regarding project partners (i.e. in case of necessary machines of different make, i.e. a palettizer) 30. Company's flexibility regarding project revisions
Satisfaction with the employees (factor 6)	31. Expertise of personnel 32. Language skills of personnel 33. Friendly appearance of personnel
Satisfaction with the execution of instructional training (factor 7)	34. Fixed price for instructional training 35. Language of instructional training 36. Quality of instructional training 37. Up-to-date topics of instructional training

Table 1. (*Continued*)

Factor	Performance Features
Satisfaction with the corporate behavior (factor 8)	38. Company's legal form (i.e. family-owned company) 39. Worldwide company presence
Satisfaction with the company's reachability and reaction time (factor 9)	40. Availability of personnel 41. Short reaction time regarding inquiries
Satisfaction with new product development (factor 10)	42. Compliance with local laws of measurement and calibration 43. Customer involvement in product development 44. Exact compliance with international standards
Satisfaction with periodic customer visits (factor 11)	45. Periodic visits by representatives of the company's local representation 46. Periodic visits by representatives of the company's head office 47. Company's offer of additional services (i.e. regular audits of the plant)
Satisfaction with the price policy (factor 12)	48. Fixed product price for the machines/systems 49. Cost/performance ratio of the machines/systems
Satisfaction with the company's credibility and reliability (factor 13)	50. Company's credit rating and reliability
Satisfaction with the offer of instructional training (factor 14)	51. Possibility of instructional training
Satisfaction with the product's compatibility with machines of different make (factor 15)	52. Product compatibility with machines of different make

model based on our questionnaire is $n = 150$. In order to meet this requirement, a second empirical study was necessary.

Data Collection for Driver Analysis

The procedure used for data collection in this study generally corresponds to the procedure of the previous study. But in order to meet the sample size requirement and due to the experiences in the first empirical study, a second business unit of the targeted manufacturer was included. The products and services sold by this business unit are very similar to the ones already examined, so that a bias caused by focusing on different kinds of machines and systems can be ruled out. The similarity of the market services and the transferability of the measurement tool to this second business were confirmed through face-to-face interviews with executives of the company's general management as well as executives in the fields of R&D, sales, production, and technical service on the business unit level.

A complete population survey in various countries was attempted. The decision criterions for market selection included their economic relevance for the building materials industry, the activity of both business units in the respective regional market and the absolute number of plants located in the country. This led to the selection of 12 countries: Austria, Brazil, Canada, France, Germany, Great Britain, Ireland, Italy, Poland, Spain, Switzerland, and the United States of America.

To prevent a potential bias provoked by predominately considering actual customers it was attempted to identify the plants via independent organizations. In the case of the business unit cement this was possible thanks to the World Cement Directory (2002), published by The European Cement Association. Since this directory is only updated every three years, the completeness and correctness of its information was checked through the subsidiary or sales representative in the respective country.

In case of the second business unit focusing on all other building materials an identification of the relevant plants via independent organizations was impossible. On this account these plants were directly identified over the sales force of the targeted manufacturer as done during scale development.

Data collection was carried out through a standardized mail questionnaire. An online survey was not attempted, because the identification of the email addresses of all relevant informants would have been extremely costly and time consuming, and because it cannot be assumed that every respondent has a (suitable) internet access to his/her disposal.

The consideration of different national markets again required a translation of the questionnaire. In order to maximize the response rate, the questionnaire was translated into each national language again using the translation-/back translation method (Douglas & Craig, 1983; Malholtra et al., 1996). The questionnaire itself contained four parts: (A) questions concerning the plant, (B) and (C) consisting of the developed measurement model (see Table 1), and (D) questions concerning the informant and the plant's investment processes.

The questionnaire was administered to 1,453 informants worldwide together with a personalized cover sheet (among others guaranteeing anonymity) and a stamped self-addressed envelop. Four weeks later, all informants who had not yet answered were again contacted with a second personalized letter, together with a replacement copy of the first cover sheet, a copy of the questionnaire, and a second self-addressed and stamped envelope.

One hundred and ninety seven questionnaires were returned, of which 25 questionnaires had to be excluded due to excessive missing data. Consequently, 172 questionnaires containing a total of 281 satisfaction evaluations (again respondents were allowed to evaluate more than one supplier) made up the analyzable database. This complies with a response rate of almost 12%. Looking at the composition of the sample it has to be noticed that 160 of the 172 respondents (93.02%) are actively involved in the investment decision process. Therefore we repeatedly succeeded in reaching those informants, who have experiences with different suppliers of custom made machinery and systems and to whom, from a supplier's perspective, it is important to induce customer satisfaction.

Data Analysis and Results

PLS-model estimation was performed using smartPLS. As the item scales are comparable, a standardization of the data is not necessary, so that model estimation was performed using the original data (Chatelin, Vinzi, & Tenenhaus, 2002). The path-weighting scheme was used for inside approximation. In this scheme, the weights are determined so that the component score for a latent variable can be well predicted and at the same time is a good predictor for subsequent dependent variables (Chin & Newsted, 1999; Fornell & Cha, 1994). This is achieved by weighting the independent variables influencing the target variable with their regression coefficients, while all dependent variables are weighted with their correlation coefficients (Chin & Newsted, 1999; Lohmöller, 1989).

Missing values are substituted using the procedure implemented in smartPLS, that is, values missing on the item level are replaced by the mean of all indicators belonging to the same factor. In case all values for the indicators of one factor are missing, the estimated value for the latent variable is treated as missing. For the inner approximation this value is then substituted with the mean over all other estimated component scores for this factor. In the outer approximation the weights are calculated using the pairwise existent data (Chatelin et al., 2002).

Bootstrapping was chosen to determine the t-values for significance evaluation (Chatelin et al., 2002; Chin, 1998). Contrary to the default of a 100 drawings set in smartPLS, the number of drawings was set to 300. Because at least 150 satisfaction evaluations were needed for model estimation, and estimated values approach the "true" scores with an increasing number of indicators and sample size (Chatelin et al., 2002), the number of cases per drawing was set to 200.

Fig. 2 shows the final parameterized PLS model for customer satisfaction with custom made machinery and systems. All factors with a significant influence on overall satisfaction are marked in bold. The *t*-values deciding about the significance of the path coefficients are given in parentheses. The influences of the single indicators on each factor are not shown due to the complexity of the model and the resulting illustration problems.

Criteria for evaluating the goodness-of-fit of a PLS model include R^2 and redundancy coefficients (Chin, 1998; Fornell & Cha, 1994; Lohmöller, 1989). Considering the values reached (0.593 in case of R^2, values between 0.577 and 0.855 in case of the redundancy coefficients) and the complexity of the model, the estimated model shows a sound goodness-of-fit.

Fig. 2 indicates that two factors only have a significant influence on customer satisfaction: s*atisfaction with the machines and systems* with a path coefficient of 0.520 (*p*-value < 0.001) and *satisfaction with the quotations* with a path coefficient of 0.104 (*p*-value < 0.005).

This is the time to have a look at descriptive results: As we can see from Table 2, respondents have stated a lot of performance indicators to be very important for them. But despite the fact that general and partial satisfaction judgements show enough variance, there is no significant influence of the majority of performance indicators on overall satisfaction.

DISCUSSION

The result that merely two factors have a significant influence on customer satisfaction is by all means surprising, considering that the 52 performance features identified are those, which from a supplier's and customer's point of view are relevant for customer satisfaction with custom made machinery and systems, and considering that Homburg and Rudolph's (2001) analysis using the inappropriate CBSEM reveals a significant influence of all factors included in their study. Thus, the question about possible reasons for this result arises. A first possible explanation lies in the characteristics of custom made machinery and systems. These products and services are individually produced or in some cases even engineered. So, in contrast to consumer goods or the product businesses studied by Homburg and Rudolph (2001), a customer has to first specify his product requirements. These requirements thereby result from the customer's situation or the targeted goals the market

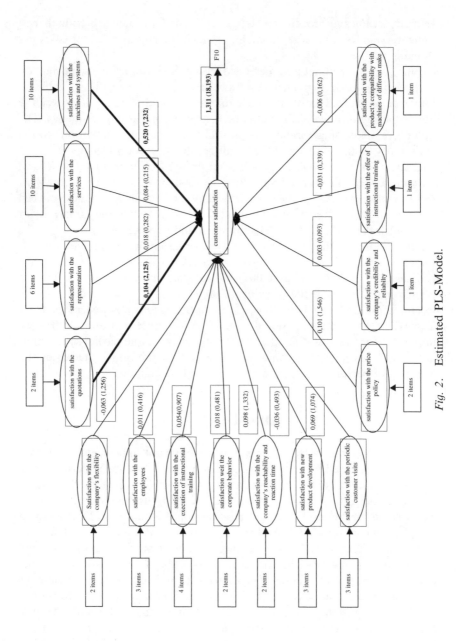

Fig. 2. Estimated PLS-Model.

Table 2.   Importance of the Performance Features.

Performance Feature	*n*	Average Importance
1. Reliability of the machines and systems	170	6.69
2. Life-time of the machines and systems	168	6.42
3. Machine's/system's first-line-maintenance capabilities	169	6.36
4. Technological advancement of the machines and systems compared to "state-of-the-art"	169	5.78
5. Capacity of the machines and systems	169	6.21
6. Functionality/user friendliness operation of the machines and systems	169	6.30
7. Appearance (design) of the machines and systems	168	4.13
8. Quality of the provided operating instructions	168	5.83
9. Cleanliness of the machine's/system's filling process	169	6.41
10. Weight accuracy of the machines and systems	169	6.56
11. Delivery time of machines and systems	164	5.43
12. Reliability of given target dates	166	6.19
13. Reliability of given statements	169	6.38
14. Quality of installation and commissioning services	171	6.41
15. Duration of installation and commissioning services	169	5.93
16. Timely availability of the after-sales services	171	6.25
17. Local availability of the after-sales services	166	5.75
18. Fast processing of complaints/problems	168	6.38
19. Price of after-sales services	167	5.84
20. Availability/delivery time of spare parts	170	6.41
21. Corporate representation by means of sales literature	167	4.33
22. Corporate representation by means of print media (i.e. periodical, professional journals)	159	3.92
23. Corporate representation by means of the internet (i.e. Web site)	153	4.37
24. Corporate representation by means of events (i.e. trade shows, conferences/symposiums)	156	4.26
25. Possibility to utilize services via e-business	145	3.82
26. Broadness of the product line	161	4.78
27. Composition of quotations	156	5.43
28. Transparency of quotations	153	5.85
29. Company's flexibility regarding project partners (i.e. in case of necessary machines of different make, i.e. a palettizer)	158	6.03
30. Company's flexibility regarding project revisions	153	5.70
31. Expertise of personnel	169	6.42
32. Language skills of personnel	153	4.76
33. Friendly appearance of personnel	166	5.23

Table 2. (*Continued*)

Performance Feature	n	Average Importance
34. Fixed price for instructional training	123	5.05
35. Language of instructional training	128	5.41
36. Quality of instructional training	127	5.99
37. Up-to-date topics of instructional training	123	5.62
38. Company's legal form (i.e. family-owned company)	159	3.41
39. Worldwide company presence	160	4.28
40. Availability of personnel	167	6.12
41. Short reaction time regarding inquiries	169	6.18
42. Compliance with local laws of measurement and calibration	157	6.09
43. Customer involvement in product development	158	5.24
44. Exact compliance with international standards	150	5.67
45. Periodic visits by representatives of the company's local representation	166	4.32
46. Periodic visits by representatives of the company's head office	160	3.86
47. Company's offer of additional services (i.e. regular audits of the plant)	157	4.28
48. Fixed product price for the machines/systems	166	5.97
49. Cost/performance ratio of the machines/systems	164	6.46
50. Company's credit rating and reliability	162	5.99
51. Possibility of instructional training	152	5.31
52. Product compatibility with machines of different make	155	5.59

service is supposed to achieve. In other words, all suppliers evaluated in our sample meet the customers' expectations considering the penalty-services, so there is no room for achieving competitive advantages. If a company did not fulfill (at least) the penalty-services, our respondents would not rate the company, because they no longer were customers to that firm. This situational dependence could explain the non-significance of many factors.

A second explanation is the possibility of methodological problems influencing the results. Especially three potential problems affecting the path coefficients and their *t*-values are possible. First, interactions between the latent variables could exist (e.g. *satisfaction with new product development* and *satisfaction with machines and systems*), violating the PLS assumption of a causal chain between the variables (Lohmöller, 1989). Second, the assumption of a linear relationship between the model's variables could be invalid (Lohmöller, 1989), and third, the use of a 7-point scale could have led to an excessive demand regarding the informants' capabilities of differentiating between the single-scale points. In this case, the informants only used a coarser segmentation of the scale to differentiate between different levels of satisfaction (Bortz & Döring, 2002).

In order to check for these potential problems a binary-logistic regression analysis was conducted. Owing to its capability of analyzing causal relationships between binary variables, allowing interactions between the variables and assuming a non-linear relationship between the independent variables and the dependent variable (Kleinbaum & Klein, 2002), this statistical methods allow to simultaneously check for all potential problems described.

In order to use logistic regression analysis for this purpose, it was necessary to subdivide the respondents into two groups. Looking at the overall satisfaction it can be noted that with a mean of 5.007 the informants are quite satisfied in general with their suppliers. Therefore, all informants whose overall satisfaction ratings marked 6 or 7 were assigned to the group "completely satisfied customers." Consequently, all others were defined as "less satisfied customers." After this segmentation the sample consists of 162 (57.7%) completely and 119 (42.3%) less satisfied customers. On the factor level, the sample was segmented using a median-split of the estimated component scores. A respondent is thus defined as completely (less) satisfied referring to a certain factor, if his component score lied above (below) the corresponding median.

According to an exploratory procedure, different models allowing different interrelations between the factors were built based on plausibility arguments and then compared with one another on the basis of goodness-of-fit criteria. These criteria include R^2 according to Cox and Snell, R^2 according to Nagelkerke, and the classification matrix (Kleinbaum & Klein, 2002; Norušis, 2005).

With a correct classification rate of 81.5%, an R^2 according to Cox and Snell of 0.384 and a R^2 according to Nagelkerke of 0.516 the model allowing no interrelations between the independent variables achieved the best goodness-of-fit values. This allows the conclusion that possible interactions between the independent variables did not influence the PLS results. Table 3 shows the regression results for this model.

According to Table 3, two factors – *satisfaction with the machines and systems as well as satisfaction with the quotations* – show a significant influence on customer satisfaction at the 5% level. The strongest influence comes from the *satisfaction with machines and systems*. The corresponding "EXP(B)" value of 8.745 states that if the customer's satisfaction with the

Table 3. Results of the Binary Logistic Regression.

	Regression-Coefficient B	Standard Error	Wald	df	Significance	EXP(B)	95.0% Confidence-Interval for EXP(B)	
							Lower Value	Upper Value
Machines and systems	2.168	0.367	34.967	1	0.000	8.745	4.262	17.944
Services	0.388	0.410	0.897	1	0.344	1.474	0.660	3.293
Quotation	1.111	0.345	10.351	1	0.001	3.038	1.544	5.978
Company's flexibility	0.177	0.362	0.239	1	0.625	1.194	0.587	2.428
Representation	0.260	0.352	0.545	1	0.460	1.297	0.650	2.586
Employers	0.580	0.396	2.151	1	0.142	1.786	0.823	3.879
Execution of instructional training	−0.213	0.381	0.314	1	0.575	0.808	0.383	1.704
Corporate behavior	0.055	0.355	0.024	1	0.878	1.056	0.527	2.117
Company's reachability and response time	−0.188	0.393	0.229	1	0.632	0.829	0.384	1.789
Product development	−0.286	0.396	0.520	1	0.471	0.751	0.345	1.634
Periodical customer visits	0.560	0.362	2.402	1	0.121	1.751	0.862	3.557
Price policy	0.497	0.392	1.608	1	0.205	1.645	0.762	3.548
Company's credibility and reliability	−0.132	0.371	0.126	1	0.723	0.877	0.423	1.815
Offer of instructional training	0.229	0.401	0.325	1	0.569	1.257	0.573	2.758
Product's compatibility with machines of different make	0.729	0.404	3.261	1	0.071	2.073	0.940	4.571
Constant term	−3.595	0.526	46.722	1	0.000	0.027		

machines and systems raises one-scale point, the chance ratio of belonging to the group of completely satisfied customers increases by 8.745. With an "EXP(B)" value of 3.038 the *satisfaction with the quotations* shows the second strongest influence on customer satisfaction. Thus, the regression analysis in general verifies the PLS results referring to which factors have a significant influence and their order of importance. The only difference between both results bears to the role of the factor *satisfaction with the product's compatibility with machines of different make*. The binary regression analysis indeed shows a significant influence, but only at a 10% level. Therefore, we can summarize that methodological aspects did not cause problems. Hence, we have no reason to doubt about the results of the PLS estimation.

But for the manufacturers of custom made machinery and systems it is not only important to know, what factors influence customer satisfaction, but rather what role the single performance features play. To answer this, we look at the PLS results concerning the influences of the single items on their corresponding factors. The following discussion is limited to those factors showing a significant influence on customer satisfaction, penalty-services are excluded though not unimportant to survive in the market.

Of the 10 performance features determining a customer's satisfaction with the machines and systems, only the "reliability of the machines and systems" turns out to be significant (p-value < 0.001). The importance of this performance feature is not surprising, considering that industrial goods are purchased to fulfill a certain function in the customer's production process. The non-significance of the remaining performance features does not necessarily imply their general unimportance. They merely do not allow generalizing the statements of their importance for all customers.

Referring to the *satisfaction with quotations*, which is determined by the customer's satisfaction with the composition and transparency of the quotations, only the first item proves to have a significant influence (p-value < 0.001). Although seeming implausible at first, also this can be explained looking at the characteristics of custom made machinery and systems. As described earlier a customer has to specify his requirements before the business project can commence. Consequently, an intensive cooperation between the supplier and customer is necessary to begin on, so that many details concerning the project are well known to the customer, before he receives a written quotation.

As to the other factors, significant influences cannot be documented, just as in the PLS analysis.

CONCLUSIONS AND LIMITATIONS

The primary objective of this paper was the identification of the main drivers of customer satisfaction with industrial goods taking custom made machinery and systems as an example. In order to achieve this goal, the development of a new measurement model for customer satisfaction was necessary, since an application of existing ones, as for instance INDSAT, was not possible due to methodological and content-related problems. The results of this study have numerous theoretical and managerial implications. From a theoretical perspective, the major contribution of this paper lies in the identification of customer satisfaction as a formative rather than a reflective construct. A formative understanding of customer satisfaction implies not only that Churchill's (1979) scale development procedure, in which an item pool is purified using reliability and validity criteria, is not applicable, but also questions the validity of existing measurement models. Moreover, eliminating items because of their lack of correlation (domain-sampling model) could have led to the elimination of important aspects. Future research projects, especially aiming at measuring customer satisfaction, should bear this in mind and forbear from a scale purifying procedure based on item-to-total correlations. The theoretical discussion in this paper concerning the procedure of scale development for formative constructs revealed that, until today, no consensus on how to develop such a measurement model is reached (see, e.g. Diamantopoulos, 2005; Diamantopoulos & Winklhofer, 2001; Finn & Kayande, 2005; Rossiter, 2002, 2005). The two main streams in this area differ regarding the role of statistical methods for reliability and validity evaluation. Future research should therefore concentrate on reaching a pragmatic consensus regarding scale development for formative constructs.

At the same time, identifying customer satisfaction as a formative construct also affects the possibility of using covariance-based structural equation models for driver identification. Despite the fact that structural equation models have proven themselves in research and therefore have often been used in customer satisfaction studies, in most cases they are not suitable for formative constructs (Chin & Newsted, 1999). An attractive alternative for analyzing causal relationships between formative constructs is the PLS method, because it treats an unobservable variable as the weighted sum of its indicators (Fornell & Bookstein, 1982). Erroneously applying a covariance-based structural equation model to formative constructs will severely influence the results. Comparing, for example, our results with those of Homburg and Rudolph (2001), significant differences are to be noticed. First, Homburg and Rudolph (2001) show that all seven dimensions of the INDSAT have a significant influence on customer satisfaction. Our study indicates that only two factors exist, which significantly contribute to a customer's satisfaction. Second, according to Homburg and Rudolph (2001), especially aspects concerning customer orientated processes (e.g. satisfaction with salespeople, satisfaction with order handling) play an important role in customer satisfaction with industrial products. In contrast, the results obtained in this study show that a high level of customer satisfaction can especially be achieved through high product quality. To what extent these contradictory results come from methodological differences or from different types of industrial goods can only be answered through a replication study.

Let us now discuss managerial implications. Because customer satisfaction tools in the past were predominantly developed using Churchill's (1979) suggested procedure and its potential risk of omitting important aspects of the construct, managers should carefully evaluate and, if necessary, revise their measurement tools already in use.

We recommend specifying a model according to the process applied in this study. Using our scale for measuring customer satisfaction enables suppliers of custom made machinery and systems to gain an in-depth insight on how well companies fulfill the customer's expectations. Since we assume that the performance features making up a customer's satisfaction differ depending on the type of industrial goods, it can be necessary to supplement, exclude, or rephrase single items, if the market services of the supplier are different from the machines and systems examined in this study.

Admittedly, the developed scale is fairly complex and therefore bears the risk of an unsatisfying response rate. A possible solution for this problem is measuring customer satisfaction using 15 items relating to the factor levels (e.g. satisfaction with the machines and systems).

Referring to the drivers of customer satisfaction our results clearly state that only a few factors exist, over which a supplier can generally influence his customer satisfaction level. These include the *satisfaction with the machines and systems* and the *satisfaction with quotations*. Interestingly, the factor *satisfaction with the price policy* has no significant influence. This indicates that a price strategy is not promising for the goals of a high level of customer satisfaction and consequently a high level of customer loyalty, customer retention, or positive word-to-mouth recommendation. These goals can rather be achieved by offering customers products of high quality, especially of high reliability.

At this point a word of caution seems appropriate: The non-significance of the other factors does not necessarily mean that these factors are generally irrelevant for inducing customer satisfaction. For example, a company's flexibility regarding project partners or project revisions will only play a significant role in a customer's satisfaction, if such a flexibility is expected or required. So, our results seem to confirm the necessity of "adaptive selling" (Spiro & Weitz, 1990; Weitz, Sujan, & Sujan, 1986), meaning that different selling approaches are required for different selling situations. Therefore, consequential customer orientation is a necessary requirement for achieving a high level of customer satisfaction.

Despite the care taken in every step of this study, there are some possible issues that could have influenced the results. First of all, Rossiter's (2002) C-OAR-SE procedure has the disadvantage of not being able to evaluate a scale's reliability and validity using statistical criteria. Therefore, the developed scale could be criticized of being subject to a high level of interpretational subjectivity. Another limitation concerns the single informant technique used throughout the study, all the more as Homburg and Rudolph (2001) show that the importance of the seven INDSAT dimensions varies across different roles of buying-center members. The different roles buying-center members play during the decision processes is a well-known, but yet unsolved problem in studies concerning industrial goods (McQuiston, 1989; Sheth, 1973). In most cases researchers try to solve this problem by identifying the buying-center members according to their function in the organization (see, e.g. Homburg & Rudolph, 2001). But also this method does not sufficiently solve the problem, since a member's function does neither necessarily reflect his actual role nor his power in the decision process (Nicosia & Wind, 1977). Nevertheless, analyzing the importance of the different drivers of customer satisfaction with custom made machines and systems for different buying-center members could give interesting insights for recommendations with respect to "adaptive selling."

The last limitation to be mentioned is the fact that the present study bases on cross-sectional data and therefore only gives a static view of customer satisfaction with custom made machinery and systems. Analyzing customer satisfaction in a longitudinal study could give interesting insights on how the importance of the different drivers changes over time, and what role they play in different situations.

Although the importance of customer satisfaction is well-known for several years, merely a few studies exploring customer satisfaction with industrial goods exist. Despite its limitations, this study provides a valuable guidance for future empirical research concerning customer satisfaction in general and especially with industrial goods.

The generalizability of our results may be seen ambiguous: On one hand, we provide a valid and reliable tool that may easily be transferred to other sectors of capital goods, not denying that several items may be added or eliminated due to sector particularities. On the other hand, we do not have any proof that expectations and attitudes of people working in the field of custom designed machinery and systems are similar to those of other branches as, say, standard machinery and systems. Hence, identifying drivers of and monitoring the level of customer satisfaction remains at least an industry-specific if not a company-specific task.

NOTE

1. Simple imputation substitutes a value for each missing value. If possible we imputed the mean condition on observed values of other variables, otherwise each missing value was imputed with the variable mean of the complete cases.

REFERENCES

Aaker, D. A., & Joachimsthaler, E. (2000). *Brand leadership*. New York: The Free Press.

Albrecht, K., & Zemke, R. (1985). *Service America*. Homewood, IL: Dow Jones-Irwin.

Anderson, E., Chu, W., & Weitz, B. (1987). Industrial purchasing: An empirical exploration of the buyclass framework. *Journal of Marketing, 51*(3), 71–86.

Anderson, E. W. (1996). Customer satisfaction and price tolerance. *Marketing Letters, 7*(3), 265–274.

Anderson, E. W., & Sullivan, M. W. (1993). The antecedents and consequences of customer satisfaction for firms. *Marketing Science, 12*(2), 125–143.

Babakus, E., & Boller, G. W. (1992). An empirical assessment of the SERVQUAL scale. *Journal of Business Research, 24*(3), 253–268.

Backhaus, K., & Günter, B. (1976). A phase-differentiated interaction approach to industrial marketing decisions. *Industrial Marketing Management, 5*(5), 255–270.

Bagozzi, R. P., & Baumgartner, H. (1994). The evaluation of structural equation models and hypothesis testing. In: R. P. Bagozzi (Ed.), *Principles of marketing research* (pp. 386–422). Cambridge: Blackwell Publishers.

Bingham, F. G., & Raffield, B. T. (1990). *Business-to-business marketing management*. Homewood, IL: Irwin.

Biong, H. (1993). Satisfaction and loyalty to suppliers within the grocery trade. *European Journal of Marketing, 27*(7), 21–38.

Blalock, H. M. (1969). *Theory construction: From verbal to mathematical formulation*. Englewood Cliffs, New York.

Bollen, K. A. (1989). *Structural equations with latent variables*. New York: John Wiley & Sons.

Bollen, K. A., & Lennox, R. (1991). Conventional wisdom in measurement: A structural equation perspective. *Psychological Bulletin, 110*(2), 305–314.

Bortz, J., & Döring, N. (2002). *Forschungsmethoden und evaluation: für human- und sozialwissenschaftler* (3rd ed.). Berlin: Springer.
Chatelin, Y.-M., Vinzi, V. E., & Tenenhaus, M. (2002). *State-of-art on PLS modeling through the available software*. HEC Business School, Jouy-en-Josas. URL: http://ideas.repec.org/p/ebg/heccah/0764.html [last access 2006/04/03].
Chin, W. W. (1998). The partial least squares approach to structural equation modeling. In: G. A. Marcoulides (Ed.), *Modern methods for business research* (pp. 295–336). Mahwah: Lawrence Erlbaum Associates.
Chin, W. W., & Newsted, P. R. (1999). Structural equation modelling: Analysis with small samples using partial least squares. In: R. H. Hoyle (Ed.), *Statistical strategies for small sample research* (pp. 307–341). Thousand Oaks, CA: Sage.
Churchill, G. A. (1979). A paradigm for developing better measures of marketing constructs. *Journal of Marketing Research, 16*(1), 64–73.
Churchill, G. A., & Surprenant, C. (1982). An Investigation into the determinants of customer satisfaction. *Journal of Marketing Research, 19*(4), 491–504.
Cronbach, L. J. (1951). Coefficient alpha and the internal structure of tests. *Psychometrika, 16*(3), 297–334.
Cronin, J., & Taylor, S. (1992). Measuring service quality: A re-examination and extension. *Journal of Marketing, 56*(3), 55–68.
Diamantopoulos, A. (2005). The C-OAR-SE procedure for scale development in marketing: A comment. *International Journal of Research in Marketing, 22*(1), 1–9.
Diamantopoulos, A., & Winklhofer, H. M. (2001). Index construction with formative indicators: An alternative to scale development. *Journal of Marketing Research, 38*(2), 269–277.
Douglas, S. P., & Craig, C. S. (1983). *International marketing research*. Englewood Cliffs: Prentice-Hall College Division.
Edwards, J. R., & Bagozzi, R. P. (2000). On the nature and direction of relationships between constructs and measures. *Psychological Methods, 5*(2), 155–174.
Finn, A., & Kayande, U. (2005). How fine is C-OAR-SE? A generalizability theory perspective on Rossiter's procedure. *International Journal of Research in Marketing, 22*(1), 11–21.
Fornell, C., & Bookstein, F. L. (1982). Two structural equation models: LISREL and PLS applied to consumer exit-voice theory. *Journal of Marketing Research, 19*(4), 440–452.
Fornell, C., & Cha, J. (1994). Partial least squares. In: R. P. Bagozzi (Ed.), *Advanced methods of marketing research* (pp. 52–78). Oxford: Blackwell.
Fornell, C., Johnson, M. D., Anderson, E. W., Cha, J., & Bryant, B. E. (1996). The American customer satisfaction index: Nature, purpose, and findings. *Journal of Marketing, 60*(4), 7–18.
Garbarino, E., & Johnson, M. S. (1999). The different roles of satisfaction, trust, and commitment in customer relationships. *Journal of Marketing, 63*(2), 70–87.
Grönroos, C. (1993). Toward a third phase in service quality research: Challenges and future directions. In: T. Swartz, D. Bowen & S. Brown (Eds), *Advances in services marketing and management: Research and practice, 2* (pp. 49–64). London, Greenwich, CT: JAI Press.
Halstead, D., & Page, T. J. (1992). The effects of satisfaction and complaining behavior on consumer repurchase intentions. *Journal of Consumer Satisfaction, Dissatisfaction and Complaining Behavior, 5*, 1–11.
Hart, C. W. L., Heskett, J. L., & Sasser, W. E. (1990). The profitable art of service recovery. *Harvard Business Review, 68*(4), 148–156.

Herzberg, F., Mausner, B., & Snyderman, B. (1959). *The motivation to work*. New York: John Wiley & Sons.

Homburg, C., Koschate, N., & Hoyer, W. D. (2004). Do satisfied customers really pay more? A study of the relationship between customer satisfaction and willingness to pay. Universität Mannheim, Institut für Marktorientierte Unternehmensführung, Reihe Wissenschaftliche Papiere, No. W79. Mannheim.

Homburg, C., & Rudolph, B. (2001). Customer satisfaction in industrial markets: Dimensional and multiple role issues. *Journal of Business Research, 52*(1), 15–33.

Jarvis, C. B., Mackenzie, S. B., & Podsakoff, P. M. (2003). A critical review of construct indicators and measurement model misspecification in marketing and consumer research. *Journal of Consumer Research, 30*(3), 199–218.

John, G., & Reve, T. (1982). The reliability and validity of key informant data from dyadic relationships in marketing channels. *Journal of Marketing Research, 19*(4), 517–524.

Kaiser, H. (1974). An index to factorial simplicity. *Psychometrika, 39*(1), 31–36.

Kleinbaum, D. G., & Klein, M. (2002). *Logistic regression: A self-learning text* (2nd ed.). New York: Springer.

Kohli, A. K., & Jaworski, B. J. (1990). Market orientation: The construct, research propositions and managerial implications. *Journal of Marketing, 54*(2), 1–18.

Kohli, A. K., Jaworski, B. J., & Kumar, A. (1993). MARKOR: A measure of market orientation. *Journal of Marketing Research, 30*(4), 467–477.

LaBarbera, P. A., & Mazursky, D. (1983). A longitudinal assessment of consumer satisfaction/dissatisfaction: The dynamic aspect of the cognitive process. *Journal of Marketing Research, 20*(3), 393–404.

Little, R. J. A., & Rubin, D. B. (2002). *Statistical analysis with missing data* (2nd ed.). New York: John Wiley & Sons.

Lohmöller, J.-B. (1989). *Latent variable path modeling with partial least squares*. New York: Springer.

Malholtra, N. K., Agarwal, J., & Peterson, M. (1996). Methodological issues in cross-cultural marketing research: A state-of-the-art review. *International Marketing Review, 13*(5), 7–43.

McQuiston, D. H. (1989). Novelty, complexity and importance of casual determinants of industrial buying behavior. *Journal of Marketing, 53*(2), 66–79.

Meffert, H. (1998). Kundenorientierung und kundenzufriedenheit im investitonsgütermarketing – zwei seiten einer medaille? In: J. Büschken, M. Meyer & R. Weiber (Eds), *Entwicklungen des Investitionsgütermarketing* (pp. 69–115). Wiesbaden: Deutscher Universitäts-Verlag.

Mittal, V., & Kamakura, W. A. (2001). Satisfaction, repurchase intent, and repurchase behavior: Investigating the moderating effect of consumer characteristics. *Journal of Marketing Research, 38*(1), 131–142.

Nicosia, F. M., & Wind, Y. (1977). Emerging models of organizational buying processes. *Industrial Marketing Management, 6*(5), 353–369.

Norušis, M. J. (2005). *SPSS 13.0: Statistical procedures companion*. New Jersey: Prentice-Hall.

Oliver, R. L. (1993). A conceptual model of service quality and service satisfaction: Compatible goals, different concepts. In: T. A. Swartz et al. (Eds), *Advances in service marketing management 2* (pp. 65–85). Greenwich, Conn.: JAI Press.

Oliver, R. L. (1997). *Satisfaction: A behavioral perspective on the consumer*. New York: McGraw Hill.

Parasuraman, A., Zeithaml, V. A., & Berry, L. L. (1988). SERVQUAL: A multiple item scale for measuring consumer perceptions of service quality. *Journal of Retailing, 64*(1), 12–40.

Parasuraman, A., Zeithaml, V. A., & Berry, L. L. (1991). Refinement and reassessment of the SERVQUAL scale. *Journal of Retailing, 67*(4), 420–450.

Parasuraman, A., Zeithaml, V. A., & Berry, L. L. (1994). Alternative scales for measuring service quality: A comparative assessment based on psychometric and diagnostic criteria. *Journal of Retailing, 70*(3), 201–230.

Phillips, L. W. (1981). Assessing measurement error in key informant reports: A methodological note on organizational analysis in marketing. *Journal of Marketing Research, 18*(4), 395–415.

Reichheld, F. (1996). *The loyalty effect.* Boston: Harvard Business School Press.

Reynolds, K. E., & Beatty, S. E. (1999). Customer benefits and company consequences of customer-salesperson relationships in retailing. *Journal of Retailing, 75*(1), 11–32.

Rossiter, J. R. (2002). The C-OAR-SE procedure for scale development in marketing. *International Journal of Research in Marketing, 19*(4), 305–335.

Rossiter, J. R. (2005). Reminder: A horse is a horse. *International Journal of Research in Marketing, 22*(1), 23–25.

Rudolph, B. (1998). *Kundenzufriedenheit im industriegüterbereich.* Wiesbaden: Gabler.

Rust, R. T., Inman, J. J., Jia, J., & Zahorik, A. (1999). What you *don't* know about customer-perceived quality: The role of customer expectation distributions. *Marketing Science, 18*(1), 77–92.

Schwaiger, M. (2004). Components and parameters of corporate reputation – an empirical study. *Schmalenbach Business Review, 56*(1), 46–71.

Schwaiger, M., & Cannon, H. M. (2004). Exploring company brand equity. In: P. Rose (Ed.), *Proceedings of the 2004 conference of the American academy of advertising* (pp. 67–73), Florida International University, North Miami.

Sheth, J. N. (1973). A model of industrial buyer behavior. *Journal of Marketing, 37*(3), 50–56.

Spiro, R. L., & Weitz, B. A. (1990). Adaptive selling: Conceptionalization, measurement and nomological validity. *Journal of Marketing Research, 60*(3), 61–69.

Stock, R. (2005). Can customer satisfaction decrease price sensitivity in business-to-business Markets? *Journal of Business-to-Business Marketing, 12*(3), 59–87.

Swan, J. E., & Combs, L. J. (1976). Product performance and consumer satisfaction: A new concept. *Journal of Marketing, 40*(2), 25–33.

TARP/Technical Assistance Research Program. (1979). *Consumer complaint handling in America: Summary of findings and recommendations.* Washington, DC: White House Office of Consumer Affairs.

TARP/Technical Assistance Research Program. (1986). *Consumer complaint handling in America: An updated study, Part 2.* Washington, DC: White House Office of Consumer Affairs.

Taylor, S. A., & Baker, T. L. (1994). An assessment of the relationship between service quality and customer satisfaction in the formation of consumers' purchase intentions. *Journal of Retailing, 70*(2), 163–178.

Weitz, B. A., Sujan, H., & Sujan, M. (1986). Knowledge, motivation and adaptive behavior: A framework for improving selling effectiveness. *Journal of Marketing, 50*(4), 174–191.

Wold, H. (1975). Path models with latent variables: The NIPALS approach. In: H. M. Blalock, A. Aganbegian, F. M. Borodkin, R. Boudon & V. Cappecchi (Eds), *Quantitative sociology: International perspective on mathematical and statistical modelling* (pp. 47–74). New York: Academic Press.

Wold, H. (1982). Systems under indirect observation using PLS. In: C. Fornell (Ed.), *A second generation of multivariate analysis, Vol. 1: Methods* (pp. 325–347). New York: Praeger.

Woodside, A. G., Frey, L. L., & Daly, R. T. (1989). Linking service quality, customer satisfaction, and behavioral intention. *Journal of Health Care Marketing, 9*(4), 5–17.

World Cement Directory. (2002). *Ed. by Cembureau – The European Cement Association, 1.* Brüssel: World Cement Directory.

Yoon, T.-H., & Ekinci, Y. (2003). An examination of the SERVQUAL dimensions using the Guttman scaling procedure. *Journal of Hospitality and Tourism Research, 27*(1), 3–23.

PART IV:
BUYER BEHAVIOR IN
INTERACTIVE CONTEXTS

THE EXPOSURE EFFECT OF UNCLICKED BANNER ADVERTISEMENTS

Hee-Sook Yoon and Doo-Hee Lee

ABSTRACT

Very low click-through rates (CTR) raise serious questions about the effectiveness of banner advertisements. However, we believe that the effect of a banner ad is not limited by clicks. Banner ad information itself can be processed by the audience.

We propose that the exposure effect of a banner ad exists even when the banner is not clicked. The results of our experiments strongly support this effect. Analyses also revealed that a non-clicked banner ad can create as strong of an exposure effect as clicked banner ads. Also, audiences that are able to recall the existence of the banner ad on a web page develop stronger implicit memory than those who cannot. Researchers are invited to re-test these interesting findings in various cultures with differing levels of Internet penetration and experience.

INTRODUCTION

The Internet is an interactive medium through which people can meet a variety of their needs. Sometimes it is used for goal-driven web surfing, such

Cross-Cultural Buyer Behavior
Advances in International Marketing, Volume 18, 211–229
ISSN: 1474-7979/doi:10.1016/S1474-7979(06)18009-6

as shopping and Internet banking, but in many cases it is used for leisure or to overcome ennui, especially in portal web sites. In either case, the analysis of Internet behavior requires more attention than traditional mass media.

Under these web-use situations, a banner advertisement that is located as a part of a main web page often does not receive adequate attention. This low attention naturally leads to a low click-through rate (CTR). It is known that in Korea the average CTR is less than 1 percent. Since most advertisers consider banner advertisement as a gateway to target content (content advertisement), the effectiveness of banner advertisement has been questioned. The assumption is that a low CTR indicates the poor performance of a banner ad.

This phenomenon is typical in Korea. Korea is well known as a country with one of the highest penetration rates of super high-speed Internet in the world. About 75 percent of households subscribe to ADSL or to a similar type of high-speed Internet service. This has developed due to decisive government policies, convenient installation of Internet in apartment complex residences, and Korean's, in general, eagerness to adopt new technologies. Korean Internet users can, therefore, be considered an ideal study group, having had the longest and the most varied of experiences. Studying Korean's Internet behavior is ideal because of their diverse and wide range of experiences and their high level of computer skills.

Advertisers are sensitive to CTR because they consider banner ads only as a gateway to the target web page. Research has focused on clicking behavior, and, in particular, on the situations that promote clicking (Chatterjee, Hoffman, & Novak, 1998; Stern, 1997) and any antecedent variables (Cho, Lee, & Tharp, 2001; Dahlen, 2001; Hofacker & Murphy, 2000; Shamdasani, Stanaland, & Tan, 2001). Due to these works, we are able to understand clicking behavior in more depth. However, these studies are limited in explaining how a banner ad is clicked and they do not contribute to the understanding of the banner ad's effect.

We posit that the role of banners is not limited to the gateway function, but extends to building brands through increased awareness. Two studies are particularly relevant. Briggs and Hollis (1997) proposed that a banner ad works with or without the added benefit of click-through. They reported that only one exposure to a banner ad increases advertisement awareness, brand perception, and purchase intention. They even stated that advertising on the web appeared to work in the same way as print advertisement. Dahlen (2001) argued that no difference exists in brand awareness and brand attitude between two groups of people – those exposed to and those not exposed to banner advertisements. Based on this analysis he emphasized the importance of CTR. We, however, suspect that this argument may be overstated because Dahlen's survey may not have been controlled for other influences and because the dependent variables – brand awareness and brand attitude – may not tap the banner ad exposure effect. We believe that the exposure effect of banner ads needs to be more correctly measured.

This poses a question: does a banner advertisement play important roles even without being clicked? Is it possible that a banner ad can be effective without being clicked? We believe that this issue is very interesting and significant in terms of academic theory as well as managerial implications. We will propose a conceptual framework for banner ad information processing and then rigorously investigate the exposure effect of a banner ad.

LITERATURE REVIEW

The studies on banner advertising can be summarized into two categories. One group focuses on the Internet as a new medium and the other empirically tests its effectiveness.

A few studies identify the characteristics of Internet advertising and its relationship to traditional media (Berthon, Pitt, & Watson, 1996; Bezjian-Avery, Calder, & Iacobucci, 1998; Hoffman & Novak, 1996). It is reported that verbal messages are more effective than visual expression in Internet advertising, which is contrary to the traditional media (Bezjian-Avery et al., 1998). Considering the interactivity of the Internet, Berthon et al. (1996) pointed out that conversion efficiency (number of purchases/number of active visitors) needs to be managed. Internet advertising is better suited for highly involved and/or rationally oriented consumers and should be recognized as an important communication method (Yoon & Kim, 2001).

A number of observed studies on Internet advertising focus on CTR and exposure effects. Stern (1997) discovered several factors that can affect CTR: position of the banner, humor, a "click here" message, interrogative sentence type, and bright colors and animation. Regarding repeated exposure to a banner and the probability of being clicked, Chatterjee et al. (1998) posit a *U*-curve relationship. According to them, the click probability drops to zero after three repetitions and then bounces back (Hofacker & Murphy, 2000). Dahlen (2001) reported that Internet novices record higher CTR and tend to change brand awareness and brand attitude more positively than more experienced Internet users do.

Briggs and Hollis (1997) opened a door to a discussion of the exposure effect of banner ads. They report that only one exposure to a banner can increase brand loyalty, brand perception, and advertisement awareness, even without being clicked. Although the study provides good insights, its exploratory nature means that the results need to be viewed conservatively. Cho et al. (2001) reported that the degree of forced exposure to banner ads has a significantly positive relationship to advertisement perception and to the clicking of banners. The effectiveness of a banner also depends on the characteristics of the website where it is exposed. There seems to be a positive relationship between the attitude toward the website and the attitude toward both a banner ad and a brand, as well as the attitude toward the website and purchase intention (Bruner II & Kumar, 2000). The effect of a banner can also be influenced by web page complexity. When the web page is quite simple, the banner ad has more effect on attitude toward the banner, the brand, and the website as well as on purchase intention (Stevenson, Bruner II, & Kumar, 2000). In the case of high-involvement products, a website relevant to the product can create higher banner advertisement effects ("relevance-driven"). For low-involvement products, a website with a high reputation results in higher effects ("reputation-driven") (Shamdasani et al., 2001).

Earlier studies explain many aspects of banner advertisements. However, most of them share the common limitation that CTR is considered the main measure of banner effect (Bhat, Bevans, & Sengupta, 2002). This assumes the gateway role of a banner ad, while ignoring the fact that a banner itself may create an exposure effect. Another limitation related to this method is that some studies collected data from voluntary subjects through pop-up window announcements. A possible flaw in this case is that the subjects may notice the object of the study and give too much attention to the advertisement. In a few studies that employ existing brands, a more tightly controlled research design is needed to detect genuine effects.

Internet is a hybrid medium that has characteristics of a personal medium and a mass medium (Berthon et al., 1996; Dreze & Zufryden, 1997), and possiblility of immediate and interactive one-to-one communication. As such, its effect can be measured exactly in various levels, compared to existing media. We believe a conceptual model of banner ad information processing needs to be incorporated in both the clicking and exposure effects.

A banner ad on the Internet also has the characteristics of a hybrid, so its effects need to be discussed from both points of view. We believe a conceptual model of banner ad information processing needs to incorporate both the clicking and the exposure effects.

METHOD

Conceptual Framework

One major objective of advertising is to form, change, or maintain attitudes toward an advertised brand. Traditionally, therefore, the effects of an advertisement are measured by attitude toward a brand, attitude toward an advertisement, memories of advertised messages and brand name, beliefs about the advertised attributes, and behavioral intentions (BIs).

Numerous studies have examined the relationship among these variables. It is also thought that advertising information is processed through cognition of brand (C_b), shapes attitude toward an advertisement (A_{ad}), and is used to form attitude toward a brand (A_b). Furthermore, we may conclude that BI is affected by brand attitude (Brown & Stayman, 1992; Gardner, 1985; Homer, 1990; Miniard, Bhatla, & Rose, 1990; Mitchell & Olson, 1981; MacKenzie, Lutz, & Belch, 1986; MacKenzie & Spreng, 1992; Moore & Hutchinson, 1983, 1985; Park & Young, 1984).

We posit that the information processing of a banner ad is similar to that of mass media advertisements, but is slightly modified due to clicking behavior. Our banner information processing (BIP) model is presented in Fig. 1. It explains how an audience processes information after being exposed to a banner ad and it incorporates both clicking and non-clicking situations. In the BIP framework, A_b is affected by both the banner and by the content advertisement that is exposed after clicking. Exposure to banner forms cognition of a brand through banner advertisement (C_{bb}) and attitude toward banner advertisement (A_{bad}); both affect A_b directly. When the banner is clicked, both the cognition of brand formed by content advertisement (C_{bc}) and attitude toward content advertisement (A_{cad}) affect A_b. That is, a banner affects A_b both directly and indirectly via content advertisement.

When a banner is clicked, information processing can be explained as follows. Exposure to a banner forms C_{bb} and A_{bad}, which simultaneously affect the clicking decision and A_b. After being exposed to a banner, an audience processes the message cognitively and the advertisement itself affectively. Then they decide whether the banner is worth clicking. If it is, the click leads to the target web page and to content advertisement. Since a content ad usually contains detailed information, the audience exerts more effort to process it. The content is then processed in the same manner as the banner ad. The combined effects of C_{bc} and A_{cad} influence A_b, which at same time is influenced by C_{bb} and A_{bad}.

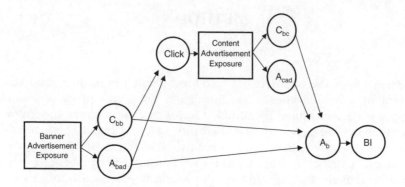

C_{bb} = Cognition of brand formed by banner advertisement exposure

C_{bc} = Cognition of brand formed by content advertisement exposure

A_{bad} = Attitude toward banner advertisement A_{cad} = Attitude toward content advertisement

A_b = Attitude toward brand   BI   = Behavior Intention

Fig. 1.   Banner Information Processing Model.

After being exposed to a banner ad, a person may decide it is not worth clicking. In this case, C_{bb} and A_{bad} directly affect A_b. In the case of a non-clicking situation, a banner ad may affect the formation of attitudes toward advertisement in concurrence with cognition on advertisement messages and ultimately affect attitudes toward a brand.

Exposure Effects of Internet Advertisement on Brand Attitude

A banner should be considered a stand-alone, or an independent, advertisement as well as a gateway to content ads. In both cases, the exposure may be intentional or incidental. The former is purposive exposure to stimuli in order to achieve an individual's goal while the latter occurs by chance (Shapiro, 1999; Shapiro, MacInnis, & Heckler, 1997). When the audience is motivated to process information in incidental situations, this information may be processed with very little or no awareness of advertising stimuli. Traditionally, the classical conditioning theory and the mere exposure effect have been used to explain the process.

Numerous studies focus on direct affect transfer through classical conditioning (Allen & Madden, 1985; Bierley, McSweeney, & Vannieuwkerk,

1985; Gorn, 1982; Gresham & Shimp, 1985; Stuart, Shimp, & Engle, 1987). The supposition is that an unconditioned stimulus (US) will arouse an affective response. When the US is systematically paired with a conditioned stimulus (CS), the subjects become aware of the contingency relations and the generated affect will then transfer from the US to the CS (Allen & Madden, 1985; Zajonc, 1980; Zajonc, Pietromonaco, & Bargh, 1982).

Repeated exposure can shape preference without awareness of the stimulus (Bornstein, 1989) and can create a positive attitude toward the object (Janiszewski, 1993). Mere exposure may explain consumer attitude formation in low involvement situations. A positive attitude can be formed even without intentional information processing (Vanhule, 1994).

When a banner is not clicked, it is likely that the advertisement is incidentally exposed to the audience. When an individual concentrates on a certain task, other information can be processed without getting attention. Even incidental exposure to an advertisement can affect attitudes toward the brand and the advertisement (Janiszewski, 1993); the possibility of including the brand in the consideration set is higher (Shapiro et al., 1997). This incidental exposure effect occurs not through intentional but pre-attentive information processing (Janiszewski, 1993) and passive learning (Krugman, 1986). The effect occurs despite the fact that subjects show no explicit memory of the ads (Shapiro, 1999). Based on this research stream, we speculate that an unclicked banner is an incidental situation and can have an exposure effect.

H1. The cognition of brand formed by banner advertisement exposure (C_{bb}) is stronger than that of the control group.

H2. The attitude toward brand (A_b) that is formed by banner advertisement exposure is more positive than that of the control group.

It is widely accepted that cognition of brand attributes and attitude toward advertisements affect attitudes toward the advertised brand (Brown & Stayman, 1992; Gardner, 1985; Homer, 1990; MacKenzie et al., 1986; MacKenzie & Spreng, 1992; Miniard et al., 1990; Mitchell & Olson, 1981; Moore & Hutchison, 1983; Shimp, 1981). We expect a similar relationship among C_{bb}, A_{bad}, and A_b.

H3. The cognition of brand formed by banner advertisement exposure (C_{bb}) and attitude toward brand (A_b) are positively related.

H4. The attitude toward banner advertisement (A_{bad}) and attitude toward brand (A_b) are positively related.

The Effect of Banner Advertisement on Memory

An exposure to banners is expected to affect the audience's memory. Researchers generally measure explicit memory, such as recall and recognition, which requires intentional efforts to retrieve information about a stimulus. Because most banner ads are exposed incidentally and do not get much attention, the explicit memory effect can be marginal. Recall and recognition measurement have limited use in measuring the incidental process. Yet, we believe that incidentally exposed banners still can affect implicit memory about the advertised brand.

H5. Implicit memory among subjects exposed to a banner advertisement, although they did not click it, is higher than that of the control group.

PILOT STUDY

We initially conducted a pilot study to test the hypotheses.

Banner Advertisement

In the pilot study we simply manipulated a banner ad not to be opened even if it is clicked. The banner was for a non-existent virtual brand and was located on a consulting company web site that was not yet open to the public at the time. Our intent was to prevent undesirable confounding effects due to prior web experience, attitude toward a web site, and attitude toward an existing brand. The test product category – a beverage – was selected based on a pre-test ($n = 20$), because involvement with this category was found to be below middle level. High involvement products were avoided because they draw too much deliberate attention (Petty, Cacioppo, & Schuman, 1983). An existing brand was avoided because prior experience, knowledge, and attitudes may have affected the experiment. The virtual brand name, Tropical, was selected by another pretest ($n = 25$), which yielded a familiarity score in the middle range (4.8 on a 7-point scale). If familiarity is high, then the brand name intrinsically can create high preference for the brand.

Subjects in the experiment group navigated the web site and were exposed to a target banner ad. The banner ad was located at the top of each web page. On the contrary, subjects of the control group navigated web pages with no banner ad. The time of navigation allowed was 15 min in both groups. Although they navigated the same web site, exposure and non-exposure to a banner ad between the experimental group and the control group were manipulated in this manner.

Experiment Process

Subjects were selected from undergraduate students enrolled in an Internet marketing class. The 70 subjects were randomly assigned to either the manipulated (exposure) group or to the control (non-exposure) group. The experiment was conducted in a computer laboratory.

Subjects were asked to navigate the web site as if they visited it by chance while surfing. They were notified that they had 15 min for navigation and should try to look at the overall aspect of the site, including content, structure, and design. They were told that the object of the experiment was to observe the navigation response of people who visited a site by chance. Navigation behavior of a web site can differ depending on the goal (Hoffman & Novak, 1996), so no goal was given to the subjects. After completing a hard copy questionnaire, subjects were debriefed on the real object of the experiment.

The advertisement was prepared by a professional banner design company. The location of the ad was at the top center of each page of the web site. A 700×45 pixel banner ad was designed to roll three animated pages. The banner contained attribute messages and pictures so that it promoted cognitive as well as affective information processing. The messages were "Natural fruit juice 100%," "Unique tropical fruit taste," and the brand name "Tropical." The pictures were of tropical fruits and a beach.

Measurement

The dependent variables were cognition of brand attributes through banner advertisement (C_{bb}), attitude toward banner advertisement (A_{bad}), attitude toward brand (A_b), and implicit memory. C_{bb} was measured by a 7-point Likert type scale for the two messages and the brand name. A_{bad} and A_b were measured by a 7-point semantic differential scale ("dislike–like" and "bad–good") that was modified from a previous study (MacKenzie, Spreng, & Olshavsky, 1996).

Memory for messages involved both implicit and explicit memory. Implicit memory usually is measured by a word fragment completion task or a word stem completion task (Graf, Mandler, & Haden, 1982), by free association (Schacter, 1985), by word identification (Jacoby, 1983), or by reading of an inverted script (Kolers, 1975). In this study, considering the characteristics of the message, we used both word stem completion and word fragment completion tasks. The former requires completing a word when only the first letter is given. The latter requires completing a message in which some words are missing (i.e., "_____ fruit juice _____ %"). One point was given for each correct answer.

For the control group, since they were not exposed to banner advertisement, implicit memory, brand cognition (C_{bb}), and attitude toward brand (A_b) were measured excluding attitude toward banner advertisement (A_{bad}). The method of measurement for brand cognition (C_{bb}) and attitude toward brand (A_b) was the same with that for the experiment group.

Results

Among the 70 questionnaires, 65 were analyzed after discarding unusable submissions. The scales were found to be reliable regarding Cronbach's alpha for $A_{bad} = 0.948$, for $A_b = 0.895$. In order to test Hypothesis 1, cognitions of brand between the exposure group and the control group were compared. A t-test revealed that the difference was not statistically significant (exposure group 4.90, control group 4.37). Hypothesis 2 concerns any difference in attitude toward brand (A_b) between the two groups, and the t-test revealed no difference of statistical significance (exposure group 4.19, control group 4.37). Hypotheses 3 and 4 involve positive relationships among C_{bb}, A_{bad}, and A_b. To test the hypotheses, two simple regression analyses were done. In each, A_b was the dependent variable and either C_{bb} or A_{bad} was the independent variable. It was found that both C_{bb}, ($\beta = 0.487$, $p < 0.001$) and A_{bad} ($\beta = 0.778$, $p < 0.001$) were positively related to A_b. Hypothesis 5, regarding implicit memory effects of banners, was supported by a t-test (exposure group 2.32, control group 1.40, $p < 0.001$). That is, the implicit memory of subjects exposed to the banner, although they did not click, was greater than that of the control group. Since the difference is due to incidental exposure to the banner, this finding indicates an exposure effect.

Limitations of the Pilot Study

The pilot study revealed that C_{bb} and A_{bad} may be positively related to A_b. However, from a conservative perspective, it may not be sufficient to show that C_{bb} and A_{bad} are formed by banner ad exposure. Consequently, it may not follow that A_b is affected by such exposure.

This result may be due to an unnatural experimental process. In the pilot, an un-clickable banner was used. That is, when a subject clicked the advertisement there was no response. Subjects could consider this situation unrealistic and develop negative feelings because they still had to wait 15 min until the experimenter stopped the navigation. Those feelings could contaminate the exposure effect of the banner ad. To avoid these problems, in the main experiment we used a more natural banner and more appropriate methods.

MAIN EXPERIMENT

Experimental Design and Process

The experimental design and the measured variables for this experiment were the same as those of the pilot test. However, the experimental process and banner ad were more sophisticated and designed to be more natural. On the contrary, during the pilot test, when one clicked the banner ad, a content ad was programmed to appear on the screen. The content ad consisted of three attribute-related messages and a picture of the advertised product. The picture of the product was located on the left side of the web page, while messages were on the right side.

The subjects who clicked the banner ad were exposed to a content advertisement and those who did not were exposed to only web contents with the banner ad. The subjects in the control group were not exposed to a banner ad, and were merely exposed to web contents.

The web site was the same as in the pilot study and the location of the banner remained at the top and the center of each web page. The brand name and messages were the same, though visual elements were modified because the A_{bad} score in the pilot was below average (3.2 on a 7-point scale). To make the banner more neutral, the banner ad used in the pilot experiment was improved with colors and background pictures.

Subjects in the main experiment were students who enrolled in an introduction to business or in principles of marketing class. These subjects were considered to be more neutral and less involved with the Internet than those in the pilot study. By doing so, we could reduce a potential response bias due to the characteristics of subjects (Bezjian-Avery et al., 1998).

In all, 161 subjects were randomly assigned to the experiment and the control group. Experimental design consisted of a group exposed to a banner ad and of a control group without a banner ad. The experiment group exposed to a banner ad was later divided into two sub groups based on clicking and non-clicking behavior. The decision to click was a free act of the subject. The valid numbers used in the final analyses were 38 subjects in the control group, 39 subjects who clicked the banner ad, and 38 subjects who did not click the ad.

The subjects were told the same falsified objective as the pilot study and were asked to navigate for 15 min. Subjects who were exposed to, but did not click the banner, answered a questionnaire regarding C_{bb}, A_{bad}, A_b, implicit memory, and general Internet usage behavior after the navigation. If subjects clicked the banner, an electronic questionnaire appeared in a pop-up window right away. It contained questions on C_{bb}, A_{bad}, A_b, and on implicit memory affected by the banner ad. When these subjects clicked the "completed" button after answering the questionnaire, the content ad appeared on the screen. After viewing the content ad, they were returned to a previous web page by clicking an end button. The pop-up questionnaire that appeared between the banner ad and the content ad was designed to measure pure effect of the banner ad without a possible confounding effect by the content ad. Subjects who clicked the banner also answered a paper questionnaire about general Internet usage behavior after finishing the navigation.

For dependent variables, C_{bb}, A_{bad}, A_b, implicit memory, recall, and recognition were measured. For implicit memory, more rigorous methods than in the pilot study were used in order to ensure higher accuracy of the responses. The measure items for implicit memory were modified to make it more difficult to make random guesses.

In most previous studies, subjects were situated in unnatural experimental settings and, as such, too much attention could be given to the stimuli, which may have resulted in a demand artifact. In our study, the banner exposure occurred more naturally while the subjects were navigating a real site. We also could collect log file data that recorded the actual navigation behavior of the subjects.

RESULTS AND DISCUSSION

Before analyzing the results, the reliability of the measures was checked. Cronbach alpha's for all variables were high enough to warrant further analyses: A_{bad} of control group = 0.901, A_{bad} of click group after exposure = 0.675, A_b of click group after exposure = 0.867, A_{bad} of non-click group after exposure = 0.937, and A_b of non-click group after exposure = 0.972.

Hypothesis 1 states that the cognition of brand formed by a banner advertisement exposure (C_{bb}) is stronger than that of the control group. A t-test strongly supported the hypothesis ($p = 0.009$) that the mean of the exposure group (4.66) was statistically greater than that of the control group (3.85). Hypothesis 2 concerns the fact that the attitude toward brand (A_b) that is formed by a banner advertisement exposure is more positive than that of the control group. A t-test did not show enough statistical evidence of support (exposure group = 4.16, control group = 4.46, $p = 0.252$). Hypotheses 3 and 4 are about positive relationships among C_{bb}, A_{bad}, and A_b. A multiple regression analysis was conducted with A_b as the dependent variable and with the other two as independent variables. The results revealed a marginal support for Hypothesis 3 ($\beta = 0.309$, $p = 0.055$) and strong support for Hypothesis 4 ($\beta = 0.761$, $p < 0.001$). The implicit memory effect posited in Hypothesis 5 also was strongly supported (experiment group = 0.760, control group = 0.105, $p = 0.004$). That is, even in the case where people are exposed to banner ads but do not click it, they retain an implicit memory of the message.

With these stimulating results, we began to explore the non-click situation. We conceived two reasons people do not click a banner advertisement. One is that they do not choose to do so although they are aware of its existence; the other is that they are unaware of it due to lack of attention. We were curious about any differences in the effect of banner ads in these two cases. To pursue the matter, we classified the non-click data into two categories – subjects who remembered the existence of the banner and those who did not. The classification was based on the answers to a question item about their recall of the banner ad existence. If the answer was "yes" the subject was classified as a recall group, and if "no," or "do not know," as a non-recall group. Although the number in each group was small (recall group = 11, non-recall group = 19) with the exception of missing data ($n = 8$), we decided to continue the analysis to obtain some further insights.

We conducted ANOVAs to compare implicit memory, cognition of brand (C_b), and attitude toward brand (A_b) in the recall, the non-recall, and the control groups. The results are given in Table 1 and strongly indicate that statistical differences were found for implicit memory ($p < 0.001$) and a support for C_b ($p = 0.010$). A_bs among the three groups were not significantly different, however ($p = 0.200$). With the two significant test results, we further conducted Scheffe tests to compare the means of the recall and non-recall groups with that of control group. The analyses revealed that implicit memory and cognition of brand (C_b) of recall group were statistically greater than those of the control group ($p < 0.001$). Although

Table 1. ANOVA Results for Non-Click and Control Group.

Dependent Variable	Condition	N	Mean	Standard Deviation	F	p-Value
Cognition of brand by	Non-recall	19	4.44	1.41		
banner advertisement	Recall	11	5.18	1.42	4.95	0.010
exposure (C_{bb})	Control	38	3.85	1.16		
Attitude toward brand	Non-recall	19	3.84	1.01		
(A_b)	Recall	11	4.36	1.27	1.65	0.200
	Control	38	4.46	1.16		
Implicit memory	Non-recall	19	0.32	0.95		
	Recall	11	1.73	1.42	14.27	0.000
	Control	38	0.11	0.65		

cognition of brand (C_b) shows a very marginal significance ($p = 0.104$), all measures of the non-recall group were not different from those of the control group at alpha level of 0.05.

In summary, these additional analyses support that the banner ad exposure effect exists even without being clicked, particularly when people are able to recall the banner ad's existence. We also, despite of the poor statistical results, posit that the possibility of the exposure effect could exist even when people cannot recall the existence of the banner ad. We think that if the analyses were conducted with more sufficient degrees of freedom, the p-value would be much smaller. In this context, further research on this issue should be done.

Post Analyses and Discussion

Is there a banner ad exposure effect? If we combine all the statistical results for the hypotheses, we may be able to support the existence of the effect. The exposure of a banner ad created stronger cognition of brand than the controlled one. Implicit memory formed by banner ad exposure is higher than that of the control group even without clicking it. Also, the cognition of brand and the attitude toward the banner ad, formed by banner ad exposure, positively lead to the attitude toward brand. Although this may be good empirical evidence to support the effect, we still investigated additional evidence. We attempted to witness if the exposure effect of a non-clicked banner ad is at least similar to that of clicked banner ad. If this is the case, we could say that the exposure effect, without the banner ad being clicked, is as strong as when it is clicked.

Table 2. *T*-Test Results for Non-Click and Click Group.

Dependent Variable	Condition	N	Mean	Standard Deviation	*p*-Value
Cognition of brand by banner advertisement exposure (C_{bb})	Non-click	38	4.66	1.41	0.507
	Click	39	4.44	1.55	
Attitude toward banner advertisement (A_{bad})	Non-click	38	4.24	1.12	0.346
	Click	39	4.00	1.03	
Attitude Toward brand (A_b)	Non-click	38	4.16	1.06	0.921
	Click	39	4.13	1.12	
Implicit memory	Non-click	38	0.76	1.20	0.005
	Click	39	1.72	1.69	

To investigate this issue, exposure effects between the click group and non-click group were compared and analyzed. Prior to analyzing the data, we excluded subjects who opened the banner ad more than once during the experiment. After reviewing the log file of the subjects' surfing behavior, we believe that these subjects returned to the banner ad thinking they made an error in opening the banner ad or they attempted to study the banner ad to answer the pop-up questionnaire. In either instance, if a subject viewed the banner twice or more, the questionnaire was discarded.

As shown in Table 2, with the exception of implicit memory ($p = 0.005$), *t*-tests did not support the differences between the two groups in cognition of brand formed by banner advertisement exposure (C_{bb}), attitude toward banner advertisement (A_{bad}), and attitude toward brand (A_b). These results provide additional evidence to support that the exposure effect of a non-clicked banner ad is as strong as that of clicked banner ad. Hence, considering the analyses in this research, we finally conclude that an exposure effect of a banner ad exists even in the case that the banner ad is not clicked.

CONCLUSION

Compared to traditional mass media, the Internet is, by nature, a much more interactive medium. When using the Internet, audiences control their behavior. They navigate a web site in order to achieve their goals. They might actively search for specific information with attention, or they may simply use the Internet for entertainment. In either case, their activity requires more attention than passive exposure to mass media. In this kind of web environment, a banner ad which is located on the same page of main contents is very difficult to draw attention. Most banner ads are exposed to their audience very passively and incidentally. Less than 1 percent of CTR on average is a good evidence of this. And, some argue that in this context the effectiveness of banner ads is questionable.

However, lower CTR does not necessarily mean the banner ads are ineffectual. As revealed in this study, a banner ad can create the exposure effect even when the ad is not clicked. Also, stronger implicit memory is formed by audiences that are able to recall the existence of the banner ad on the web page, than those who cannot. Furthermore, we suggest that the exposure effect may exist even when audiences are not able to recall the existences of a banner when they navigate a web site. Although the power of the analysis to support this was not strong enough, we posit the existence of the effect. We recommend further well-designed research, with more degrees of freedom to investigate and confirm this conclusion.

This study also revealed that a non-clicked banner ad is able to create as strong of an exposure effect as a clicked banner ad. A non-clicked banner and a clicked banner created similar levels of cognition of brand formed by banner advertisement exposure (C_{bb}), attitude toward banner advertisement (A_{bad}), and attitude toward brand (A_b). The magnitude of the exposure effect can be influenced by whether the existence of the banner ad can be recalled rather than by the clicking behavior.

We believe that this study contributes uniquely to the general understanding of banner ad exposure effect, particularly when it is not clicked. Also, it opened a wide avenue toward future study of the effect. We also proposed a conceptual BIP model to explain banner advertisement information processing. In the model, the exposure process of an Internet banner ad is divided into sub-levels, clicking and non-clicking routes, and then their respective exposure effects are systematically analyzed for the first time in this study. This model needs to be tested more rigorously in the follow-up studies.

This study has some limitations. Although the internal validity is secured by the experiment design and tightly controlled experimental procedure, external validity is still limited. In future research, diverse replications need to be conducted with diverse products, websites and subjects.

Another possible limitation of this study is due to the cultural characteristics of the subjects. The experiment was conducted in a society where Internet penetration is very high. This means that the subjects were well experienced with computers and very skillful in using Internet. Also, perhaps multiple information processing could be possible when the subjects navigate the web, although they themselves would not be aware of it. Subjects might also have the ability to process banner ad information while they are surfing the web for their main goals. Korea can be considered as an ideal country to study Internet behavior because a variety of Internet experiences co-exist. On the other hand, the subjects' behaviors may create some difficulty in generalizing for other societies. We, therefore, suggest that this study be repeated with different subjects to compare the exposure effects among countries of different levels of Internet experience. Discussions on this issue should be continued by further study in countries having different levels of Internet penetration.

REFERENCES

Allen, C. T., & Madden, T. J. (1985). A closer look at classical conditioning. *Journal of Consumer Research, 13*(March), 301–315.

Berthon, P., Pitt, L. F., & Watson, R. T. (1996). The World Wide Web as an advertising medium. *Journal of Advertising Research, 36*(1), 43–54.

Bezjian-Avery, A., Calder, B., & Iacobucci, D. (1998). New media interactive advertising vs. traditional advertising. *Journal of Advertising Research, 38*(4), 23–32.

Bhat, S., Bevans, M., & Sengupta, S. (2002). Measuring users' web activity to evaluate and enhance advertising effectiveness. *Journal of Advertising, 16*(3), 97–106.

Bierley, C., McSweeney, F. K., & Vannieuwkerk, R. (1985). Classical conditioning of preferences for stimuli. *Journal of Consumer Research, 12*(December), 316–323.

Bornstein, R. F. (1989). Exposure and affect: Overview and meta-analysis of research. *Psychological Bulletin, 106*(2), 265–289.

Briggs, R., & Hollis, N. (1997). Adverting on the web: Is there response before click through. *Journal of Advertising Research, 37*(2), 33–45.

Brown, S. P., & Stayman, D. M. (1992). Antecedents and consequences of attitude toward the ad: A meta-analysis. *Journal of Consumer Research, 19*(June), 34–51.

Bruner, G. C., & Kumar, A. (2000). Web commercials and advertising hierarchy-of-effects. *Journal of Advertising Research, 40*(1/2), 35–42.

Chatterjee, P., Hoffman, D. L., & Novak, T. P. (1998). *Modeling the clickstream: Implications for web-based advertising efforts.* http://elab.vanderbilt.edu/research/manuscripts/index.htm

Cho, C. H., Lee, J.-G., & Tharp, M. (2001). Different forced-exposure levels to banner advertising. *Journal of Advertising Research, 41*(4), 45–56.

Dahlen, M. (2001). Banner advertisements through a new lens. *Journal of Advertising Research, 41*(4), 23–30.

Dreze, X., & Zufryden, F. (1997). Testing web site design and promotion content. *Journal of Advertising Research, 37*(2), 77–91.

Gardner, M. P. (1985). Does attitude toward the ad affect brand attitude under a brand evaluation set. *Journal of Marketing Research, 22*(May), 192–198.

Gorn, G. J. (1982). The effects of music in advertising of choice behavior: A classical conditioning approach. *Journal of Marketing, 46*(Winter), 94–101.

Graf, P., Mandler, G., & Haden, P. (1982). Simulating amnesic symptoms in normal subjects.
Science, 218, 1243–1244.

Gresham, L. G., & Shimp, T. A. (1985). Attitude toward the advertisement and brand attitudes.
Journal of Advertising, 14(1), 10–18.

Hofacker, C. F., & Murphy, J. (2000). Clickable world wide web banner ads and content sites.
Journal of Interactive Marketing, 14(1), 49–59.

Hoffman, D., & Novak, T. D. (1996). Marketing in hypermedia computer mediated environments. *Journal of Marketing, 60*(July), 50–68.

Homer, P. M. (1990). The mediating role of attitude toward the ad: Some additional evidence.
Journal of Marketing Research, 27(February), 78–86.

Jacoby, L. L. (1983). Perceptual enhancement: Persistent effects of an experience. *Journal of
Experimental Psychology: Learning, Memory and Cognition, 9*(January), 21–38.

Janiszewski, C. (1993). Pre-attentive mere exposure effects. *Journal of Consumer Research,
20*(December), 376–392.

Kolers, P. A. (1975). Memorial consequences of automized encoding. *Journal of Experimental
Psychology: Human Learning and Memory, 1,* 689–701.

Krugman, H. E. (1986). Low recall and high recognition advertising. *Journal of Advertising
Research, 26*(1), 79–86.

MacKenzie, S. B., Lutz, R. J., & Belch, G. E. (1986). The role attitude toward the ad as a
mediator of advertising effectiveness: A test of competing explanations. *Journal of Marketing Research, 23*(May), 130–143.

MacKenzie, S. B., & Spreng, R. A. (1992). How does motivation moderate the impact of central
and peripheral processing on brand attitudes and intentions? *Journal of Consumer
Research, 18*(March), 519–529.

MacKenzie, S. B., Spreng, R. A., & Olshavsky, R. W. (1996). A re-examination of the determinants of consumer satisfaction. *Journal of Marketing, 60*(July), 15–32.

Miniard, P. W., Bhatla, S., & Rose, R. L. (1990). On the formation and relationship of ad and
brand attitudes: An experimental and causal analysis. *Journal of Marketing Research,
27*(August), 290–303.

Mitchell, A. A., & Olson, J. C. (1981). Are product attribute beliefs the only mediators
of advertising effects on brand attitudes? *Journal of Marketing Research, 18*(August),
318–322.

Moore, D. L., & Hutchinson, J. W. (1983). The effects of ad affect on advertising effectiveness.
Advances in Consumer Research, 10, 526–531.

Moore, D. L., & Hutchinson, J. W. (1985). The influence of affective reactions to advertising:
Direct and indirect mechanisms of attitude changes, In: L. F. Alwitt & A. A. Mitchell
(Eds), *Psychological processes and advertising effects: Theory, research and applications*
(pp. 65–87). Hillsdale, NJ: Lawrence Erlbaum Associates.

Park, C. W., & Young, S. M. (1984). *The effects of involvement and executional factors of a
television commercial on brand attitude formation.* Report no. 84-100. Cambridge, MA:
Marketing Science Institute.

Petty, R. E., Cacioppo, J. T., & Schuman, D. (1983). Central and peripheral routes to advertising effectiveness: The moderating role of involvement. *Journal of Consumer
Research, 10*(September), 135–146.

Schacter, D. L. (1985). Priming of old and new knowledge in amnesic patients and normal subjects. *Annals of the New York Academy of Science, 444*(January), 41–53.

Shamdasani, P. N., Stanaland, A. J. S., & Tan, J. (2001). Location, location, location: Insights for advertising placement on the Web. *Journal of Advertising Research, 41*(4), 7–21.

Shapiro, S. (1999). When an ad's influence is beyond our conscious control: Perceptual and conceptual fluency effects caused by incidental ad exposure. *Journal of Consumer Research, 26*(June), 16–36.

Shapiro, S., MacInnis, D. J., & Heckler, S. E. (1997). The effects of incidental ad exposure on the formation of consideration sets. *Journal of Consumer Research, 24*(June), 94–104.

Shimp, T. A. (1981). Attitude toward the ad as a mediator of consumer brand choice. *Journal of Advertising, 10*(2), 9–15.

Stern, J. (1997). *Advertising on the web: What makes people click.* Indianapolis, IN: Que Corporation.

Stevenson, J. S., Bruner, G. C., & Kumar, A. (2000). Webpage background viewer attitudes. *Journal of Advertising Research, 40*(1/2), 29–34.

Stuart, E. W., Shimp, T. A., & Engle, R. W. (1987). Classical conditioning of consumer attitudes: Four experiments in an advertising context. *Journal of Consumer Research, 14*(December), 334–349.

Vanhule, M. (1994). Mere exposure and the cognitive–affective debate revisited. *Advances in Consumer Research, 21*, 264–269.

Yoon, S.-J., & Kim, J.-H. (2001). Is the Internet more effective than traditional media? Factors affecting the choice of media. *Journal of Advertising Research, 41*(6), 53–60.

Zajonc, R. B. (1980). Feeling and thinking: Preferences need no inferences. *American Psychologist, 35*(2), 151–175.

Zajonc, R. B., Pietromonaco, P., & Bargh, J. (1982). Independence and interaction of affect and cognition. In: M. S. Clark & S. T. Fiske (Eds), *Affect and cognition* (pp. 211–227). Hillsdale, NJ: Lawrence Erlbaum.

WEBSITE EVALUATION FACTORS AND VIRTUAL COMMUNITY LOYALTY IN KOREA

Kyung Hoon Kim and Yong Man Jung

ABSTRACT

With the growth of the internet, more attention is being paid to new uses of the internet. This study examines loyalty to 'virtual communities' that internet users participate in. A research model is developed to describe the relationship between website evaluation factors and virtual community loyalty. Results are consistent with the predictions of the model.

INTRODUCTION

Recent developments in internet technology and in the availability of internet access have been rapidly implemented in Korea. Many Korean websites are now appearing on the internet in order to satisfy customers' various needs. In terms of number of sites, 'virtual community' was ranked as the second biggest category in Korean websites in 2005.

In April 2005, over 12.1 million Korean subscribers were using high-speed internet broadband service. Among those subscribers, over 6.7 million Koreans used XDSL service, which ranked as the most used service and over 4.2 million Koreans used cable modem type internet services. Over 1.2 million Koreans

Cross-Cultural Buyer Behavior
Advances in International Marketing, Volume 18, 231–252
Copyright © 2007 by Elsevier Ltd.
All rights of reproduction in any form reserved
ISSN: 1474-7979/doi:10.1016/S1474-7979(06)18010-2

were using high-speed internet services provided by their own apartment complexes. Korea introduced website domains in the Korean language in August 2003. As of April 2005, 608,725 domains existed in this form. These trends of internet related development have helped to create a more favorable environment in which Korean users can access virtual communities (NIDA, 2005).

Recently, virtual communities in Korea have been rapidly increasing. As of 2005, 949 Korean websites hosted numerous virtual communities, and over 14 million people are visiting these Korean virtual communities daily. These figures suggest that virtual communities are significant tools in influencing consumer's purchase behavior (Market Cast, 2005).

Koreans are known for their collectivism which has originated from old, agricultural traditions. Even though the culture is rapidly changing now, collectivism remains as one of the most important values in Korean society. Collectivism has helped in the fast adoption of the virtual community concept in Korea. Talukder and Yeow (2006) found the impact of individualism and of collectivism on gaps of technology, of marketing, and of culture in virtual communities.

It is well documented that a virtual community can help marketers increase the performance of their marketing activities such as brand loyalty, consumer trust, promotion, relationship building, and customer loyalty (Ko, Kim, & Kwon, 2006; Farquhar & Rowley, 2006; Koh & Kim, 2004; Flavian & Guinaliu, 2005, 2006; Talukder & Yeow, 2006; Holland & Baker, 2001; Kim, Lee, & Hiemstra, 2004; Figallo, 1998; Kim, 2000).

In order to access such benefits, marketers need to understand how users evaluate virtual communities. The performance of virtual communities should be also studied along with virtual community loyalty. Customer loyalty has been one of the most important variables used to measure the performance of successful marketing programs. These issues are critical in planning and in marketing successful virtual communities.

Liu and Arnett (2000) found that the quality of information, the possibility of learning, the system quality, the system usage, and the service quality influenced customer's evaluations of websites. They concluded that the quality of information and service, the system usage, the interesting characteristics, and the system design played significant roles in making websites successful. Their findings were based upon the data collected from webmasters of Fortune 1000 companies.

Palmer (2002) studied customer orientation of websites. He found that the site design, the ease of use, the inclusion of multimedia technology, and the ease of download were significant for the success of websites.

The studies mentioned above suggest that researching evaluation factors are important in understanding the success of websites (Besty, 1999). No study has been done to analyze the relationship between website evaluation factors and virtual community loyalty. Thus, studying the relationship between website evaluation factors and its' members' loyalty toward the virtual community will help marketers to understand the dynamics involved in marketing virtual communities.

The purposes of this study were to, first, review past research on evaluation factors of Korean websites and virtual community loyalty in Korea, second, to set up a research model describing the relationship between website evaluation factors and virtual community loyalty in Korea based upon the research hypotheses generated from the literature review, and third, to test the research hypotheses and draw marketing implications from the results of the research hypotheses tests.

LITERATURE REVIEW

Virtual Community

The concept of virtual community, as with any group of people who share a common bond, is not dependent on physical interaction or on common geographic location (McDonough, 1997; Bell & Newby, 1972; Hillery, 1995; Poplin, 1979; Wellman et al., 1996). However, tools for computer-mediated communication have recently permitted the construction of low-cost, online, virtual community infrastructures with a global reach (Kim & Bang, 2005). Such technologies support virtual communities that consist of a web of complex relationships in a way that was not previously possible. Several thousand virtual communities are now accessible over the web. These typically require members to register before allowing access to discussion forums or to conferences, for example. Such subject-specific virtual meeting places are seeded with content by virtual community hosts. These hosts also mediate the postings within each conference and 'police' online behavior so that it adheres to community-accepted norms.

Hagel and Armstrong (1996, 1997) explained their concept of virtual community. They defined virtual communities as computer-mediated spaces where there was an integration of content and communication with an emphasis on member-generated content. The other three defining characteristics of a virtual community are a distinctive focus on membership, the integration of content and communication, and a choice of competing vendor offers. Such communities have social and commercial purposes. They not only serve as a marketing feedback tool and as new idea conduits, but they also act as a check on quality and social responsibility. In such communities, customers own companies, rather than companies owning customers.

Kozinets (2002) classified virtual communities based on five structures: first, boards – electronic bulletin boards, for example, USE-NET and newsgroups; second, rings – thematically linked web pages; third, lists – e-mail lists united by a common topic or interest; fourth, dungeons – themed virtual locations in which interactions are structured by role playing rules; fifth, chat rooms – unthemed virtual locations loosely organized around common interests. The boards, rings, and lists use asynchronous and time-delayed communication, whereas dungeons and chat rooms use synchronous, real-time communication. The former serves an information selling purpose, while the latter serves social and relational purposes (Carter, 2005; Catterall & Maclaran, 2001).

Fernbank (1999) classified virtual communities based on their common value systems, norm, rules, and on their sense of identity and association. Virtual communities are also classified based on their cultural composition and the unique collective sense which members share (Leimeister, Ebner, & Krcmar, 2005; Nelson & Otnes, 2005).

Moreover, virtual communities are classified by whether they are initiated by a company or formed by customers independently. In the former, many corporate websites encourage customers to form virtual communities by having a discussion list or a bulletin board (Wellman, 2005; Catterall & MacLaran, 2001; Alper, 1998; Ward, 1999). This move is motivated by a desire to provide easier company-to-customer contact and to encourage customers' loyalty. In the latter, many customers form their own virtual communities independently. As such, they are free from any company control; examples include newsgroups devoted to Harley Davidson motorcycles (Schouten & McAlexander, 1995), to Saab cars, and to Macintosh computers (Muniz & O'Guinn, 1998).

Farquhar and Rowley (2006) mentioned that creating and maintaining an online community requires resources and commitment on the part of the community host. Specific aspects of community management that need attention including:

(a) *Website content*: Content may derive from the community organizer or community members, and community sites often have elements of both. A key role for the organizer is to ensure depth, currency, and quality of content. This involves not only supplying and structuring content, but also managing member created content.

(b) *Member engagement*: Member contribution to a community is vital to its success. Too many voyeurs or lurkers who learn from other contributions but who do not make their own contribution will reduce the level of interactivity in the community. Member behavior also needs to be managed through codes of conduct, and where necessary, interventions. Both members and hosts need to respect member privacy (Suh & Kim, 2002).

(c) *Business viability*: Advertisers expect value for advertising fees and commissions. If online communities cannot deliver value, then revenue will decline, and the business viability of the community may be in question. Critical mass focus, level of member visits, and engagement are important facilitators of business viability.

Thus, in this study, to accommodate a broader range of the virtual community with consumption related purpose, we define the virtual community as a 'group of people with common interests or goals related to consumption purpose, interacting for knowledge sharing predominantly in cyberspace.'

Website Evaluation Factors

This study attempts to extract evaluation factors of websites from Hong and Jung's (2000) research. It is called the 3C-D-T model (Fig. 1).

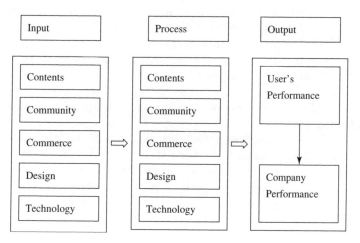

Fig. 1. 3C-D-T Model.

There are three phases in this model called input, process, and output. This model assumes that the construction and operation of websites influences the performance of the website.

Input is the evaluation of the relationships between the construction of a website and a company's business strategy. Process is the evaluation of the relationship between the company's website's strategy and the operation of the website. Output is the evaluation of the user's perceived level of performance resulting from the construction and operation of the website.

Evaluation factors of input and of process consist of contents, community, commerce, design, and technology. Variables measuring these evaluation factors consist of items for users, web specialists, and industry specialists. Factors of input are evaluated by web specialists. Factors of process are evaluated by industry specialists and web specialists. Finally, factors of output are evaluated by users, web specialists, and industry specialists (Choi, Lee, & Hwang, 2005; Kim, Kwak, & Nam, 2004; Delone & Mclean, 1992; Edwards, 1998; Spink, Bateman, & Jansen, 1999; Susan, 1997).

Constructs of evaluation factors are contents, community, commerce, design, and technology.

(1) *Contents*: It refers to the information and the related materials on websites. It is one of the most important evaluation factors for the websites. Sub-constructs of contents consist of update, easy to understand, diverse, useful, and accurate.
(2) *Community*: It refers to a group of people meeting in cyberspace where users can partake in various activities which satisfy their common interests. Sub-constructs of community consist of accommodation, incentives, communication, identity, and member's activities.
(3) *Commerce*: It is the relationship between a company's website strategy and its marketing strategy. Sub-constructs of commerce consist of transaction, business strategy, marketing, customer service, and reliability (Eighmey, 1997; Eighmey & McCord, 1998; Liu, Arnett, Capella, & Beatty, 1997).
(4) *Design*: It is the relationship between the information provided by the website and its visual factors. Sub-constructs of design consist of interaction, information structure, navigation, and visual factors.
(5) *Technology*: It refers to the technology used to construct the website and the technology used to operate the website. Sub-constructs of technology consist of security and capacity (Cho & Cheon, 2003; Davis, 1989).

Virtual Community Loyalty

Studies of loyalty toward communities on the internet have just been started. Jun (2002) studied the relationship between the lifestyle of members of any given virtual community and their loyalty toward the website. Lifestyle of virtual community members consisted of contents, commerce, community, and communication. Loyalty toward the website consisted of intention to revisit and intention to recommend the website. In his study, the type of virtual community was the mediating variable. It consisted of alumni, avatar, chatting, and same interest groups.

Oh (2002) studied the relationship between the characteristics of contents and the virtual community loyalty. Characteristics of contents consisted of three constructs: interface, information contents, and service for users. Interface consisted of structural clarity and search convenience. Information contents consisted of the basic information contents, quality of information, and interaction of information contents. Service for users consisted of only one construct called basic service quality for users.

Kwak's (2001) research in virtual communities tested the relationships among the operational factors, the reliability, and the usefulness of the virtual community and the community identity, and the loyalty toward the virtual community. Operational factors consisted of objectives, leadership, profile of member, regulation, events, closeness to reality, and small group.

Koh and Kim (2003) studied the loyalty toward the virtual community provider as community service provider's outcome. They found knowledge-sharing activity influences community participation and community promotion. Community promotion was further found to influence loyalty toward the virtual community provider.

Kim et al. (2004) found that the sense of the online virtual community influences customers' loyalty. Specifically, loyalty to the online virtual community and loyalty to the portal site was measured. Among the results, customers' loyalty was found to influence travel product purchases.

Virtual community loyalty has been tested with its relationship to contents characteristics, lifestyle of virtual community members, and operational factors of virtual communities (Flavian & Guinaliu, 2006). However, the influence of website evaluation factors on virtual community loyalty has never been tested empirically. Thus, it is worthwhile to find out if website evaluation factors influence virtual community loyalty.

RESEARCH MODEL AND HYPOTHESES

Research Model

Based upon results of literature review in related areas, the following research model (Fig. 2) was constructed. This model describes the relationships between website evaluation factors and virtual community loyalty.

Research Hypotheses

The following research hypotheses were generated from our research models based upon reviewing past research studies in order to analyze relationships between the 'website evaluation factors' and 'virtual community loyalty.'

H1. Contents of the virtual community site positively influences virtual community loyalty.

H2. Community of the virtual community site positively influences virtual community loyalty.

H3. Commerce of the virtual community site' positively influences virtual community loyalty.

H4. Design of the virtual community site positively influences virtual community loyalty.

H5. Technology of the virtual community site positively influences virtual community loyalty.

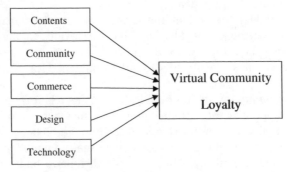

Fig. 2.   Relationships between Website Evaluation Factors and Virtual Community Loyalty.

METHOD

Measurement

Contents, community, commerce, design, and technology were measured by 5-point Likert scales (see Table 1). Contents were measured by five sub-constructs: update, easy to understand, diverse, useful, and accurate.

Table 1. Operationalization of Constructs in our Research Model.

Construct	Sub-Construct	Variables
Contents	Update	Information update, indication of updating'dates, regular update
	Easy to understand	Title, summary information, uses of graphics, charts and images
	Diverse	Variety of information, information of special fields
	Useful	Useful for the solution, number of frequency of user's visits
	Accurate	Grammar, reliability of information
Community	Accommodation	Variety of groups
	Incentives	Information (news and cases), motivation program, educational materials
	Communication	Discussion, forum, chatting room
	Identity	Vision, mission and goals of community, member registration
	Member's activities	Member's participation, off-line event
Commerce	Transaction	Order process, order information, retrieving, order carrying out/delivery
	Business strategy	Value creation, strategic alliance, relationship between website and company strategy
	Marketing	Customized marketing, market segmentation, branding website
	Customer service	Communication with customers, handling customer's needs, customization
	Reliability	Reliability of company
Design	Interaction	Dialogue between system and users, menu function
	Information structure	Structure of website
	Navigation	Easy to navigate
	Visual factors	Layout of graphics and letters
Technology	Security	Server system security, database system security, network firewall, backup recovery system
	Capacity	Connection time, loading time, transaction processing time, number of people connected at the same time, system stability (number of downloads)

Community was measured by five sub-constructs: accommodation, incentives, communication, identity, and member's activities. Commerce was measured by five sub-constructs: transaction, business strategy, marketing, customer service, and reliability. Design was measured by four sub-constructs: interaction, information structure, navigation, and visual factors. Technology was measured by two sub-constructs: security and capacity.

Data Collection

Data for this study were collected by using online questionnaires. Samples for this study consisted of members of Korean virtual communities which promote personal relationships at the following portals: Daum, Naver, iloveschool, Sayclub, Saycupid, and MSN. We posted our online questionnaire on bulletin boards of those virtual communities since no mailing list was available for sampling due to privacy restrictions. An internet coupon of US$2 was offered to respondents.

A pilot study was conducted during the first week of March 2005. Fifty questionnaires were collected in the pilot test. Based upon the results of the data analysis from the pilot study, reliability and validity of the questionnaire items were analyzed. Some of questions were improved based upon results of reliability and validity analyses.

The main data collection was conducted for one month during March and April of 2005. In all, 300 questionnaires were collected from members of Korean virtual communities of which 271 questionnaires were found to be usable for the analysis.

ANALYSIS

Sample Characteristics

Use of Website for Virtual Community
Daum was the website most frequently used as a virtual community (53.4%). Cyworld was the second most frequently used site (19.4%). Naver was the third and Say-Club was the fourth site (see Table 2).

Virtual Community Characteristics
The most frequently used characteristic of the virtual community was computer/internet (22.3%). The second most frequently used characteristic of the

Table 2.   Use of Website for Virtual Community in Korea.

Virtual Community	Number of Users	Percentage
Daum	135	53.4
Cyworld	49	19.4
Naver	21	8.3
Say-Club	18	7.0
Damoim	8	3.1
Dreamwiz	5	2.0
Yahoo	5	2.0
Birdybirdy	4	1.6
Miscellaneous	8	3.2
Total	253	100

virtual community was friendship. Hobby/recreation, broadcasting/entertainment, and school/alumni were third, fourth, and fifth, respectively (see Table 3).

Visiting Time for Virtual Community
For visiting time for the virtual community, 'less than 15 min' was found to be the most frequently cited time. '15–30 min' of visiting time for virtual community was ranked as the second most frequently cited time and 30 min to one hour was third (see Table 4).

Demographics
Regarding gender, 32.2% of the samples were males and 67.8% of the samples were females. Regarding age distribution, 69.1% of respondents were 15–24 years old, 16.7% were less than 14 years old, 10.8% were 25–29 years old, and 3.3% were 30–39 years old. Regarding occupations, 90.7% were students, 6.7% were salaried men, 1.5% were professionals, 0.7% were housewives, and 0.4% reported miscellaneous occupations. In regards to experience of internet usage, 35.9% had used the internet for 6–7 years, 31.5% had used the internet for 4–5 years, 24.1% had used the internet more than 7 years, and 7.0% had used the internet for 2–3 years, and 1.5% had used the internet for less than 1 year. Concerning the time of using virtual communities during a day, 41.4% were found to use virtual communities after 21:00. 37.3% were found to use virtual communities during 18:00–21:00. 10.4% were found to use virtual communities during 15:00–18:00. 6.3% were found to use virtual communities during 12:00–15:00, and 4.5% were found to use virtual communities during 09:00–12:00.

Table 3. Characteristics of Virtual Community in Korea.

Virtual Community Characteristics	Number of Users	Percentage
Computer/internet	58	22.3
Friendship	47	18.1
Hobby/recreation	23	8.8
Broadcasting/entertainment	20	7.7
School/alumni	18	6.9
Culture/art	15	5.8
Game	13	5.0
Fan club	13	5.0
Religion	11	4.2
Sports/leisure	10	3.8
Education/foreign language	8	3.1
Cartoon/animation	8	3.1
Region	5	1.9
Female matters	3	1.2
Living/health	3	1.2
Drama/movie	3	1.2
Politics/law	1	0.4
Economics/finance	1	0.4
Total	260	100

Table 4. Visiting Time for Virtual Community.

	Less than 15 min	15–30 min	30 min to 1 h	1–2 h	Longer than 2 h	Total
Number of users	72	99	67	22	10	270
Percentage	26.7	36.8	24.8	8.1	3.7	100

When asked about where the virtual community was used, 78.5% used virtual communities at their homes, while 8.5% used virtual communities at their school, and 8.5% used virtual communities at the PC room. 3.0% used virtual communities at their companies.

Reliability and Validity

Reliability
Cronbach's alpha was used to analyze reliability levels of the questionnaire items. Reliability analyses were done for six constructs. Cronbach's alpha's

Table 5. Reliability Analysis of Website Evaluation Factors.

Construct	Number of Items	Cronbach's Alpha
Contents	6	0.8861
Community	7	0.8432
Commerce	10	0.8809
Design	7	0.8635
Technology	6	0.8093

ranged from 0.8093 to 0.8861 (see Table 5). These alpha levels were good enough to be used for further statistical analyses in terms of Kim's (1998) reliability research.

Validity
Table 6 shows the results of the factor analysis in analyzing the validity of the questionnaire items. VARIMAX rotation was employed to clarify results of the factor analysis. Factor analysis showed 6-factor solutions. Website evaluation factors had five constructs to be measured. Factor analysis showed that the questionnaire items measuring design, contents, technology, and community were found to be valid. Only the items measuring commerce were found to be divided into two groups. Variables measuring commerce were not grouped with variables measuring other constructs. Thus, we can conclude that items measuring commerce had a high enough level of the validity to be used for the further analysis.

Testing Research Hypotheses

Relationship between Contents and Virtual Community Loyalty
Results of the multiple regression analysis indicated that the content of a website significantly influences virtual community loyalty (see Table 7). F value (15.689) of the regression model was found to be significant (p-value: 0.000). R^2 was 0.275. Diversity and reliability of member's information were found to positively influence virtual community loyalty. P-values of t-test for these two variables were less than 0.05.

Relationship between Community and Virtual Community Loyalty
Results of the multiple regression analysis indicated that the community of the website significantly influences virtual community loyalty. F value (12.543) of the regression model was found to be significant (p-value: 0.000).

Table 6.   Factor Analysis: Factor Loadings.

Variable	Factor 1	Factor 2	Factor 3	Factor 4	Factor 5	Factor 6
Design 2	*0.749*	0.109	0.152	0.159	0.164	7.618E−02
Design 4	*0.701*	0.267	0.143	0.185	5.786E−02	0.183
Design 5	*0.682*	0.102	0.190	0.234	0.275	−4.9E−02
Design 1	*0.654*	0.215	0.206	0.261	0.242	5.362E−02
Design 6	*0.641*	0.201	0.193	0.184	0.148	7.360E−02
Design 3	*0.595*	5.022E−02	−0.129	0.209	−9.7E−03	0.363
Design 7	*0.585*	0.186	0.114	8.070E−02	0.248	0.106
Contents 3	0.207	*0.797*	9.395E−02	0.175	0.201	1.305E−05
Contents 2	0.223	*0.775*	0.176	7.472E−02	0.181	9.722E−02
Contents 5	8.305E−02	*0.764*	9.659E−02	0.139	0.114	0.104
Contents 1	0.258	*0.689*	0.169	0.135	0.311	5.279E−02
Contents 4	0.138	*0.664*	5.998E−02	0.113	0.338	0.160
Contents 6	0.142	*0.594*	1.687E−02	0.174	0.128	9.119E−02
Commerce 1	0.187	0.161	*0.801*	0.165	8.921E−02	0.164
Commerce 4	0.115	−5.5E−02	*0.793*	2.738E−02	9.350E−02	7.345E−02
Commerce 2	8.084E−02	0.261	*0.756*	5.987E−02	0.131	0.139
Commerce 3	0.129	8.919E−02	*0.717*	8.668E−02	1.658E−02	0.217
Technology 2	0.198	1.299E−02	9.871E−02	*0.760*	0.146	1.244E−02
Technology 5	0.140	0.223	6.668E−02	*0.724*	8.123E−03	0.156
Technology 3	0.197	−4.1E−02	8.553E−02	*0.714*	9.685E−02	−3.1E−02
Technology 4	0.160	0.247	3.256E−02	*0.646*	0.113	0.165
Technology 1	0.221	0.228	0.213	*0.644*	0.107	−6.0E−02
Technology 6	0.145	0.157	−0.206	*0.484*	3.337E−02	0.239
Community 6	4.898E−02	0.108	0.109	7.154E−02	*0.680*	0.069
Community 7	0.148	0.215	0.127	3.715E−02	*0.658*	7.026E−04
Community 3	0.267	0.256	−9.1E−02	0.133	*0.619*	0.320
Community 2	0.199	0.339	5.674E−02	0.111	*0.587*	0.250
Community 4	0.309	0.226	5.566E−02	0.180	*0.559*	3.556E−02
Community 5	0.284	0.302	9.751E−02	0.112	*0.499*	5.068E−02
Commerce 7	9.916E−02	9.503E−02	0.180	5.977E−02	0.185	*0.793*
Commerce 8	−1.4E−02	2.889E−02	0.160	5.793E−02	0.335	*0.666*
Commerce 6	0.230	0.141	0.395	3.602E−02	1.095E−02	*0.645*
Commerce 5	0.294	0.173	0.428	0.158	5.625E−02	*0.509*
Commerce 10	0.361	0.235	0.382	9.315E−02	5.671E−02	*0.400*
Commerce 9	0.232	−1.8E−02	0.322	2.432E−02	0.292	*0.387*

R^2 was 0.259. Active member's participation was found to positively influence loyalty toward the virtual community (see Table 8). *P*-values of *t*-test for this variable was less than 0.05.

Relationship between Commerce and Virtual Community Loyalty
Results of the multiple regression analysis indicated that the commerce of the website significantly influences virtual community loyalty. *F* value (4.051) of the regression model was found to be significant (*p*-value: 0.000).

Table 7. Relationship between Contents and Virtual Community Loyalty.

Contents	Virtual Community Loyalty			
	Beta	Standard Error	t-Value	p-Value
Constant	1.410	0.205	6.893	0.000
Update	0.126	0.067	1.871	0.062
Easy to understand	−6.4E−02	0.080	−0.804	0.422
Diverse	0.221	0.078	2.849	0.005
Useful	8.830E−02	0.061	1.438	0.152
Reliability of contents	−6.5E−02	0.073	−0.886	0.377
Reliability of member's information	0.194	0.060	3.248	0.001

$R^2 = 0.275$, $F = 15.689$, Significance $= 0.000$.

Table 8. Relationship between Community and Virtual Community Loyalty.

Community	Virtual Community Loyalty			
	Beta	Standard Error	t-Value	p-Value
Constant	1.149	0.225	5.103	0.000
Variety	6.936E−02	0.056	1.234	0.218
Member's participation boundary	7.601E−02	0.059	1.284	0.200
Incentives	0.116	0.065	1.789	0.075
Communication	0.105	0.059	1.788	0.075
Identity	5.889E−02	0.055	1.064	0.288
Activation of off-line	3.656E−02	0.057	0.647	0.518
Active member's participation	0.118	0.057	2.061	0.040

$R^2 = 0.259$, $F = 12.543$, Significance $= 0.000$.

R^2 was 0.143. The variety of shopping malls and the managing of a customer service department were found to positively influence loyalty toward the virtual community (see Table 9). P-values of t-test for these two variables were less than 0.05.

Relationship between Design and Virtual Community Loyalty
Results of the multiple regression analysis indicated that the design of the website significantly influences virtual community loyalty. F value (13.587) of the regression model was found to be significant (p-value: 0.000). R^2 was 0.276. Information structure was found to positively influence loyalty

Table 9. Relationship between Commerce and Virtual Community Loyalty.

Commerce	Virtual Community Loyalty			
	Beta	Standard Error	t-Value	p-Value
Constant	1.958	0.241	8.109	0.000
Variety of products	−1.8E−02	0.078	−0.234	0.815
Variety of shopping malls	0.144	0.073	1.982	0.049
Variety of payment methods	−5.3E−03	0.063	−0.084	0.933
Order processing convenience	0.113	0.066	−1.698	0.091
Branding website	7.662E−02	0.074	1.042	0.298
Investment to website	−1.9E−02	0.073	−0.263	0.792
Customized marketing service	3.925E−02	0.074	0.531	0.596
Communication with customers	−8.6E−03	0.069	−0.124	0.902
Managing customer service department	0.143	0.068	2.096	0.037
Reliability of company	0.137	0.072	1.900	0.059

$R^2 = 0.143$, $F = 4.051$, Significance $= 0.000$.

Table 10. Relationship between Design and Virtual Community Loyalty.

Design	Virtual Community Loyalty			
	Beta	Standard Error	t-Value	p-Value
Constant	0.941	0.247	3.804	0.000
Interaction	6.176E−02	0.069	0.900	0.369
Information structure	0.166	0.072	2.319	0.021
Easy to navigate	1.682E−04	0.060	0.003	0.998
Layout of graphics and letters	0.130	0.072	1.818	0.070
Easy to locate the current page	0.119	0.063	1.884	0.061
Consistency in description	3.513E−02	0.067	0.522	0.602
Proper colors and fonts	0.103	0.061	1.708	0.089

$R^2 = 0.276$, $F = 13.587$, Significance $= 0.000$.

toward the virtual community (see Table 10). *P*-values of *t*-test for this variable was less than 0.05.

Relationship between Technology and Virtual Community Loyalty
Results of the multiple regression analysis indicated that the technology of the website significantly influences virtual community loyalty. *F* value (12.878) of the regression model was found to be significant (*p*-value: 0.000).

Table 11. Relationship between Technology and Virtual Community Loyalty.

Technology	Virtual Community Loyalty			
	Beta	Standard Error	t-Value	p-Value
Constant	1.396	0.218	6.394	0.000
Server system security	7.528E−02	0.056	1.352	0.177
Capacity of the site	0.187	0.067	2.663	0.008
Stability of the site system	−4.1E−02	0.064	−0.641	· 0.522
State of the art web technology	0.186	0.056	3.295	0.001
Mypage and storage capacity	1.888E−02	0.066	0.284	0.777
Stability of personal information	0.119	0.049	2.447	0.015

$R^2 = 0.234$, $F = 12.878$, Significance $= 0.000$.

R^2 was 0.234. Capacity of the site, state-of–the-art web technology and stability of personal information were found to positively influence loyalty toward the virtual community (see Table 11). P-values of t-test for these three variables were less than 0.05.

Results of Testing Research Hypotheses
The five research hypotheses were tested by using multiple regression analysis. Five multiple regression models for the five research hypotheses were found to be significant. T-test results for variables in the regression models revealed that there is more than one significant variable in each regression model. All of significant variables in regression models were found to influence dependent variables positively.

By analyzing R^2, design and contents constructs had the strongest influences on virtual community loyalty. Community's influence was the second strongest and technology was the third strongest. Commerce had the least influence on virtual community loyalty.

Thus, all of the research hypotheses in this study were found to be supported.

CONCLUSION

Summary

This study analyzed the relationship between evaluation factors of the website and the virtual community loyalty.

The five research hypotheses were tested by using multiple regression analysis. Five sub-constructs of evaluation factors of the website were found to positively influence virtual community loyalty.

Design and contents were found to be two most important evaluation factors for virtual community loyalty.

By analyzing individual variables in regression models, this study found the diversity and the reliability of member's information in contents, the active member's participation in community, the variety of shopping malls, and the managing of customer service departments were found to positively influence loyalty. In commerce, information structure in community and capacity of the site, state-of-the-art web technology and stability of personal information in technology were also found to positively influence virtual community loyalty.

Implications

The following marketing implications were drawn from the findings of the research hypotheses:

First, this study found that the design and the contents of a virtual community site to be the most important evaluation factors influencing virtual community loyalty in Korea. Thus, the virtual community manager should carefully monitor members' satisfaction of his or her virtual community site. Also it is critical to benchmark other virtual communities' contents and design since Korean virtual community sites are changing rapidly.

Second, marketers of a virtual community should make sure that their virtual communities have a variety of information for their members. Diversity of contents was found to positively influence virtual community loyalty in the data analysis of this study. The diversification of information provided by virtual communities will also attract more future members and also improve customer retention (Kotler & Gary, 2006).

Third, member's information should be managed reliably. This issue is related to the security of member's information. Reliability of member's information and stability of managing member's information were found to positively influence virtual community loyalty in the data analysis of this study. If members of community feel their personal information is not carefully managed by the community, then they will not continue to participate in those communities in the future. Member's confidence in a community's reliable management along with a high level of security for member's information will ensure a high number of participants and traffic in the virtual community.

Fourth, this study found that active member participation was found to positively influence virtual community loyalty. Virtual community marketers should create programs to motivate users to participate in the virtual community more actively. For example, small groups within the virtual community can be organized by the virtual community in order to satisfy the needs of those who share common interests.

Fifth, the R^2 of the multiple regression model analyzing the relationship between commerce and virtual community loyalty was found to be the smallest (0.143) compared to those of other regression models in this study. This may suggest that members may shop at specialized internet shopping malls. Marketers of virtual community should not urge their members to shop at their community. However, they can provide their members with product-related information through their virtual community sites. This may help their members to purchase products which the virtual community promotes.

Sixth, a variety of shopping malls and customer service departments were found to positively influence virtual community loyalty from the data analysis of this study. If the virtual community wants to expand their service into the shopping mall business, they should find ways to provide or to introduce various shopping malls to their members in order to satisfy their variety of needs. Customer service departments play a strategically important role in creating a positive image for the commerce side of virtual community. Customers consider a virtual community with a customer service department to be better equipped for electronic commerce.

Seventh, regarding the design of the website, the information structure and the ease of locating the current page were found to positively influence virtual community loyalty from the results of the data analysis of this study. These findings suggest that members will be more likely to visit the virtual community again if he or she can locate the information he/she wants to find more easily. Marketers of virtual community can increase the level of virtual community loyalty by providing a better menu system to visitors.

Eighth, capacity of the site, state-of-the-art web technology, and stability of personal information were found to positively influence virtual community loyalty. Security of member's personal information plays an important role in increasing a virtual community's loyalty. The virtual community should pay attention to providing a high level of security for their users. Users of a virtual community should be informed about how their personal information can be protected, for example. Also, members who navigate in a virtual community equipped with more dynamic technology will have a high level of loyalty toward the virtual community. This can be achieved by using more advanced web technology.

Suggestions for the Future Research

Suggestions for future research based upon results and marketing implications of this study are as follows:

First, the number of virtual communities should be considered when data is collected. Sampling which takes into consideration the number of members in the virtual community site will help us obtain better data collection.

Second, measures of website evaluation factors and virtual community loyalty should be improved. Measures for those constructs used in this study can be better purified in retesting for members of various types of virtual communities.

Third, sample units used for this study consisted of mainly young members of virtual communities. Studies with more generalized samples should increase validity and reliability of data for the study in this area.

REFERENCES

Alper, A. (1998). A cyber story. *Computerworld, 32*(23), 2.

Bell, C., & Newby, H. (1972). *Community studies: An introduction to the sociology of the local community.* New York: Praeger.

Besty, (1999), *Ten c's for evaluating internet sources.* http://www.uwec.edu/library/guides/tencs.html

Carter, D. (2005). Living in virtual communities: An ethnography of human relationships in cyberspace. *Information, Communication and Society, 8*(2), 148–167.

Catterall, M., & MacLaran, P. (2001). Researching consumers in virtual worlds: A cyberspace odyssey. *Journal of Consumer Behavior, 1*(3), 228–237.

Cho, C-H., & Cheon, H. J. (2003). Korean vs. American corporate websites: Interactivity, comparative appeals and use of technology. *Journal of Korean Academy of Marketing Science, 11*, 79–101.

Choi, N. H., Lee, C. W., & Hwang, Y. Y. (2005). The study of influence factors on external information search effort in online shopping malls. *Journal of Korean Academy of Marketing Science, 15*(3), 93–116.

Davis, D. F. (1989). Perceived usefulness, perceived ease of use, and user acceptance of information technology. *MIS Quarterly*, September, pp. 319–340.

Delone, W. H., & Mclean, R. E. (1992). Information system success: The quest for the dependent variable. *Information System Research, 3*(1), 60–95.

Edwards, J. (1998). *Tips for evaluating a world wide web search.* http://www.uflib.ufl.edu/hss/ref/tips.html

Eighmey, J. (1997). Profiling user responses to commercial web sites. *Journal of Advertising Research, 37*(3), 59–66.

Eighmey, J., & McCord, L. (1998). Adding value in the information age: Users and gratification of sites on the world wide web. *Journal of Business Research, 41*, 187–194.

Farquhar, J., & Rowley, J. (2006). Relationships and online consumer communities. *Business Process Management, 12*(2), 162–177.

Fernbank, J. (1999). There is a there: Notes toward a definition of cyber community. In: S. Jones (Ed.), *Doing internet research: Critical issues and methods for examining the net* (pp. 203–220). Thousand Oaks, CA: Sage.

Figallo, C. (1998). *Internet world: Hosting web communities*. Hoboken, NJ: Wiley.

Flavian, C., & Guinaliu, M. (2005). The influence of virtual communities on distribution strategies in the internet. *International Journal of Retail and Distribution Management, 33*(6), 405–425.

Flavian, C., & Guinaliu, M. (2006). Consumer trust, perceived security and privacy policy: Three basic elements of loyalty to a web site. *Industrial Management and Data Systems, 106*(5), 601–620.

Hagel, J., & Armstrong, A. G. (1996). The real value of virtual communities. *Harvard Business Review*, May–June.

Hagel, J., & Armstrong, A. G. (1997). *Net gain: Expanding markets through virtual communities*. Cambridge, MA: Harvard Business School Press.

Hillery, G. A. (1995). Definitions of community: Areas of agreement. *Rural Sociology, 20*, 111–123.

Holland, J., & Baker, S. M. (2001). Customer participation in creating site brand loyalty. *Journal of Interactive Marketing, 15*(4), 34–45.

Hong, Il. Y., & Jung, B. H. (2000). Comprehensive evaluation model of internet website. *Journal of Korean Society of Business Administration, 17*(3), 161–180.

Jun, B. S. (2002). *Relationship between lifestyle of member of virtual community and intention to revisit*. Dissertation, Changwon National University.

Kim, A. J. (2000). *Community building on the web*. Berkeley: Peachpit Press.

Kim, K. H. (1998). An analysis of the optimum number of response categories for Korean consumers. *Journal of Korean Academy of Marketing Science, 1*, 61–86.

Kim, S. H., & Bang, H. Y. (2005). A study on service quality and switching costs of instant messenger service users. *Journal of Korean Academy of Marketing Science, 15*(1), 1–20.

Kim, S. Y., Kwak, Y. S., & Nam, Y. S. (2004). Exploring navigation pattern and site evaluation variation in a community website by mixture model at segment level. *Journal of Korean Academy of Marketing Science, 13*, 209–229.

Kim, W. G., Lee, C., & Hiemstra, S. J. (2004). Effects of an online virtual community on customer loyalty and travel product purchases. *Tourism Management, 25*, 343–355.

Ko, E., Kim, K. H., & Kwon, J. H. (2006). Impact of fashion on-line community characteristics on brand loyalty: Comparisons among lifestyle groups. *Journal of Korean Academy of Marketing Science, 16*(3), 87–106.

Koh, J., & Kim, Y.-G. (2004). Knowledge sharing in virtual communities: An e-business perspective. *Expert Systems with Applications, 26*, 155–166.

Kotler, P., & Gary, A. (2006). *Principles of marketing* (11th ed.). Upper Saddle River, NJ: Prentice-Hall.

Kozinets, R. (2002). *The field behind the screen: Using the method of netnography to research market oriented vc's*. Available at www.kellog.nwu.edu/faculty/kozinets/htm

Kwak, M. S. (2001). *Influencing factors of loyalty toward the virtual community*. Dissertation, Yonsei University.

Leimeister, J., Ebner, W., & Krcmar, H. (2005). Design, implementation and evaluation of trust-supporting components in virtual communities for patients. *Journal of Management Information Systems, 21*(4), 101–135.

Liu, C., & Arnett, P. K. (2000). Exploring the factors associated with web site success in the context of electronic commerce. *Information & Management, 38*, 22–23.

Liu, C., Arnett, P. K., Capella, M. L., & Beatty, C. R. (1997). Web sites of the fortune 500 companies: Facing customers through home pages. *Information & Management, 31*, 335–345.

Market Cast (2005). Internet marketing statistics. Available at www.marketcast.co.kr

McDonough, M. (1997). Frequently asked questions: Virtual communities. Internal paper prepared for virtual community hosts at the Thomson Virtual Communities Laboratory.

Muniz, A., & O'Guinn, T. (1998). *Brand community*. Working paper, University of Illinois at Urbana-Champaign, IL.

Nelson, M., & Otnes, C. (2005). Exploring cross-cultural ambivalence: A netnography of intercultural weeding message boards. *Journal of Business Research, 58*(1), 89–95.

NIDA (2005). *Internet statistics information system*. National Internet Development Agency.

Oh, T. Y. (2002). *Contents characteristics and member's loyalty toward the on-line community*. Dissertation, Hankuk University of Foreign Studies.

Palmer, J. W. (2002). Web site usability, design and performance metric. *Information System Research, 13*(2), 151–167.

Poplin, D. E. (1979). *Communities: A survey of theories and methods of research* (2nd ed.). New York: Macmillan Publishing Co., Inc.

Schouten, J., & McAlexander, J. (1995). Subcultures of consumption: An ethnography of the new bikers. *Journal of Consumer Research, 22*(June), 43–61.

Spink, A., Bateman, J., & Jansen, J. B. (1999). Searching the web: A survey of excite user. *Internet Research: Electronic Networking Application and Policy, 9*(2), 117–128.

Suh, M. S., & Kim, Y. K. (2002). The study about influencing factors on the member's identification in online community. *Journal of Korean Academy of Marketing Science, 10*, 111–137.

Susan, E. B. (1997). *Evaluation criteria – the good, the bad & the ugly or why it is a good idea to evaluate web source*. http://lib.nmsu.edu/instruction/evalcrit.html

Talukder, M., & Yeow, P. H. P. (2006). A study of technical, marketing, and cultural differences between virtual communities in industrially developing and developed countries. *Asia Pacific Journal of Marketing, 18*(3), 184–200.

Ward, K. (1999). The cyber-ethnographic construction of two feminist online communities. *Sociological Research Online, 4*(1). Available at www.socioresonline.org.uk

Wellman, B., Salaff, J., Dimitrova, D., Garton, L., Gulia, M., & Haythornthwaite, C. (1996). Computer networks as social networks: Collaborative work, telework and virtual community. *Annual Review of Sociology, 22*(February), 213–238.

Wellman, B. (2005). Community: From neighborhood to network. *Communication of the ACM, 48*(10), 53–55.

GLOBAL YOUTH AND MOBILE GAMES: APPLYING THE EXTENDED TECHNOLOGY ACCEPTANCE MODEL IN THE U.S.A., JAPAN, SPAIN, AND THE CZECH REPUBLIC

Shintaro Okazaki, Radoslav Skapa and Ildefonso Grande

ABSTRACT

The global mobile game industry expects spectacular growth in the coming years. Ubiquitous entertainment has been drawing much attention from the "global youth" segment, which seeks innovative, efficient, and enjoyable pastimes. However, little is known about the adoption behavior of mobile games across cultures. This study aims to fill this gap by examining the factors influencing mobile game adoption in the U.S.A., Japan, Spain, and the Czech Republic. The technology acceptance model has been extended by incorporating two variables: inherent novelty seeking and social norms. Our research model received strong support from the American and Japanese samples. However, only modest support was

Cross-Cultural Buyer Behavior
Advances in International Marketing, Volume 18, 253–270
ISSN: 1474-7979/doi:10.1016/S1474-7979(06)18011-4

found for the Czech sample. In closing, after recognizing important lim-
itations, we discuss the managerial and theoretical implications.

INTRODUCTION

Mobile phones quickly opened up new dimensions of entertainment applications by blending the virtual game world with the increased ubiquity of
the communication device. According to Nokia (2006), in 2005, the mobile
gaming market surpassed $2.43 billion in worldwide revenues. Industry an-
alysts project that this figure will reach nearly $4.02 billion by 2006, and
$10.17 billion by 2010 with downloadable mobile gaming accounting for
more than 30% of the total (Mobic, 2005).

Mobile games rapidly became an attractive, as well as a practical alternative to PC-based games because mobile games do not require advanced
computing skills. Thus, sociodemographically, they can be played by a much
broader segment of Internet and of mobile users. Among mobile users, sharp
color screens and enhanced sound features appeal especially to the youth
segment, and a significant percentage of teenagers spend much time in a small
mobile "living" space. In fact, mobile games may represent one of the most
typical "global youth" cultures, in which, despite a diversity of daily activities
and lifestyles, a common interest is shared across cultures. As a result, marketers and advertisers have begun to recognize mobile games as a platform of
branded fun for the "global teens."

Mobile games are information technology applications, and, therefore, it is
both important and necessary to examine what factors influence consumers'
adoption of such technology. However, there is a dearth of academic research
in this area, especially in a cross-cultural context. This study attempts to fill
this research gap by adopting the technology acceptance model as a research
base, but with two additional factors: inherent novelty seeking and social
norms. Our target is young mobile gamers across borders. As such, a comparative study was conducted in the U.S.A., Japan, Spain, and the Czech
Republic. These countries were chosen in an attempt to make a stronger case
for the existence of a global youth culture with different cultural backgrounds.

In what follows, we first review the relevant literature regarding the mobile gaming industry in the four countries. We then establish research questions and explain the methodology in detail. Next, we describe the results
while recognizing important limitations. In closing, we attempt to draw
theoretical and managerial implications.

Mobile Gaming Industry across Countries

Japan and Korea accounted for about the half of the $2.43 billion world-wide mobile gaming revenue in 2005, while Europe and the U.S.A. were significantly behind (Nokia, 2006). This may be partially due to the difference in mobile Internet penetration. The NPD group found that just 12% of U.S. mobile users go online, as opposed to 76% of users in Japan who surf the Web through their wireless handset (NPD Techworld, 2006). Because of this high usage of mobile Internet, Japanese consumers are also more likely to demonstrate "a higher level of usage of, and interest in, advanced mobile phone features than do consumers in the U.S." (NPD Techworld, 2006). Such "features" include wireless Web browsing, mobile email, ringtone downloads, PDA functions, graphics and screensaver downloads, mobile gaming, picture messaging, digital music listening, video messaging, and mobile TV and video.

However, the U.S. mobile gaming market is growing at a rapid pace. According to Wireless World Forum (W2F), Japan's current dominance will be eclipsed by China and by the U.S.A. in 2006 (ZGroup Mobile, 2006). One senior analyst noted that "we are beginning to see operators and game companies announce greater levels of usage of these handsets for downloading games. For example, in the five months leading up to May 2004, Verizon Wireless customers (in the U.S.A.) downloaded more than 12 million games" (Phillips, 2004). In 2003, 10 million U.S. consumers spent $77 million on downloadable, mobile games, but the industry expects that this figure will grow to reach $220 million by 2009 (Phillips, 2004). In 2005, 60% of those who played mobile games in the U.S.A. were teenagers, between the ages of 13 and 17 (NPD Techworld, 2006).

In Spain, Telefónica Móviles offers mobile gaming content to *MoviStar e-moción* customers who have access to Sega Mobile's wireless games including Depth Charge, Sega Sports Mobile Golf, and Aiai's Funhouse (Sega, 2005). Sega Mobile will adapt some of its most successful video console games to mobile handsets such that customers will be able to download these *Java2ME* games on to their cell phones. Users will have easy access to content through *MoviStar e-moción* in the *juegos-videojuegos* (games-videogames) option in the browsing menu. From here, customers can download the games they require, store them in their handset, and play them as many times as they wish, at no extra charge (Sega, 2005). According to the data provided by three carriers (Amena, Telefónica Móvi, and Vodafone), more than 18 millions SMS were sent through the networks in 2003, with Telefónica leading the market with 50% of the traffic (Noticiasdot.com, 2004).

Telefónica Móvil owns Telefónica O2 Czech Republic, which was created by the 2006 merger of fixed-line operator Český Telecom and its mobile phone unit, Eurotel (Kozáková, 2006). In the Czech Republic, mobile phone penetration was 95% in 2003, which puts the Czech Republic in fourth place among the European Union (Eurostat, 2005). However, mobile commerce has been used by only 10% of mobile users. With regard to specific applications, SMS, mobile banking, and ringtone downloads are the most popular. In 2005, Czech users downloaded approximately 50,000 games per month, and spent 1.4 million euro (SIBIS, 2003). Most frequent user segments are teenagers between the ages of 13 and 19. In contrast to other countries, 65% of "regular" players are female. However, male users tend to download more games which cost 1–3 euro each, while females tend to play preinstalled games (SIBIS, 2003).

Global Youth Culture

Taylor (2002) points out that, despite an indication of the existence of the "global teen" segment, there is a lack of empirical effort in segmentation research. In fact, the notion of a youth market is rather prototypical (see, e.g., Hassan & Katsanis, 1994), while various names such as "Gen X," "Baby Busters," or "MTV Generation," embrace this arguably homogeneous segment (Kjeldgaard, 2002). Christensen (2002) conducted a large-scale qualitative survey in Europe and found that innovation and communication are two of four primary factors that commonly attract the young generation to brands across the continent. Combining these two factors, the mobile phone became a key information technology among youth because they expect interactions to be fun and spontaneous, but, at the same time, to be private and personal (de Chenecey, 2002).

SMS-based text messaging has been used more frequently than email, because it is fast, cheap, and ubiquitous (Byfield, 2002). For example, Cadbury, McDonald's, Emap, Xbox, and 20th Century Fox all successfully used SMS as a marketing channel in targeting youth (de Kerckhove, 2002). This reflects the important observation that innovative, wireless communication technology has made the mobile phone the most important possession for European, American, and Japanese teens (Arundhati, 2002).

Based on a study of 27,000 teens in 44 countries, Moses (2000) points out that global teens indeed make up a homogeneous market that includes music, fashion, film, video games, and technology. In this respect, the gaming industry has been attempting to generate new games that garner an almost global cult, following "Pokemon," "Rockstar Games," "Grand Theft Auto," and "Super Mario Sunshine" (Arundhati, 2002). Games represent an ideal industry, in which marketers can target global youth in the same way as national youth – via television and the computer. Because the message is primarily electronic, advertising or promotion can be generated in New York, London, or Paris (Moses, 2000).

Across the world, the lives of late teens appear to be synchronized. Byfield (2002) conducted a qualitative study of boys and girls ages 16–19 years old in 10 major cities (Tokyo, Shanghai, Hong Kong, Sydney, Milan, Berlin, Madrid, Paris, London, and Mexico City). She points out that

> History, economy and culture fade into insignificance in the world of global branding. The same names appear in Tokyo and Mexico as in Sydney and Berlin. This is not surprising for established, famous global names like Nike, Sony, Pepsi, Coca-Cola and McDonald's but nowadays many of the newer, less familiar international media, technology and fashion brands feature just as often. (p. 15)

In comparison with past decades, today's youth are much less rebellious or political, and are unlikely to desire any ideological change in the world. However, while they appear to remain ambivalent toward such issues, they catch and spread a new trend via the Internet, especially if it is supported by the media (Byfield, 2002).

Clearly, there are more similarities than differences among the youth (Kjeldgaard & Askegaard, 2004; Moses, 2000). Some point out that this is partially due to westernization: Asian teens hunger for Western culture via sophisticated information technology (Arundhati, 2002). Specifically, Internet and mobile communication technology appear to be a "nice-to-have" accessory among the cross-border youth segments. As yet, however, there are few empirical studies of the factors connecting youth and information technology adoption.

The Extended Technology Acceptance Model

What are the determinants of mobile gaming adoption by the global youth segment? To address this question, we focus on the technology acceptance model (TAM), which has received considerable attention in information technology adoption (Davis, 1989; Davis, Bagozzi, & Warshaw, 1989). Originally, this model was based on the theory of reasoned action (TRA). This theory suggests that an individual's belief influences their attitude, which, in turn, shapes their behavioral intention (Ajzen & Fishbein, 1980;

Fishbein & Ajzen, 1975). TAM extended this chain to the belief–attitude–
intention–behavior relationship given that consumers' behavioral intention
to use a technology depends largely on two specific beliefs: perceived ease of
use and perceived usefulness. This original TAM is depicted in Fig. 1.

This study adopts TAM as a baseline model because it has received extensive empirical support through validations, applications, and replications
across a diverse range of information technology including the Internet (Hsu
& Lu, 2004; Moon & Kim, 2001). In this study, we propose a TAM-based
attitudinal model that focuses on three primary dimensions: ease of use
(EOU), efficiency, and fun. These dimensions capture important consumer
perceptions on the use of gaming technology.

The first dimension, EOU, refers to the extent to which an individual
believes that the use of a technology will be free of effort (Venkatesh, 2000).
EOU affects the second dimension, "efficiency," which corresponds to
"usefulness" in the TAM. Here, the concept is "it fits my life." This stems
from the utilitarian component of experiential value, encompassing both
reliability and the satisfaction that the technology provides (Mathwick,
Malhotra, & Rigdon, 2001). EOU also determines the level of hedonic
component, or "fun," which has been found to be an important addition to
the technology-based service adoption (Dabholkar & Bagozzi, 2002). This is
similar to "playfulness" in mobile Internet (Cheong & Park, 2005), and

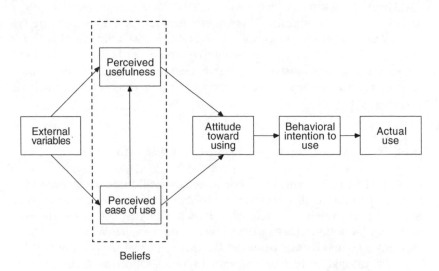

Fig. 1. Technology Acceptance Model. *Source:* Davis et al. (1989).

"perceived enjoyment" in m-commerce (Bruner & Kumar, 2005; Nysveen, Pedersen, & Thorbjørnsen, 2005). Therefore, we posit:

H1. The perceived ease of using mobile games will have a direct, positive effect on the perceived fun.

H2. The perceived ease of using mobile games will have a direct, positive effect on the perceived efficiency.

Both utilitarian and hedonic components mediate the effect of EOU and determine an overall evaluation of attitude toward mobile games. However, prior research on TAM, in various consumer contexts, indicates that EOU has only indirect effects on the attitude or intention (Bruner & Kumar, 2005; Venkatesh, 2000). On the other hand, Dabholkar and Bagozzi (2002) found that EOU acts as a direct determinant of attitude toward using technology. Our primary proposition lies in the former in that given a high usability of a mobile device, consumers are expected to have more confidence in their ability to use mobile games. Thus, EOU will not pose much influence on their attitudes. Instead, consumers' trials will depend more on psychological motives in that affective as well as cognitive components will directly influence on the attitude formation. Thus

H3. The perceived fun will have a direct, positive effect on attitude toward mobile games.

H4. The perceived efficiency will have a direct, positive effect on attitude toward mobile games.

Prior research attempts to incorporate additional factors in TAM such as perceived playfulness (Moon & Kim, 2001) and flow experience (Hsu & Lu, 2004), among others. Such extension generally improves the amount of variance explained by the model, thus, this study chooses to extend TAM by incorporating two external variables: inherent novelty seeking and social norms. First, inherent novelty seeking can be defined as the desire to seek out new stimuli (Dabholkar & Bagozzi, 2002). Here, what drives the youth to adopt mobile games is their innate propensity to seek innovative technology. This is similar to Rogers's (1995) concept of "venturesomeness." The literature suggests, as a generalized predisposition, that there is a significant relationship between new product adoption behavior and innate consumer innovativeness (Im, Bayus, & Mason, 2003). We believe that the propensity of novelty seeking among the youth will be one of the primary determinants of attitude toward mobile games. Furthermore, it affects its antecedents such as EOU and as perceived fun. This advances the following hypotheses:

H5. The inherent novelty seeking will have a direct, positive effect on the perceived ease of using mobile games.

H6. The inherent novelty seeking among the youth will have a direct, positive effect on the perceived fun.

H7. The inherent novelty seeking among the youth will have a direct, positive effect on attitude toward mobile games.

Next, social norms encompass the notion of conformity which can take three forms: informational, normative, and identification. Informational influence occurs when consumers use the behaviors and the opinions of reference group members as a potentially useful information source. Normative influence occurs when consumers fulfill group expectations in order to gain a direct reward or to avoid a sanction. Identification influence occurs when an individual has accepted the group's values as his or her own (Hawkins, Best, & Coney, 2001). Given a significant reference group influence among the youth, it is expected that individuals attempt to adopt mobile gaming to strengthen their membership or to win approval from colleagues. Thus, this factor affects not only attitude toward mobile games, but also intention to play the games. More formally

H8. The social norms will have a direct, positive effect on attitude toward mobile games.

H9. The social norms will have a direct, positive effect on the intention to play mobile games.

Finally, when people develop positive attitudes, they are likely to use the technology. However, in Davis et al.'s (1989) original model, the attitude toward using a technology was omitted because of partial mediation of the impact of beliefs on intention by attitude (Venkatesh, 2000). That is, people intend to use a technology if it is useful even if they do not have a positive attitude. However, prior research suggests that enjoyment significantly, and directly, affects online shoppers' attitude (Childers, Carr, Peck, & Carson, 2001), while the attitude mediates the effects of fun on behavioral intention to use technology-based self-service (Dabholkar & Bagozzi, 2002). Therefore, we posit

H10. The attitude toward mobile games will have a direct, positive effect on the intention to play games.

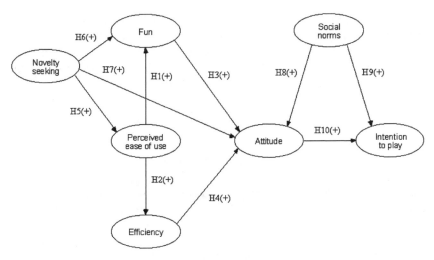

Fig. 2. Research Model.

Fig. 2 shows our research model in which the above hypotheses are summarized. In the following section, the methodology of our empirical investigations is explained in detail.

METHOD

The questionnaire consisted of two parts. In the first part, we collected demographic data, such as gender, age, monthly allowance, monthly family income, mobile phone experience, and mobile game usage. In the second part, we included question items regarding the constructs we proposed in our research model. The majority of the scale items are adopted from the existing literature, but are adapted to the mobile gaming context. All the questions were asked using a 7-point Likert scale from 1 (completely disagree) to 7 (completely agree), with 4 as an anchoring point.

The questionnaire was first prepared in English, and later translated into the respective languages by the translation–back translation method to ensure cross-cultural equivalency. The sample consisted of college students in the U.S.A., Japan, Spain, and the Czech Republic. Because the majority of mobile game users are between 16 and 25 years old, the use of a student sample was deemed to be adequate in this study. After completing the survey, we carefully examined the questionnaires and removed the incomplete questionnaires because missing data seriously distort the statistical analysis. After that, we also removed extreme outliers via box-plot analysis. As a result, we obtained 100, 165, 181, and 153 usable responses in the U.S.A., Japan, Spain, and the Czech Republic, respectively.

FINDINGS

Descriptive Statistics

Table 1 summarizes the demographic information of the respondents in each country. The gender distribution differs considerably across countries. Except for Spain, males generally outweigh females. In Japan, only one fourth of the sample was female. As the respondents consist of college students, the vast majority was between 18 and 25 years old. With regard to mobile usage experience, Japanese respondents appear to have longer experience than the others. That is, the percentage that has used mobile phone for more than six years is notably higher in Japan than in the other countries.

Concerning the actual use of mobile games, Tables 2 and 3 show the weekly usage frequency of preinstalled and of downloaded mobile games,

Table 1. Descriptive Statistics of the Respondents (%).

Demographics	U.S.A. (n = 100)	Japan (n = 165)	Spain (n = 181)	Czech Republic (n = 153)
Gender				
Male	56.1	75.2	47.0	56.9
Female	43.9	24.8	53.0	43.1
Age				
<20 years old	42.9	37.6	39.2	2.0
20–25 years old	56.1	61.2	59.7	96.1
>25 years old	1.0	1.2	1.1	2.0
Years of mobile phone use				
<1 years	8.2	0.6	3.3	0.7
1–2 years	30.6	1.8	12.7	2.6
3–4 years	28.6	22.4	37.6	23.5
5–6 years	16.3	34.5	29.8	43.1
>6 years	16.3	40.6	14.9	29.4

Table 2. Weekly Usage of Preinstalled Mobile Games (%).

Times/Week	U.S.A.	Japan	Spain	Czech Republic	Total
0	60.2	66.7	60.2	65.4	63.3
1	20.4	11.5	14.9	9.8	13.6
2	8.2	5.5	11.0	10.5	8.9
3	3.1	6.1	6.6	6.5	5.9
4	2.0	1.8	1.7	1.3	1.7
5	3.1	1.2	1.1	2.0	1.7
6	0.0	1.2	1.1	0.7	0.8
7	3.1	6.1	3.3	3.9	4.2
Total	100.0	100.0	100.0	100.0	100.0

Table 3. Weekly Usage of Downloaded Mobile Games (%).

Times/Week	U.S.A.	Japan	Spain	Czech Republic	Total
0	83.7	55.2	81.2	83.0	74.9
1	5.1	12.1	5.5	5.9	7.4
2	3.1	6.1	6.6	1.3	4.5
3	1.0	6.1	3.3	2.6	3.5
4	3.1	5.5	2.2	2.0	3.2
5	1.0	2.4	0.6	1.3	1.3
6	1.0	0.0	0.0	0.0	0.2
7	2.0	12.7	0.6	3.9	5.0
Total	100.0	100.0	100.0	100.0	100.0

respectively. For the former, the general tendency does not differ much across the countries. However, for the latter, and for the use of downloaded mobile games, Japan shows much higher usage than the other countries. Specifically, almost half of the respondents (44.8%) are likely to play downloaded mobile games at least once a week. This frequency is notably higher when compared to the other countries: 16.3% in the U.S.A., 18.8% in Spain, and 17% in the Czech Republic. Furthermore, more than 20% of the respondents in Japan play downloaded games more than four times a week (7.1% in the U.S.A., 3.4% in Spain, 7.2% in the Czech Republic). These figures appear to correspond to mobile gaming penetration, as described in our literature review, and thus justify the adequacy of our four-country samples.

Measurement Model Assessment

Following the recommendations by Anderson and Gerbing (1988), we used a two-stage data analysis approach. First, we performed a confirmatory factor analysis (CFA) on the basis of the combined data from all four countries. AMOS 5.0 was used with maximum likelihood method (Byrne, 2001). This procedure was appropriate to indicate the lowest level of reliability and validity of our measurement model. The CFA produced significant χ^2 value (χ^2_{168} = 450.57, $p < 0.001$), which was likely due to a large sample size. However, more pragmatic indices indicate an acceptable fit: goodness of fit index (GFI) = 0.93, comparative fit index (CFI) = 0.95, Tucker–Lewis index (TLI) = 0.94, and root mean square error of approximation (RMSEA) = 0.053. On this basis, we calculated the composite reliability for each score. As Table 4 shows, the scores were very high for all scales, exceeding the minimum recommended 0.50 by Hair, Black, Babin, Anderson, and Tatham (2006).

Next, we estimated the measurement model fit for all four countries separately. The results are as follows: for the U.S.A., CFI = 0.90, TLI = 0.88, RMSEA = 0.086; for Japan, CFI = 0.95, TLI = 0.94, RMSEA = 0.054; for Spain, CFI = 0.91, TLI = 0.89, RMSEA = 0.071; and for the Czech Republic, CFI = 0.94, TLI = 0.93, RMSEA = 0.053. Thus, the fit of the measurement model is deemed to be acceptable in all countries.

Finally, to compare the models cross-culturally, we also performed tests for measurement invariance because the scale intervals of the latent constructs must be comparable across countries (Steenkamp & Baumgartner, 1998). Specifically, we assessed the measurement invariance by comparing nested complete measurement models in terms of the χ^2 difference with corresponding degrees of freedom. The results show that χ^2 difference was insignificant between all six pairs of countries. On this basis, we now turn to the hypotheses testing, and compare the focal paths of interest across countries.

Table 4. Reliability of the Constructs Examined.

Constructs	No. of Items	Cronbach's α	Composite Reliability
Efficiency	3	0.71	0.88
Ease of use	3	0.70	0.88
Fun	3	0.75	0.91
Novelty seeking	3	0.71	0.86
Social norms	3	0.85	0.97
Attitude	3	0.85	0.96
Intention	3	0.93	0.99

Hypotheses Testing

We performed a structural equation modeling for each sample using the maximum likelihood method via AMOS 5.0 (Byrne, 2001). Table 5 summarizes the parameter estimates, the *t*-value and the goodness-of-fit indexes, of the structural equation models for the four countries. Except for χ^2 statistics, the fit measures were within acceptable intervals in Japan and in the Czech Republic. The χ^2 test is sensitive to the number of observed variables, and may be inappropriate as an indicator of a more complex model. Therefore, the fit measures in the U.S.A. and Spain seem to reflect somewhat misspecified models.

Hypotheses 1 and 2 posit that the perceived EOU will directly and positively affect perceived fun and perceived efficiency, respectively. To our surprise, the path from EOU to fun was not significant in any of the countries examined. On the other hand, the path from EOU to efficiency was significant in all countries except in the Czech Republic. That is, unlike previous studies on TAM in an Internet context, the perceived EOU seem to have direct effects only on the utilitarian component and not on the hedonic component.

Hypotheses 3 and 4 predict that both perceived efficiency and fun will directly, and positively, affect attitude toward mobile games. The path from fun to attitude was supported in the U.S.A. and Japan, while the path from fun was supported in the U.S.A. and Spain. That is, American youth seem to formulate their positive attitude toward mobile games when they perceive greater efficiency and fun about the games.

Hypotheses 5–7 are related to the role of inherent novelty seeking in a mobile gaming context. The path from this variable to EOU, which corresponds to Hypothesis 5, was significant in the U.S.A. and Japan, but insignificant in the others. On the other hand, the path from inherent novelty seeking to fun, encapsulated by Hypothesis 6, was significant only in Japan and Spain. By contrast, stronger support was found for Hypothesis 7 which posits the path from novelty seeking to attitude toward mobile games. This path was significant in all countries except in the Czech Republic.

Turning now to Hypotheses 8 and 9, we examine the effects of social norms on attitude toward, and on intention to play, mobile games. The first path was found to be significant in all countries except Japan, while the second was significant in Japan and the Czech Republic. Hence, the Czech Republic seems to exhibit stronger effects of social norms among the youth in terms of attitude and intention.

Finally, Hypothesis 10 anticipates that a more positive attitude toward mobile games will lead to a greater intention to play such games. This path

Table 5. Standardized Coefficient Estimates in Each Country.

			U.S.A.		Japan		Spain		Czech Republic	
			Estimate	t	Estimate	t	Estimate	t	Estimate	t
H1	Ease of use	→ Fun	0.294	1.76	0.030	0.30	0.084	0.73	0.781	1.46
H2	Ease of use	→ Efficiency	0.738	4.10***	0.362	3.12**	0.702	2.89**	1.000	1.44
H3	Fun	→ Attitude	0.263	2.19**	0.409	3.78***	0.119	1.47	0.056	0.22
H4	Efficiency	→ Attitude	0.238	2.40**	0.118	1.54	0.550	5.04***	0.528	1.84
H5	Novelty seeking	→ Ease of use	0.515	2.93**	0.350	3.03**	0.562	1.92	0.536	1.36
H6	Novelty seeking	→ Fun	0.325	1.95	0.498	3.51***	0.517	2.21**	−0.009	0.18
H7	Novelty seeking	→ Attitude	0.264	2.23**	0.551	4.07***	0.483	2.24**	0.145	1.09
H8	Social norms	→ Attitude	0.532	5.64***	0.052	0.75	0.130	2.17**	0.284	3.21**
H9	Social norms	→ Intention to play	−0.125	−1.31	0.364	4.44***	0.133	1.95	0.287	3.63***
H10	Attitude	→ Intention to play	0.918	7.52***	0.359	4.51***	0.695	8.18***	0.640	6.56***
			$n = 100$		$n = 165$		$n = 181$		$n = 153$	
			$\chi^2_{178} = 341.17$		$\chi^2_{178} = 354.57$		$\chi^2_{178} = 435.13$		$\chi^2_{178} = 290.40$	
			CFI = 0.87		CFI = 0.90		CFI = 0.85		CFI = 0.91	
			TLI = 0.84		TLI = 0.88		TLI = 0.83		TLI = 0.89	
			RMSEA = 0.097		RMSEA = 0.078		RMSEA = 0.090		RMSEA = 0.064	

Note:
**$p < 0.01$.
***$p < 0.001$.

was significant in all countries examined, thus providing the strongest support in all the hypothesized paths.

LIMITATIONS

To make our findings more objective, important limitations should be recognized. First, this study did not distinguish online versus offline mobile gamers because of the small sample size. The number of online gamers was large in Japan, but moderate in the other countries, and as such was insufficient to perform multigroup analysis. Given potential differences in online consumer behavior, the adoption model for online and for offline gamers may be different. Future research should address this issue further. Second, in our proposed model, actual behavior was not included. However, the attitude-intention chain of TAM should end with the behavioral consequence. This limitation should be overcome in the future.

DISCUSSION

In this study, we examined factors influencing mobile gaming adoption among the youth in the U.S.A., Japan, Spain, and the Czech Republic. A research model based on TAM was proposed and tested across countries.

First, this study makes an important contribution to the consumer behavior literature; it is one of the first attempts to explain mobile gaming adoption in a cross-cultural context. Despite increasing empirical research, there is a serious lack of studies that examine specific mobile service application, and cross-cultural exploration in mobile commerce research hardly exists. This study serves as one of the pioneering attempts in this area.

Second, our proposed model received the strongest support from the American and Japanese samples, in which 7 out of 10 hypotheses were supported. The Spanish sample corroborated six hypotheses. In contrast, only three hypotheses were supported by the Czech sample. One of the most likely reasons for this may lie in the differences in mobile gaming penetration across the countries. On the one hand, situational variables associated with mobile games, including distribution channel, operator support, and 3G environments, may be similar in the U.S.A. and Japan, but may differ significantly in Europe. On the other hand, Spain may be in a unique position because its largest mobile operator, Telefónica, adopted i-mode technology in 2002, and has collaborated with Sega in marketing Japanese mobile games in Spain. In this regard, the Czech mobile market has a clearly distinct structure, which may have led to the rejection of the majority of our hypotheses.

Third, it was surprising that none of the countries supported the path from EOU to fun. That is, it appears that fun does not mediate the relationship between EOU and attitude. Instead, EOU affects attitude toward mobile games only through efficiency. This originates from people having a positive affect or attitude toward mobile games because it looks easy to use, practical, and thus, "fitting into my life." This mediation effect was supported in the U.S.A. and Japan. Furthermore, EOU mediates the effect of inherent novelty seeking on efficiency. This is consistent with prior research that shows a weak direct link between EOU and attitude.

Fourth, the findings of this study provide empirical evidence of the existence of a "world youth segment" in the U.S.A., Japan, and Spain. It is reasonable to assume that a somewhat homogeneous youth segment may exist in these countries. This segment seeks innovative technology that provides efficient and enjoyable pastimes. In this context, social norms appear to affect attitude, or intention, in adopting such innovative entertainment. That is, conforming to the reference group, communication within groups, or opinion leadership, appears to play a significant role in the diffusion of innovation among the youth (Hawkins et al., 2001). This is also parallel to mobile-based "word-of-mouth" effects in which young users are likely to use this device to establish a social network (Nysveen et al., 2005).

ACKNOWLEDGMENTS

The authors gratefully acknowledge the financial support provided by the Telecommunications Advancement Foundation (Japan). They also thank Morikazu Hirose, Fumiko Nakamura, Yoshie Sano, and Kazue Shimamura for their data collection.

REFERENCES

Ajzen, I., & Fishbein, M. (1980). *Understanding attitudes and predicting social behavior*. Englewood Cliffs, NJ: Prentice-Hall.

Anderson, J. C., & Gerbing, D. W. (1988). Structural equation modeling in practice: A review and recommended two-step approach. *Psychological Bulletin, 103*, 411–423.

Arundhati, P. (2002). Global youth united. *Marketing News, 36*(22), 1, 49.

Bruner, G. C., & Kumar, A. (2005). Explaining consumer acceptance of handheld Internet devices. *Journal of Business Research, 58,* 553–558.

Byfield, S. (2002). Snapshots of youth: The lives of late teens across the world. *Young Consumers, 3*(4), 15–21.

Byrne, B. M. (2001). *Structural equation modeling with AMOS: Basic concepts, applications, and programming.* Mahwah, NJ: Lawrence Erlbaum Associates.

Cheong, J. H., & Park, M. C. (2005). Mobile Internet acceptance in Korea. *Internet Research, 15*(2), 125–140.

Childers, T., Carr, C., Peck, J., & Carson, S. (2001). Hedonic and utilitarian motivations for online retail shopping behavior. *Journal of Retailing, 77*(4), 511–535.

Christensen, O. (2002). Changing attitudes of European youth. *Young Consumers, 3*(3), 19–32.

Dabholkar, P. A., & Bagozzi, R. P. (2002). An attitudinal model of technology-based self-service: Moderating effects of consumer traits and situational factors. *Journal of the Academy of Marketing Science, 30*(3), 184–201.

Davis, F. D. (1989). Perceived usefulness. Perceived ease of use. And user acceptance of information technology. *MIS Quarterly, 13*(3), 319–339.

Davis, F. D., Bagozzi, R. P., & Warshaw, P. R. (1989). User acceptance of computer technology: A comparison of two theoretical models. *Management Science, 35*(8), 982–1003.

de Chenecey, S. P. (2002). Putting brands in their place. *Young Consumers, 4*(2), 47–50.

de Kerckhove, A. (2002). Building brand dialogue with mobile marketing. *Young Consumers, 3*(4), 37–43.

Eurostat (2005). Around 80 mobile subscriptions per 100 inhabitants in the EU25 in 2003. *Eurostat News Release 20/2005,* February 7.

Fishbein, M., & Ajzen, I. (1975). *Belief, attitude, intention and behavior: An introduction to theory and research.* Reading, MA: Addison-Wesley.

Hair, J. F., Black, W. C., Babin, B. J., Anderson, R. E., & Tatham, R. L. (2006). *Multivariate data analysis* (6th Ed.). Upper Saddle River, NJ: Prentice-Hall International.

Hassan, S. S., & Katsanis, L. P. (1994). Identification of global consumer segments. *Journal of International Consumer Marketing, 3*(2), 11–28.

Hawkins, D. I., Best, R. J., & Coney, K. A. (2001). *Consumer behavior: Building marketing strategy.* New York: McGraw-Hill.

Hsu, C. L., & Lu, H. P. (2004). Why do people play on-line games? An extended TAM with social influences and flow experience. *Information and Management, 41*(7), 853–868.

Im, S., Bayus, B. L., & Mason, C. H. (2003). An empirical study of innate consumer innovativeness, personal characteristics, and new-product adoption behavior. *Journal of the Academy of Marketing Science, 32*(1), 61–73.

Kjeldgaard, D. (2002). Youth identities and consumer culture: Navigating local landscapes of global symbols. *Advances in Consumer Research, 29,* 387–392.

Kozáková, P. (2006). Phone merger breathes new O2 into market. *Czech Business Weekly.* http://www.cbw.cz/phprs/2006030628.html

Mathwick, C., Malhotra, N., & Rigdon, E. (2001). Experiential value: Conceptualization. Measurement and application in the catalogue and Internet shopping environment. *Journal of Retailing, 77,* 39–56.

Mobic (2005). *The mobile gaming market is growing around the World with sales of $2.5 billion.* January 25. http://www.mobic.com/news/publisher/view.do?id = 3684

Moon, J. W., & Kim, Y. G. (2001). Extending the TAM for a world-wide-web context. *Information & Management, 38*(4), 217–230.

Moses, E. (2000). *The $100 billion allowance: Accessing the global teen market.* London: Wiley.

Nokia (2006). Forum Nokia PRO games zone to provide advanced support for next generation of Nokia mobile gaming. *Nokia Snap Mobile News,* March 20. http://snapmobile.nokia.com/n-gage/web/en/snapmobile/pr_03202006.jsp

Noticiasdot.com (2004). *Los españoles mandamos 18.000 millones de SMS durante el 2003.* February 23. http://www2.noticiasdot.com/publicaciones/2004/0204/2302/noticias230204/noticias230204-6.htm

NPD Techworld (2006). *Japan offers key lessons for wireless market innovation in the U.S. says the NPD group.* February 13. http://www.tekrati.com/research/News.asp?id = 6488

Nysveen, H., Pedersen, P. E., & Thorbjørnsen, H. (2005). Intention to use mobile services: Antecedents and cross-service comparisons. *Journal of the Academy of Marketing Science, 33*(3), 330–347.

Phillips, L. (2004). *Mobile games market worth €6.7bn by 2009-report.* August 30. http://www.dmeurope.com/default.asp?ArticleID = 2854

Rogers, E. M. (1995). *The diffusion of innovations* (4th Ed.). New York: Free Press.

Sega (2005). Spanish carrier Telefónica Móviles and Sega mobile. *Press Release,* May 5. http://www.segamobile.com/about.php?PageID = 58

SIBIS (Statistical Indicators Benchmarking the Information Society) (2003). *Czech Republic Country Report 2,* 44.

Steenkamp, J. B. E. M., & Baumgartner, H. (1998). Assessing measurement invariance in cross-national consumer research. *Journal of Consumer Research, 25*(1), 78–90.

Taylor, C. R. (2002). What is wrong with international advertising research? *Journal of Advertising Research, 42*(6), 48–54.

Venkatesh, V. (2000). Determinants of perceived ease of use: Integrating control, intrinsic motivation, and emotion into the technology acceptance model. *Information Systems Research, 11*(4), 342–365.

ZGroup Mobile (2006). *Mobile games market report. Games.* http://www.zgroup-mobile.com/published_games/realtimestrategy/massivedestruction/massivedestruction.html

EMPIRICAL CLASSIFICATION OF WEB SITE STRUCTURE: A CROSS-NATIONAL COMPARISON

Koo-Won Suh, Charles R. Taylor and Doo-Hee Lee

ABSTRACT

This study develops a typology of web site structure and then makes a cross-national comparison between Korea and Australia. Using a content analysis method, the study classifies 383 corporate web sites based on the typology. The study identifies two general types of web site structure: the hypermedia type and static image type and uses cluster analysis and discriminant analysis to verify the results. The study then tests predictions as to which type of web site will be more prominent in Australia versus Korea based on cultural factors. Results show that Korean firms employ the hypermedia type more frequently, whereas Australian companies are more prone to use the static image type. Cultural factors and industry-based factors are used to explain the results.

INTRODUCTION

The Web is clearly an important integrated marketing communications tool. There is no doubt that a corporate web site can provide advantages by

Cross-Cultural Buyer Behavior
Advances in International Marketing, Volume 18, 271–292
Copyright © 2007 by Elsevier Ltd.
All rights of reproduction in any form reserved
ISSN: 1474-7979/doi:10.1016/S1474-7979(06)18012-6

facilitating real-time, two-way communication. As a new and increasingly pervasive marketing communication medium, the Web has two distinctive features. The first is its hyperlink capability through which users navigate and obtain information on the Web. In contrast to traditional media, web users engage in interactive activity. Furthermore, web users can choose what information they access and where they access it, as well as determine their viewing time. In other words, web users dictate communication. As a result, web users can experience the feeling that they are in control (Markham, 1998). Additionally, the Web provides a real-time feedback function, and web users can control the communication environment.

A second distinctive feature of the web is its multi-modality (i.e., its multi-media nature involving the use of text, images, sound, and moving images including video), which can provide a richer means of information presentation. When marketing information is presented using this multimodal capability, customers may become more interested in and engaged with the message.

The importance of interactivity and multimodality in web-mediated communications (WMC) lies in their ability to enhance learning, understanding, mental engagement, and satisfaction (e.g., Dennis & Kinney, 1998; Kerpedjiev, Carenini, Green, Moore, & Roth, 1998; Oviatt & Cohen, 2000; Spector, 1995; Street & Manning, 1997). More specifically, hypermedia can enrich the quality of information and its presentation, stimulate sensory perception in a synergistic way, and enhance the experience of accessing information (e.g., Nisbett & Ross, 1980). Although traditional advertising seems to generate a kind of emotional interaction (Huff, Sproull, & Kiesler, 1989), web sites generate a virtual community where firms and consumers exchange information and interact socially (Suh, Couchman, & Park, 2003). It has, thus, been argued that a web site delivers not only "symbolic content" (i.e., multimedia) but also "sensory content" (i.e., virtual reality) (Fogg, 1999).

In light of the potential advantages of the Web in communications, the question of how to design the corporate web site is very important. Unfortunately, there are very few empirical studies providing a clear picture of how to effectively design a web site for integrated marketing communications purposes. Many researchers (e.g., Dalal, Quible, & Wyatt, 2000; Huizingh, 2000) have observed that most web site design guidelines have been based on experience and anecdotes of designers, and suggest that theoretical and empirical studies are needed.

The development of a new classification scheme may be the first step in the web site design study. A classification scheme enables researchers to divide web sites into mutually exclusive groups based upon distinctive features. One of the most important functions of a classification system is to establish a basis of measurement (e.g., Kerlinger, 1964). Another function is to facilitate the use of standard terminology in the study of web site design. An empirically driven classificatory taxonomy has the advantage of better explaining real world phenomena than an artificial typology.

This study has two main goals. The primary goal is to classify corporate web sites in terms of their structure. To do this, we first develop a framework for studying web site structure. We then propose taxonomy of a corporate web site based on conspicuous features of structural elements. The secondary goal of the study is to test hypotheses as to whether there are differences in Korean and Australian web sites.

Although cross-cultural study is necessary because a corporate web site is inherently a global communication medium, only a limited number of studies have been performed in a cross-cultural context. This study tries to fill the gap by comparing Australian and Korean web sites. The inclusion of both Australian and Korean web sites reflects not only the international nature of the Web, but also allows the study to encompass a wide range of industries and company sizes. Australia and Korea were chosen because these two countries play important roles in the Asia Pacific region and they represent different perspectives on markets, competition, culture, and industry structure (Suh, Taylor, & Lee, 2005).

LITERATURE REVIEW

Web Site Structure

Content and structure are two basic elements that determine type of web site (e.g., Huizingh, 2000; McCready, 1997). In a communications context, it is frequently said that content is "what is said" while structure is "how it is said". In other words, content refers to the communication message and structure refers to the manner of organization of a web site. As a web site utilizes a wider range of content and structural elements than traditional advertising, a typical advertising typology (e.g., slice-of-life, comparison, and demonstration) cannot be applied to a web site. This study draws on the traditional advertising literature as well as on WMC literature in order to develop a systematic basis for formulating a web site typology.

It has been argued that different types of web site content (i.e., what is said) and web site structure (i.e., how it is said) will create different effects on consumer's interaction with a corporate web site (e.g., Escalas, Jain, &

Strebel, 2001). Thus, several scholars have focused on the effectiveness of web site type (e.g., Choi, 2000; Dalal et al., 2000; Escalas et al., 2001; Huizingh, 2000; Li & Bukovac, 1999). Generally, different web site types have yielded different effects on consumer attitudes. For example, Escalas et al. (2001) have reported that a well-organized web site increased consumer satisfaction. Choi (2000) has found that a web site with an animated human character generated higher social presence than a web site without an animated character.

For the last two decades, the effect of advertisement types has been the main interest of marketing scholars. Traditional advertising studies have dominantly focused on whether a specific element is present or absent in advertisements (e.g., McQuarrie & Mick, 1999; Scott, 1994; Stewart & Koslow, 1989). However, past research on traditional advertising often has yielded different conclusions about the effectiveness of a particular element (Laskey, Fox, & Crask, 1994). Alternatively, many researchers (e.g., Dyer, 1982; Laskey et al., 1994) have argued that the traditional approach (i.e., atomistic) is problematic and have thus suggested adopting a holist approach, rather than an atomistic approach, in classifying advertising types. Here, it would be beneficial to examine the difference between two approaches.

There are two competing approaches to investigate a typology of web sites: atomistic (or mechanistic) and holistic approaches. First of all, an atomistic approach has emphasized the presence or absence of a particular element of a web site (such as text, sound, image, etc.). A considerable amount of advertising effectiveness studies has been done on the atomistic basis, and verbal (or text-based) versus visual (or graphic-based) message types have been a very popular approach. Based on this approach, traditional advertising studies have generally found that a visual type is more effective than a verbal type (e.g., Landoni & Gibb, 2000; McQuarrie & Mick, 1999), although there have been some controversies. This approach is still applied to web site typology studies (e.g., Choi, 2000; Li & Bukovac, 1999).

To the contrary, a holistic approach has been based on the Gestalt psychology, which has asserted that people understand the universe as an organized whole, not an elementary part (Gray, 1991). This approach, therefore, seeks to identify a pattern of a web site, which is a group of elements as a whole Laskey et al. (1994, p. 9) explains that a holistic approach, which focuses on executional style, rather than executional elements, is analogous to investigating personality types, rather than personal traits.

Recently, many researchers have adopted this approach in classifying advertising types (e.g., Laskey et al., 1994; Suh, 1994). Based on this approach, they have classified the televisional commercial into many different categories such as narration, demonstration, fantasy, and so forth. While several researchers (e.g., Berners-Lee, 1989; Jackson, 1997) have suggested adopting holistic approach in WMC, there are only few studies relating to web site structure (e.g., Dalal et al., 2000; Hamilton & Luo, 1999; Koehler, 1999). For instance, Koehler (1999) has classified a web site into six types: text dominant, graphic dominant, multimedia dominant, FTP/gopher dominant, e-mail dominant, and no dominant. However, these studies generally have lacked systematic investigation of web sites. Furthermore, the hybrid nature of a web site (i.e., a web site including various hypermedia elements and functions at the same time) has been neglected (Cappel & Myerscough, 1997). More studies should, thus, be concentrated in this area.

Structural Elements: Hypermedia

Hypermedia is the most distinctive feature of web site structure. Here, hypermedia is defined as the dynamic elements of a web site, which include hyperlink and multimedia. Although there have been many studies on hypermedia (e.g., Bouvin, 2000; Cockburn & Wilson, 1996; Dholakia & Rego, 1998; Palmer & Griffith, 1998), there has been some confusion with the term. Hence, it is useful here to more clearly define the elements of hypermedia.

For the categorization of multimedia, three dimensions of classification are considered: (1) linguistic or non-linguistic, (2) auditory or visual, and (3) dynamic or static properties. Previous research (e.g., Littlejohn, 1983; Krech & Crutchfield, 1965; Moriarty, 1994; Rada & Tochtermann, 1995; Ross, 1973) indicates that those three dimensions can facilitate the understanding of consumer's perception and feelings. Based on these criteria, four categories of web-based multimedia are identified. Text, as the written language including alphabets and numbers, is expressed in static and visual forms. Audio is any kind of sound that is a naturally dynamic, auditory medium. An image refers to the non-lingual, static, and visual element of a web site. It includes photographs, paintings, drawings, graphics, etc. Video refers to dynamic visual elements including both linguistic and non-linguistic. The simplest form of video is animation. Some other examples include flickering icons, spinning logos, and scrolling text (King, Knight, & Mason, 1997). More complicated forms of video are full motion video clips such as films.

A hyperlink is an important concept that distinguishes a web site from all other traditional mass media. A hyperlink refers to a connection between two or more sets of information. The prefix "hyper" emphasizes multidirectional links, which enable the user to move or jump in any direction while they are navigating a web site. This differs from the sequential nature of traditional mass media advertising. In this sense, a hyperlink is a crucial factor in determining the non-linear nature of a web site (e.g., Jackson, 1997). A hyperlink can be classified into two categories of links, an internal and external link. An internal link allows the user to move to another place within the same web site or even on the same page. An external link, however, takes users to another web site. External links are created for various purposes. For instance, by linking to external resources, a company can provide users with additional information related to the industry. Some sites facilitate external links to affiliated companies in order to enhance brand and corporate image.

THEORETICAL FRAMEWORK: CULTURAL DIMENSIONS

Our research hypothesis is drawn from cultural dimensions that vary between Australia and Korea. As the sum of attitude, behaviour, and norms collectively shared by a homogeneous group, culture may help us to understand the difference of web site structure between Australia and Korea. This study compares cross-cultural differences based on high–low context, monochromic–polychronic conceptions of time (Hall, 1976, 1983, 1990), and uncertainty avoidance (Hofstede, 1991).

According to Hall, a high context culture emphasizes non-verbal messages, whereas a low-context culture focuses on explicit verbal messages. This argument has been supported by various cross-national communication studies. For instance, Becker and Mottay (2001) identified that Asian web sites used more animation than U.S. and European sites. Javalgi, Culter, and Malhotra (1995) found that Japanese advertising emphasized more symbols and emotional appeal than U.S. advertising. Similarly, Choi, Lee, Kim, and Jeon (2005) and Honold (1999) found that users from a high-context culture (e.g., Koreans, Japanese, and Chinese) preferred icons and animations rather than text-based information in mobile communication. In contrast, users from a low-context culture (e.g., Finnish and Germans) preferred text-based explanatory information in mobile communication. Choong and Salvendy (1998) also identified that Chinese software developers showed high performance in a graphic mode, whereas Americans were more successful in a text mode. In general, studies on cross-national comparison between Asian and Western (e.g., U.S.A., U.K., and Australia) countries showed that Asian countries had a tendency to use non-verbal elements (e.g., animation and graphics) while Western countries utilized verbal messages. Korea belongs to a high-context culture and Australia is included in a low-context culture. Thus:

H1. Korean web sites will tend to include more visual elements than Australian web sites, which will focus on verbal elements.

Uncertainty avoidance can identify the cultural differences in communication. Uncertainty avoidance refers to the degree of feeling threatened in uncertain or unknown situations (Hofstede, 1991). In a high uncertainty avoidance culture, people have a tendency to distrust uncertain information and to seek truth or expertise. On the other hand, people from a low uncertainty avoidance culture tend to be risk-takers and are easily satisfied with vague information.

There are significant differences in the perceived risks of online shopping; therefore, a trust-related issue is an important cultural factor in e-commerce. Accordingly, firms, especially from a high uncertainty avoidance culture, try to reduce risk and ambiguity, and to ultimately enhance customer trust in many ways (Suh et al., 2005). Previous research has found that hyperlinks reduce risk and ambiguity by connecting a specific web site to many useful and believable sources. Hyperlinks facilitate customer trust among online consumers (Davenport & Cronin, 2000; Krebs, 2000; Palmer, Bailey, & Faraj, 2000), enhance the credibility of the web site (Park, 2000; Park, Barnett, & Nam, 2002), and provide a high-quality image (Terveen & Hill, 1998). A cross-cultural study identified that mobile phone users from Korea and Japan preferred hyperlinks more than Finnish users (Choi et al., 2005).

Based on these results, we can conclude that firms from high uncertainty avoidance cultures are likely to provide more hyperlinks than firms from low uncertainty avoidance cultures. According to Hofstede (1991), Korea is high on uncertainty avoidance, while Australia is relatively low. Hence, we would expect that:

H2. Korean web sites will include more hyperlinks than Australian web sites.

While a monochronic approach concerns the single task at hand, a polychronic culture prefers multitasking activities. In general, Australia belongs to a monochronic culture while Korea is classified into a polychronic culture (Hall, 1976, 1983, 1990). A similar approach is holistic versus piecemeal (Suh et al., 2005). A holistic approach (e.g., Eastern cultures, polychronic time orientation) has a tendency to include many structural elements in the web site while a piecemeal approach (e.g., Western culture, monochromic time orientation) utilizes only a couple of important elements. As Korea is classified as a polychronic culture, it is assumed that Korea would prefer a holistic approach to their web sites and would adopt many structural elements. To the contrary, it is expected that firms from a monochromic culture, such as Australia, would use a piecemeal approach and would therefore include fewer elements.

Based on the cultural differences we have identified, it is expected that there will be significant differences between Australian and Korean web sites. In detail, we expect Korean web sites to be consistent with a more high-context, polychronic, and holistic culture, while Australian web sites will be more consistent with the expectations of a low-context, monochromic, and piecemeal culture. Therefore:

H3. Korean web sites will tend to include more structural elements than Australian web sites, which will focus on fewer elements.

METHOD

Content Analysis

To develop the typology, the web sites of a sample of Australian and of Korean companies were content analysed. A corporate web site is an outcome of a firm's effort to communicate with customers and, as such, a study of the web site can provide useful insights into how communication activities are used to provide information for customers. Understanding what kinds of messages are presented and the hypermedia used on corporate web sites is a necessary step toward the evaluation of consumer attitudes toward these marketing activities. Content analysis is one of the best approaches for this purpose.

Content analysis is a descriptive technique that enables the systematic evaluation of communication contents (Palmer & Griffith, 1998; Rourke & Anderson, 2002). It is one of the most widely used methods for evaluating communication media including advertising (e.g., Yale & Gilly, 1988).

As web sites range in size from one page to thousands of pages (Nowak, Shamp, Hollander, & Cameron, 1999; Shneiderman, 1997), this study has focused on the home page (i.e., the first page of a web site that users encounter). The homepage is the "gateway" to a web site and, as such, plays a critical role for users much like an index or a table of contents in a book

(Dalal et al., 2000; Esrock & Leichty, 2000). Focusing on the home page allows the standardized comparison of web sites of different companies.

Two judges who were experienced web users and were bilingual Korean-English speakers evaluated each web site. One judge was trained by the other to increase inter-coder reliability (e.g., Kolbe & Burnett, 1991). The two judges coded the sampled sites independently. Inter-coder reliability was determined through pre-testing.

On the basis of a literature review of WMC studies (e.g., Cockburn & Wilson, 1996; Dholakia & Rego, 1998; Huizingh, 2000; McNaughton, 2001; Palmer & Griffith, 1998; Perry & Bodkin, 2000; Simeon, 1999), a coding frame of categories for web site structure (i.e., text, images, video, audio, and links) was generated as shown in Table 1. All categories were mutually exclusive with precise and unambiguous definitions (e.g., Holsti, 1969). As shown in Table 1, the web site structure typology includes five general

Table 1. Classification Results[a,b].

Variable		Types (Yes, %)		Mann–Whitney U Test
		Type 1 ($n = 211$)	Type 2 ($n = 172$)	
Text	Headline	86.7	0.0	***
	Description	4.7	78.5	***
Static image	Logo	94.3	89.5	NS
	Photo	95.3	84.3	***
Video/animation	Moving text	76.8	34.9	***
	Moving image	73.9	31.4	***
	Video	0.9	0.0	NS
	Video icon	17.1	7.6	**
Audio	Music	4.3	0.0	**
	Sound	5.7	1.2	*
	Audio icon	18.0	7.0	**
Links	Internal links	67.3	44.8	***
	External links	45.5	48.8	NS

Note: NS = Not significant.
*$p < 0.05$.
**$p < 0.01$.
***$p < 0.001$.
[a]94.3% of original grouped cases correctly classified.
[b]93.7% of cross-validated grouped cases correctly classified.

categories (i.e., text, images, video, audio, and links) with 13 items. The coding of web site structure was completed in 2002.

Sampling

Wright Investors' Service (http://www.corporateinformation.com) was used to locate and examine corporate home pages. This directory has listings of over 22,000 major companies around the world, including 644 Korean and 446 Australian companies at the time of the preliminary study. Since the directory excludes foreign companies in each country, local companies (i.e., locally operated and owned) could be compared. Furthermore, most of the companies listed in this directory had web addresses.

The preliminary study utilized cluster analysis, which involves a large sample with more than 100 units (Malhotra, Hall, Shaw, & Crisp, 1996). To ensure a wide variation in company sizes and in types of industries, approximately 200 web sites were selected from each country with equal numbers of Australian and Korean companies (e.g., Carney, 1972). 383 companies were selected by systematic sampling (every second company was selected from the Australian list and every third from the Korean list). For the companies that had no web site addresses (URLs) in the *Wright Investors' Service* directory, local search engines were used to try to find their corporate web sites. The Australian search engines used were *Webwombat* (http://www. webwombat.com.au) and *OzSearch* (http://www.ozsearch.com.au), whereas the Korean search engines were *Simmani* (http://www.simmani.com) and *Yahoo! Korea* (http://kr.yahoo.com). A total of 383 web site homepages were identified, including 190 Australian (43% of the Australian companies) and 193 Korean web sites (30% of the Korean companies). All web sites were treated as one sample in cluster analysis.

The distribution of company size and industry were examined. First of all, company size was measured by annual sales, which varied from under US $1,000 to over $1 billion. Around half of the Australian firms had annual sales of over $50 million, compared with 83.6% of the Korean companies. In terms of industry classification, the International Standard Industrial Classification (ISIC) was adopted. More of the firms in the Korean sample were in the manufacturing sectors than were in the Australian sample (68% versus 14%), and the distribution of firms in each sample broadly reflected the industry structure in the two countries. That is, the Australian economy is dominated by the service sector while the Korean economy is much more focused on the secondary sector, especially manufacturing (Korea Federation of Industries, 2001; The World Bank Group, 2001a, 2001b). Overall, the manufacturing sector was the largest in the sample (41.5%), followed by mining (12.4%) and finance (11.4%). Agriculture (0.8%), hotel (0.5%), education (0.5%), and health (0.2%) showed very low rates. Concerning the two countries, Korean firms were dominantly linked to manufacturing (68.7%). On the contrary, Australian companies were dispersed across various sectors such as mining (24.9%), real estate (18.0%), manufacturing (13.8%), and finance (13.8%). In terms of company size and industry, the sample appeared to be representative of the population of interest.

Pre-test of the Coding Procedure

After developing a codebook to provide a general guide for the coding procedure (Thompsen, 1994), a series of pre-tests were conducted. The importance of pre-testing has been emphasized by many researchers (e.g., Gorden, 1992; Miles & Huberman, 1994; Perreault & Leigh, 1989; Weber, 1985; Wimmer & Dominick, 1997). Pre-testing allows the researchers to identify and correct unclear definitions and coding rules, thereby enhancing the level of inter-coder agreement.

Inter-coder reliability is defined as the degree to which different coders, coding independently, reach the same coding decisions (Rourke, Anderson, Garrison, & Archer, 2001). For estimating inter-coder reliability, Thompsen (1994) suggests that at least 10 percent of the total sample should be analysed by multiple coders, while Wimmer and Dominick (1997) insist that between 10 and 25 percent should be coded. For this study, 75 sites for web site structure were analysed, accounting approximately 20 percent of the total sample.

For the test of inter-coder reliability, Perreault and Leigh's (1989) approach was adopted, which is one of the most often used measures of inter-coder reliability. Perreault and Leigh's (1989) lambda was 0.96, which demonstrate good levels of inter-coder reliability.

RESULTS

To develop the structural typologies of corporate web sites, the content analysis results were subjected to a cluster analysis in order to identify meaningful homogeneous groupings of web sites. The differences between the groups so obtained were tested for statistical significance using the non-parametric Mann–Whitney U test and crosstab analysis. For this test, the significance was set at the 0.05 level for a two-tailed test of significance. All analyses were performed using SPSS for 11.0 Windows.

Classification of Web Site Structure

The grouping of the Web site structure type was examined by cluster analysis, based on 13 web variables. As there was no predetermined number of clusters, a hierarchical clustering method was utilized (Malhotra et al., 1996). The average linkage (within group) method, based on the squared Euclidean distance between the variables, produced the closest and most stable solution. A two-cluster solution was selected as most appropriate because a dendrogram showed a big jump in the distance between clusters (see Fig. 1). The larger cluster included short text (HEA), moving images (i.e., MTE and MIM), static images (i.e., LOG and PHO), and internal links (ILI). In contrast, the smaller group contained descriptive text (i.e., DES), audio (i.e., SIC, MUS, and SOU), video (i.e., VIC and VID), and external links (i.e., ELI).

Actual Group		Predicted Group Membership		Total
		1	2	
Original 1 2	Count (%)	189 (89.6) 0 (.0)	22 (10.4) 172 (100.0)	211 172
Cross-validated[a] 1 2	Count (%)	187 (88.6) 0 (.0)	24 (11.4) 172 (100.0)	211 172

[a]Cross validation is done only for those cases in the analysis. In cross validation, each case is classified by the functions derived from all cases other than that case.

Fig. 1. Dendrogram using Average Linkage (Within Group).

```
                    Rescaled Distance Cluster Combine

   C A S E     0         5        10        15        20        25
   Label    Num  +---------+---------+---------+---------+---------+

   VIC        8   -+-------+
   SIC       11   -+       +-----------+
   VID        7   -+-+     I           I
   MUS        9   -+ +-----+           +-------+
   SOU       10   ---+           I           +-------------------+
   DES        2   -------------------+       I                   I
   ELI       13   -------------------------+                     I
   MTE        5   ----------------------+---------+              I
   MIM        6   ----------------------+         +-------+      I
   HEA        1   --------------------------------+       +---------+
   LOG        3   -------------+-----------------+    I
   PHO        4   -------------+                 +-----+
   ILI       12   ------------------------------+
```

To verify the results of the cluster analysis, a discriminant analysis was conducted. A stepwise discriminant analysis confirmed a single function (Wilk's lambda $= 0.178$, $p < 0.001$) clearly discriminating between two clusters (canonical $r = 0.907$). As shown in Table 1, the results showed that 94.3% of original grouped cases and 93.7% of cross-validated grouped cases were correctly classified.

The Mann–Whitney U test was used to test significance between each pair. As shown in Table 2, "type 1" represented 55.1% and "type 2" 44.9% of the total sample. While type 1 used all the hypermedia items except descriptive text, type 2 utilized mainly descriptive text. Therefore, type 1 sites are likely to have more central features than type 2 sites. For three items (i.e., logos, video, and external links) there was no statistically significant difference in usage between the two clusters. Logos and external links were commonly used, whereas video was not commonly used.

Reflecting the results of the Mann–Whitney U test, type 1 was named the "hypermedia" type (55.1%), which includes almost all the hypermedia elements (i.e., text, static images, animated images, audio, and internal links) except for some items description (from text) and video (from video). Type 2

Table 2. Results of Mann–Whitney U Tests.

Variable		Yes (%)		Mann–Whitney U Test	
		Australia ($n = 190$)	Korea ($n = 193$)	z-value	Significance (2-tailed)
Text	Headline	26.8	68.4	−8.129	0.000***
	Description	56.3	19.7	−7.379	0.000***
Static image	Logo	91.1	93.3	−0.804	0.421
	Photo	83.7	96.9	−4.369	0.000***
Video/animation	Moving text	35.8	79.8	−8.711	0.000***
	Moving image	31.1	78.2	−9.265	0.000***
	Video	0.0	1.0	−1.405	0.160
	Video icon	6.8	18.7	−3.455	0.001***
Audio	Music	0.5	4.1	−2.334	0.020*
	Sound	2.1	5.2	−1.602	0.109
	Audio icon	6.3	19.7	−3.879	0.000***
Links	Internal links	42.6	71.5	−5.702	0.000***
	External links	38.9	54.9	−3.128	0.002**

*$p < 0.05$.
**$p < 0.01$.
***$p < 0.001$.

was called the "static image" type (44.9%), which mainly utilizes descriptive text and static images. Logos, photographs, and external links were commonly included in both types.

Hypothesis Test: Comparative Analysis between Korea and Australia

The results of Mann–Whitney U test revealed that Korean firms used short text (headline, $z = -8.129$, $p < 0.001$), more static image (i.e., photo, $z = -7.379$, $p < 0.001$), video (i.e., moving text, $z = -87.11$, $p < 0.001$; moving image, $z = -9.265$, $p < 0.001$; video icon, $z = -3.455$, $p < 0.001$), audio (music, $z = -2.334$, $p < 0.05$; audio icon, $z = -3.879$, $p < 0.001$), and links (internal link, $z = -5.702$, $p < 0.001$; external link, $z = -3.128$, $p < 0.01$), while Australian firms utilized more descriptive text (description, $z = -7.379$, $p < 0.001$). Both Korean and Australian firms frequently used company logos but there was no statistical difference between countries. Video and sound were not frequently used and there was no difference between countries.

Next, crosstab analysis was performed to compare the use of the web site structure type between the two countries. The result showed that while the majority of Australian firms were classified into the static image type (68.4%), most of the Korean firms fell into the hypermedia type (78.2%, $\chi^2 = 84.251$, $p < 0.001$). As a result, it can be concluded that Korean web sites have a tendency to include more structural elements than Australian web sites, which focus on fewer elements. Therefore, the hypothesis was supported.

DISCUSSION

This empirical study of web site structure provided a number of interesting findings. To begin with, the study found that while static images and text are dominantly used, videos/animated images and hyperlinks are still not broadly used. In particular, the use of sound is very rarely used for corporate web sites.

This result can be explained in two ways. One explanation is based on the notion that simple design along with static elements, such as text and static image, is more effective because it facilitates shorter download time than animated images and sound (e.g., Shneiderman, 1997; Briones, 1998). Another explanation considers the fact that a corporate web is still in the early stage of development. The first introduction of the Web was in 1990 and web software and technology are still developing (e.g., Coda, Ghezzi,

Vigna, & Garzotto, 1998). Therefore, it is not surprising that a large number of corporate web sites are static and have limited hyperlinks.

Technology is not a major problem, however. The true problem is scholars and practitioners' common notion mentioned above, which is strongly based on their limited knowledge and experience (e.g., Coda et al., 1998). Web site design is different from the design of traditional advertising. Two most distinctive characteristics of the Web are interactivity and multimodality as discussed before. The capacity of the Web can be achieved through the use of hyperlinks and dynamic multimedia elements. Many researchers emphasize the importance of hyperlinks in the Web site design. Hyperlinks provide more control of information to web users. User's feeling of control ultimately enhances high degree of social interaction (Suh, Hasan, Couchman, & Lee, 2003). Social interaction cannot be sacrificed for download time and bandwidth. Accordingly, it is recommended for practitioners to use more hypermedia elements for their web sites.

The result of cluster analysis found that web site structure could be classified into two types: the hypermedia type and static image type. It seems that only two minimal types exist since a corporate web site is still in the early stage of development. Although the hypermedia type (55.1%) was slightly more frequently used than the static image type (44.9%), the usage rate of the hypermedia type is very low, considering the importance of hypermedia in WMC.

As web site design involves a wider range of design elements than traditional communication media (e.g., television, radio, newspaper, and magazine), a typical advertising typology, or simple research on the presence or the absence of a specific element, cannot be applied to web site design. The typology of web site structure derived from an empirical study provides understanding of the structure of a web site as a whole and of the elements of a web site at the same time. Therefore, the web site typology proposed in this study provides a conceptual base for establishing and developing theories related to communication and information systems.

The study also provides practitioners with useful insights into web site design, which requires well-prepared plans to select and combine various structural elements. From a structural point of view, it is expected that a change of structural elements will cause a change of overall structure (e.g., Neisser, 1967). Considering that consumers perceive web sites not just by the structural elements, but by the overall structure of the web site, this holistic approach view is the more essential approach in studying a corporate web site (e.g., Dyer, 1982).

A cross-national comparison between Korea and Australia provides a number of interesting differences. The results of the study showed that Korean firms more frequently used the hypermedia type of web site that focused on dynamic hypermedia elements (i.e., moving image, sound, and links). To the contrary, Australian firms were inclined to use the static image type, which mainly depended on descriptive test and static images (i.e., photographs and pictures). This result can be explained by a high- versus low-context culture. As Korea is a high-context culture, Korean web sites preferred more non-verbal elements, while Australia, representing a low-context culture, utilized more descriptive text. This is supported by cross-national web site study. For instance, Becker and Mottay (2001) identified that Asian web sites used more animation than U.S. and European sites. Javalgi et al. (1995) found that Japanese advertising emphasized more symbols and emotional appeal than U.S. advertising. In general, studies on cross-national comparison between Asian and Western (e.g., U.S.A., U.K., and Australia) countries showed that Asian countries had a tendency to use non-verbal elements (e.g., animation and graphics) and Western countries utilized verbal messages.

The tendency of Korean web sites to include more structural elements than Australian web sites can be explained by a monochronic versus polychronic approach. Korea, belonging to a polychronic culture, has web sites that include more structural elements, while Australian web sites, reflecting a monochronic culture, utilized less structural elements. Based on these results, it can be concluded that Korea adopted a holistic approach and has a tendency to include many structural elements in the web site, while Australia reflected a piecemeal approach and utilizes very limited elements.

Caution should be taken when interpreting the results in this study. There were differences across company size and industry types. In terms of company size, small-sized companies preferred the static image type (58.7%). On the other hand, large-sized companies utilized the hypermedia type more frequently (62.7%, $\chi^2 = 24.616$, $p < 0.001$). Coincidently, Korean firms dominated large-sized companies, while small-sized companies, dominated by Australian firms, more frequently used the static image type. We further investigated whether there was any difference in the use of web site structure in terms of industry type. The results showed significant differences across industries ($\chi^2 = 34.542$, $p < 0.001$). Consumer goods industries (e.g., manufacturing) preferred the hypermedia type, whereas business-to-business industries (e.g., mining) showed more frequent use of the static image type. Wholesale and finance sectors used both types equally (47.4% versus 52.6%, 52.3% versus 47.7%, respectively). Interestingly, Korean firms dominated the consumer goods industries, while Australian firms dominated the business-to-business industries. This implies that industry factors, such as company size and industry types, might have an effect on web site structure. The influence of industry factors on communication is supported by some cross-national studies (e.g., Katz & Lee, 1992; Koudelova & Whitelock, 2001).

Given these results, it cannot be clearly said which is the most influential factors of country difference among cultural factor and industry factors (i.e., company size, industry types, and product categories), though the evidence across these categories does point to Korean firms being at least somewhat more likely to use hypermedia web sites.

CONCLUSION

In summary, the major findings of this study are (1) web site structure can be classified, based on a holistic approach, into two types: the hypermedia type and the static image type and (2) there are cross-national differences between Korea and Australia in the use of web site structure, which are influenced by a cultural and industry factors (e.g., company size and industry types).

The use of web-based or Internet marketing is growing rapidly in today's increasingly globalized "networked economy". An increase in the importance of corporate web sites (Mohammed, Fisher, Jaworski, & Cahill, 2002) is also a result of the global "networked economy". However, while more and more companies are establishing a presence on the World Wide Web through their web sites, our understanding of the effectiveness of such corporate web sites is still at a rudimentary stage.

At this stage, the clear definition of web site structure and hypermedia can play a critical role in not only designing an effective corporate web site but also in establishing a measurement system for web site effectiveness. At present, one of the most urgent problems to be solved is an assessment of the effectiveness of a web site. The empirical typology of a corporate web site we proposed can serve as independent variables in a measurement system. In addition, although there have been many empirical studies on the Web, the results of these cannot be compared due to the application of different terms and definitions. Inconsistent definition is also a big hindrance to the development of theory. In this respect, the classification schemes and definitions in this study can be a cornerstone for building sound communication theories.

This study has several limitations. First, this study included only one type of web site (i.e., a corporate web site). Web sites can be classified into five main groups: (1) personal web sites run by individuals or groups of people, (2) corporate web sites for profit-oriented firms, (3) public sector web sites run by government agencies, (4) non-profit organization web sites for universities, and (5) web sites for voluntary organization such as the Salvation Army. Accordingly, the results of this research cannot be generalized to other types of web site. Future research needs to include other types of web site.

Another limitation is that only two countries were included in this study. Although Korea belongs to Asian culture and Australia belongs to European culture, there are cultural differences among countries that belong to the same cultural group. Moreover, each country has unique industry structure. Further study should include other countries that have various cultural and industry differences.

Finally, this is an exploratory research in nature. Accordingly, the current study does not provide information about causality between web typology and effect. We recommend that experiments should be undertaken in order to study which type is more effective and what factors have an effect on web effectiveness based on the proposed typology.

REFERENCES

Becker, S. A., & Mottay, F. E. (2001). A global perspective on web site usability. *IEEE Software,* January/February, *18*(1), 54–61.

Berners-Lee, T. (1989). *Information management: A proposal.* Available from http://www.w3.org/History/1989/proposal.html

Bouvin, D. D. (2000). *Web site design: A comparison of perceptions for a simulated university's web-based intranet.* Unpublished doctoral dissertation, University of Sarasota.

Briones, M. G. (1998). Customer service the key to on-line relationship. *Marketing News, 32*(24), 21–23.

Cappel, J. J., & Myerscough, M. A. (1997). Using the World Wide Web to gain a competitive advantage. *Information Strategy: The Executive's Journal,* Spring, 6–13.

Carney, T. F. (1972). *Content analysis: A technique for systematic inference from communications.* London: B. T. Batsford.

Choi, B., Lee, I., Kim, J., & Jeon, Y (2005). Qualitative cross-national study of cultural influences on mobile data service design. *Proceedings of the 2005 conference on human factors in computing systems (CHI 2005).*

Choi, Y. K. (2000). *Effects of presence on the effectiveness of web site advertising.* Unpublished doctoral dissertation, Michigan State University.

Choong, Y. Y., & Salvendy, G. (1998). Design of icons for use by Chinese in mainland China. *Interacting with Computers, 9*(4), 417–430.

Cockburn, C., & Wilson, T. D. (1996). Business use of the World Wide Web. *International Journal of Information Management, 16*(2), 83–102.

Coda, F., Ghezzi, C., Vigna, G., & Garzotto, F. (1998). Towards a software engineering approach to web site development. *Proceedings of the 9th international workshop on software specification and design*, April 16–18.

Dalal, N. P., Quible, Z., & Wyatt, K. (2000). Cognitive design of home pages: An experimental study of comprehension on the World Wide Web. *Information Processing and Management*, *36*, 607–621.

Davenport, E., & Cronin, B. (2000). The citation network as a prototype for representing trust in virtual environments. In: B. Cronin & H. B. Atkins (Eds), *The web of knowledge: A festschrift in honor of Eugene Garfield* (pp. 517–534). ASIS Monograph Series. Metford, NJ: Information Today Inc.

Dennis, A. R., & Kinney, S. T. (1998). Testing media richness theory in the new media: The effects of cues, feedback and task equivocality. *Information Systems Research*, *9*(3), 256–274.

Dholakia, U. M., & Rego, L. L. (1998). What makes commercial web pages popular? An empirical investigation of web page effectiveness. *European Journal of Marketing*, *32*(7/8), 724–736.

Dyer, G. (1982). *Advertising as communication*. London: Routledge.

Escalas, J. E., Jain, K., & Strebel, J. E. (2001). Satisfaction, frustration, and delight: A framework for understanding how consumers interact with web sites. In: O. Lee (Ed.), *Internet marketing research: Theory and practice* (pp. 231–251). Melbourne: IDEA Group Publishing.

Esrock, S. L., & Leichty, G. B. (2000). Organization of corporate web pages: Publics and functions. *Public Relations Review*, *26*(3), 327–344.

Fogg, B. J. (1999). Persuasive technologies. *Communication of the ACM*, *42*(5), 26–29.

Gorden, R. (1992). *Basic interviewing skills*. Itasca, IL: F. E. Peacock.

Gray, P. (1991). *Psychology*. New York: Worth Publishers.

Hall, E. T. (1976). *Beyond culture*. Garden City, NY: Anchor Press/Doubleday.

Hall, E. T. (1983). *The dance of life: The other dimension of time*. Garden City, NY: Anchor.

Hall, E. T., & Hall, M. R. (1990). *Understanding Cultural Differences*. New York: Intercultural Press.

Hamilton, M., & Luo, R. (1999). Impact of animation and complexity on web site effectiveness. *Proceedings of the third international cognitive technology conference, CT '99*, San Francisco/Silicon Valley, August 11–14.

Hofstede, G. (1991). *Cultures and organizations: Software of the mind*. New York: McGraw-Hill.

Holsti, O. R. (1969). *Content analysis for the social sciences and humanities*. Sydney: Addison-Wesley Publishing.

Honold, P. (1999). Learning how to use a cellular phone: Comparison between German and Chinese users. *Technical Communication*, *46*(2), 196–205.

Huff, C., Sproull, L., & Kiesler, S. (1989). Computer communication and organizational commitment: Tracing the relationship in a city government. *Journal of Applied Social Psychology*, *19*(16), 1371–1391.

Huizingh, E. K. R. E. (2000). The content and design of web sites: An empirical study. *Information and Management*, *37*, 123–134.

Jackson, M. H. (1997). Assessing the structure of communication on the World Wide Web. *Journal of Computer-Mediated Communication*, *3*(1) at http://www.ascusc.org/jcmc/vol3/issue1/jackson.html#abstract, accessed August 5, 2006.

Javalgi, R. G., Culter, B. D., & Malhotra, N. K. (1995). Print advertising at the component level: A cross-cultural comparison of the United States and Japan. *Journal of Business Research, 34*, 117–124.

Katz, H., & Lee, W. (1992). Oceans apart: An initial exploration of social communication differences in U.S. and U.K. prime-time television advertising. *International Journal of Advertising, 11*(1), 69–82.

Kerlinger, F. N. (1964). *Foundations of behavioral research: Educational and psychological inquiry.* New York: Holt, Rinehart and Winston.

Kerpedjiev, S., Carenini, G., Green, N., Moore, J., & Roth, S. (1998). Saying it in graphics: From intentions to visualizations. *Proceedings of the IEEE symposium on information visualization* (pp. 97–101), Research Triangle Park, NC, October 19–20.

King, J. M., Knight, P., & Mason, J. H. (1997). *Web marketing cookbook.* New York: Wiley Computer Publishing.

Koehler, W. (1999). An analysis of web page and web site constancy and permanence. *Journal of the American Society for Information Science, 50*(2), 162–180.

Kolbe, R. H., & Burnett, M. S. (1991). Content-analysis research: An examination of applications with directives for improving research reliability and objectivity. *Journal of Consumer Research, 18*(September), 243–250.

Korea Federation of Industries (KFI). (2001). *Korean economic yearbook 2001.* Seoul, Korea: FKI Media.

Koudelova, R., & Whitelock, J. (2001). A cross-cultural analysis of television advertising in the UK and the Czech Republic. *International Marketing Review, 18*(3), 286–300.

Krebs, V. (2000). Working in the connected world book network. *IHRIM (International Association for Human Resource Information Management) Journal, 4*(1), 87–90.

Krech, D., & Crutchfield, R. S. (1965). *Elements of psychology.* New York: Alfred A. Knopf.

Landoni, M., & Gibb, F. (2000). The role of visual rhetoric in the design and production of electronic books: The visual book. *The Electronic Library, 18*(3), 190–201.

Laskey, H. A., Fox, R. J., & Crask, M. R. (1994). Investigating the impact of executional style on television commercial effectiveness. *Journal of Advertising Research, 34*(6), 9–16.

Li, H., & Bukovac, J. L. (1999). Cognitive impact of banner ad characteristics: An experimental study. *Journalism and Mass Communication Quarterly, 76*(2), 341–353.

Littlejohn, S. W. (1983). *Theories of human communication* (2nd ed.). Belmont, CA: Wadsworth Publishing.

Malhotra, N. K., Hall, J., Shaw, M., & Crisp, M. (1996). *Marketing research: An applied orientation.* Sydney: Prentice-Hall.

Markham, A. (1998). *Life online: Researching real experience in virtual space.* Walnut Creek, CA: Altamira Press.

McCready, K. (1997). Designing and redesigning: Marquette libraries' web site. *Library Hi Tech, 15*(3–4), 83–89.

McNaughton, R. B. (2001). A typology of the web site objectives in high technology business markets. *Marketing Intelligence and Planning, 19*(2), 82–87.

McQuarrie, E. F., & Mick, D. G. (1999). Visual rhetoric in advertising: Text-interpretive, experimental, and reader-response analyses. *Journal of Consumer Research, 26*(June), 37–54.

Miles, M. B., & Huberman, A. M. (1994). *Qualitative data analysis* (2nd ed.). Thousand Oaks, CA: Sage Publications.

Mohammed, R. A., Fisher, R. J., Jaworski, B. J., & Cahill, A. M. (2002). *Internet marketing: Building advantage in a networked economy.* New York: McGraw-Hill.

Moriarty, S. (1994). Visual communication as a primary system. *Journal of Visual Literacy, 14*(2), 11–21.

Neisser, U. (1967). *Cognitive psychology.* New York: Appleton-Century-Crofts.

Nisbett, R., & Ross, L. (1980). *Human inference: Strategies and shortcomings of social judgment.* Englewood Cliffs, NJ: Prentice-Hall.

Nowak, G. J., Shamp, S., Hollander, B., & Cameron, G. T. (1999). Interactive media: A means for more meaningful advertising? In: D. W. Schumann & E. Thorson (Eds), *Advertising and the World Wide Web* (pp. 99–117). Mahwah, NJ: Lawrence Erlbaum Associates Publishers.

Oviatt, S. L., & Cohen, P. R. (2000). Multimodal interfaces that process what comes naturally. *Communications of the ACM, 43*(3), 45–53.

Palmer J. W., Bailey, J. P., & Faraj. S. (2000). The role of intermediaries in the development of trust on the WWW: The use and prominence of trusted third parties and privacy statements. *Journal of Computer-Mediated Communication, 5*(3). Retrieved June 22, 2000, from http://www.ascusc.org/jcmc/vol5/issue3/palmer.html

Palmer, J. W., & Griffith, D. A. (1998). An emerging model of web site design for marketing. *Communications of the ACM, 41*(3), 45–51.

Park, H. W., Barnett, G. A., & Nam, I. Y. (2002). Interorganizational hyperlink networks among websites in South Korea. *NETCOM: Networks and Communications Studies, 16*(3/4, Special issue on the Internet development in Asia), 155–173.

Perreault, W. D. J., & Leigh, L. E. (1989). Reliability of nominal data based on qualitative judgments. *Journal of Marketing Research, 26*(2), 135–148.

Perry, M., & Bodkin, C. (2000). Content analysis of Fortune 100 Company web sites. *Corporate Communications: An International Journal, 5*(2), 87–96.

Rada, R., & Tochtermann, K. (1995). Introduction to expertmedia. In: R. Rada & K. Tochtermann (Eds), *Expertmedia: Expert systems and hypermedia* (pp. 3–27). London: World Scientific.

Ross, R. (1973). Communication, symbols, and society. In: J. D. Cardwell (Ed.), *Readings in social psychology: A symbolic interaction perspective* (pp. 3–18). Philadelphia: F. A. Davis Company.

Rourke, L., & Anderson, T. (2002). Using peer teams to lead online discussions. *Journal of Interactive Media in Education, 1*, 1–21.

Rourke, L., Anderson, T., Garrison, D. R., & Archer, W. (2001). Methodological issues in the content analysis of computer conference transcripts. *International Journal of Artificial Intelligence in Education, 12*, 8–22.

Scott, L. M. (1994). Images in advertising: The need for a theory of visual rhetoric. *Journal of Consumer Research, 21*(December), 461–480.

Shneiderman, B. (1997). Designing information-abundant web sites: Issues and recommendations. *International Journal of Human-Computer Studies, 47*, 5–29.

Simeon, R. (1999). Evaluating domestic and international web site strategies. *Internet Research: Electronic Networking Applications and Policy, 9*(4), 297–308.

Spector, L. (1995). Evolving control structures with automatically defined macros. *Proceedings of the working notes of the AAAI fall symposium on genetic programming,* November 10–12, Cambridge, MA.

Stewart, D. W., & Koslow, S. (1989). Executional factors and advertising effectiveness: A replication. *Journal of Advertising, 18*(3), 21–32.

Street, R. L., & Manning, T. (1997). Information environments for breast cancer education. In: R. L. Street, W. R. Gold & T. Manning (Eds), *Health promotion and interactive technology: Theoretical applications and future directions* (pp. 121–139). Mahwah, NJ: Lawrence Erlbaum Associates.

Suh, K. (1994). *The influence of claim types and execution types on advertising effect.* Unpublished Masters thesis, Korea University, Seoul, Korea (in Korean).

Suh, K., Couchman, P. K., & Park, J. (2003). A web-mediated communication (WMC) model based on activity theory. *Proceedings of the 7th World multiconference on systemics, cybernetic and informatics (SCI 2003)*, July 27–29, Orlando, Florida, U.S.A and TT21C (transformational tools for 21st century minds), Gold Coast, Australia, July 27–29.

Suh, K., Hasan, H., Couchman, P. K., & Lee, D. (2003). Exploring social interaction in web-mediated communication. In: H. Hasan, E. Gould & I. Verenikina (Eds), *Information systems and activity theory volume 3: Expanding the horizon* (Vol. 3, pp. 141–155). Wollongong, Australia: University of Wollongong Press.

Suh, K., Taylor, C. R., & Lee, D. (2005). *A typology of the marketing communications functions of web sites: A cross-national comparison.* Working paper.

Terveen, L., & Hill, W. (1998). *Evaluating emergent collaboration on the web.* Conference of Computer Supported Cooperative Work, Seattle, Washington.

The World Bank Group (2001a). *Australia at a glance.* Available at http://www.worldbank.org/data/countrydata/aag/aus_aag.pdf

The World Bank Group (2001b). *Korea, Rep. at a glance.* Available at http://www.worldbank.org/data/countrydata/aag/kor_aag.pdf

Thompsen, P. A. (1994). *Toward a public lane on the information superhighway: A media performance analysis of the community-wide education and information service initiative.* Unpublished doctoral dissertation, The University of Utah.

Weber, R. P. (1985). *Basic content analysis.* London: Sage.

Wimmer, R. D., & Dominick, J. R. (1997). *Mass media research: An introduction* (5th ed.). New York: Wadsworth Publishing Company.

Yale, L., & Gilly, M. C. (1988). Trends in advertising research: A look at the content of marketing-oriented journals from 1976 to 1985. *Journal of Advertising, 17*(1), 12–22.

SET UP A CONTINUATION ORDER TODAY!

Did you know that you can set up a continuation order on all Elsevier-JAI series and have each new volume sent directly to you upon publication? For details on how to set up a **continuation order**, contact your nearest regional sales office listed below.

To view related series in Business & Management, please visit:

www.elsevier.com/businessandmanagement

The Americas
Customer Service Department
11830 Westline Industrial Drive
St. Louis, MO 63146
USA
US customers:
Tel: +1 800 545 2522 (Toll-free number)
Fax: +1 800 535 9935
For Customers outside US:
Tel: +1 800 460 3110 (Toll-free number).
Fax: +1 314 453 7095
usbkinfo@elsevier.com

Europe, Middle East & Africa
Customer Service Department
Linacre House
Jordan Hill
Oxford OX2 8DP
UK
Tel: +44 (0) 1865 474140
Fax: +44 (0) 1865 474141
eurobkinfo@elsevier.com

Japan
Customer Service Department
2F Higashi Azabu, 1 Chome Bldg
1-9-15 Higashi Azabu, Minato-ku
Tokyo 106-0044
Japan
Tel: +81 3 3589 6370
Fax: +81 3 3589 6371
books@elsevierjapan.com

APAC
Customer Service Department
3 Killiney Road #08-01
Winsland House I
Singapore 239519
Tel: +65 6349 0222
Fax: +65 6733 1510
asiainfo@elsevier.com

Australia & New Zealand
Customer Service Department
30-52 Smidmore Street
Marrickville, New South Wales 2204
Australia
Tel: +61 (02) 9517 8999
Fax: +61 (02) 9517 2249
service@elsevier.com.au

30% Discount for Authors on All Books!

A 30% discount is available to Elsevier book and journal contributors on all books (except multi-volume reference works).

To claim your discount, full payment is required with your order, which must be sent directly to the publisher at the nearest regional sales office above.